What Birdo is That?

A Field Guide to Bird-people

LIBBY ROBIN

MELBOURNE
UNIVERSITY
PRESS

An imprint of Melbourne University Publishing Limited
Level 1, 715 Swanston Street, Carlton, Victoria 3053, Australia
mup-contact@unimelb.edu.au
www.mup.com.au

First published 2023
Text © Libby Robin, 2023
Design and typography © Melbourne University Publishing Limited, 2023

Cover design by Alex Ross Creative
Typeset by Megan Ellis
Cover images courtesy Shutterstock
Printed in Australia by McPherson's Printing Group

A catalogue record for this book is available from the National Library of Australia

9780522879346 (paperback)
9780522879353 (ebook)

For Adela and Henry,
already keen bird watchers

CONTENTS

ABBREVIATIONS

AAAS	Australasian Association for the Advancement of Science
AAS	Australian Academy of Science
ABBS	Australian Bird Banding Scheme
ABBBS	Australian Bird and Bat Banding Scheme
ABC	Australian Bird Count; Australian Broadcasting Commission; Australian Broadcasting Corporation
AFO	*Australian Field Ornithology*
ANU	Australian National University
AOU	Australasian Ornithologists' Union
AWC	Australian Wildlife Conservancy
AWSG	Australasian Wader Studies Group
BA	Birds Australia
BINGO	big international non-government organisation
BOC	Bird Observers' Club (Australia)
BOCA	Bird Observation & Conservation Australia
CALM	Department of Conservation and Land Management (WA)
CI	Conservation International
COG	Canberra Ornithologists Group
CSIR	Council for Scientific and Industrial Research
CSIRO	Commonwealth Scientific and Industrial Research Organisation
CSU	Charles Sturt University
EDGE	Evolutionarily Distinct and Globally Endangered
FIC	Field Investigation Committee (RAOU)
HANZAB	*Handbook of Australian, New Zealand and Antarctic Birds*
IBP	International Biological Program
ICBP	International Council for Bird Preservation
IOC	International Ornithological Congress
IPA	Indigenous Protected Area
ISC	International Science Council
IUCN	International Union for Conservation of Nature
KBA	Key Biodiversity Area

LTERN	Long Term Ecological Research Network
MAB	Man and the Biosphere
MAPS	Migratory Animal Pathological Survey
NAA	National Archives of Australia
NGO	non-governmental organisation
NLA	National Library of Australia
NRCL	Natural Resources Conservation League (Victoria)
NRS	Nest Record Scheme
RAOU	Royal Australasian Ornithologists' Union
RBG	Royal Botanic Gardens (Victoria)
RN	*RAOU Newsletter*
RZSNSW	Royal Zoological Society of New South Wales
SAOA	South Australian Ornithological Association
SHOC	Southern Hemisphere Ornithological Congress
SLV	State Library Victoria
TAC	Tasmanian Aboriginal Centre
TERN	Terrestrial Ecosystem Research Network
UNESCO	United Nations Educational, Scientific and Cultural Organization
VORG	Victorian Ornithological Research Group
WCS	Wildlife Conservation Society
WEA	Workers' Educational Association (South Australia)
WWF	World Wide Fund for Nature

PROLOGUE
THIS ECCENTRIC
FIELD GUIDE

Some years ago, I had the opportunity to talk about ornithology in Alice Springs on a local radio station. A 'scientific study' was clearly a very strange way for Indigenous people to talk about understanding the creatures of Country that ushered in new seasons, guided people to food and were central to daily business.

However, my Indigenous host revealed quickly that *watching ornithologists watch birds* was a popular and widespread sport among his listeners. 'Ornithologists—you know the ones, the ones with the binoculars around their necks,' he periodically interjected, barely stifling a guffaw each time. His listeners knew the bird-people who came to Alice Springs from all over the world to add to their 'life list'. The locals may not have kept lists and certainly didn't count how many they had seen, but they knew all about birds and what they do, when and where. Watching 'newbies' come in and make a mess of watching birds was thoroughly entertaining.

The radio interview, initially supposed to be a ten-minute slot, went on for forty-five minutes, with callers and their yarns. It was an unusually long and discursive conversation. My radio host and his Indigenous listeners were not so much interested in *what* we know about birds, but *how* we know things. They were curious about what bird-facts people count and collate into field guides to identify birds. They really wanted to know why and how birds get their English names. Why this way and not another? These people were not ornithologists, but they were definitely *birdos*. They cared about birds, and wanted to know everything they could about them.

The practice of identifying a bird can be about noticing a friend and knowing who else is likely to be around with that friend, as much as sorting the stunning array of body shapes and adaptations into an official 'Order of Nature', particularly one shaped by elite thinkers in faraway places. Naming and classifying birds into systems has absorbed hundreds of years of intellectual endeavour, including by Greek philosophers such as Aristotle and Swedish polymaths such as Carl Linnaeus (1707–78), whose global system has been the backbone of the nerdy, scientific classifications of several centuries. Sorting birds into families can be about evolutionary theory and, depending on your scientific inclinations, different family patterns sometimes emerge, but not always in line with morphology—the observed shape of the bird and its behaviour. Naming is often competitive and contested. Yet most ornithologists share a love of birds, and thrill at a rare find in the field, alive and singing, just like the rest of us who listen when we walk in the bush or in a local park.

The twentieth century saw a steady separation of the language of the professional ornithologist and the amateur birdo, yet many people are both. The field guide, the technical tricks of the sound recorder and now apps have changed how we watch birds, and how we classify them, but *noticing* them is still important for humans. Nature, for some, is a mental health activity. Some even talk about *forest bathing*. Listening to birdsong and immersing oneself in bird-worlds is urgent as so many of our birds become rarer as their habitats change. Noticing the absence of local birds is important, too, as local extinctions sometimes herald trouble further afield. Birds new to an area may be cues to a warming world as ecological niches shift south (in Australia) or further up a mountain. For millennia, humans have watched birds, and birds have watched humans. What we call each other depends on our language, our syrinx, our world views.

What Birdo is That? plays with the title of Neville Cayley's original field guide, *What Bird is That?*, first published in 1931 by the New South Wales branch of the Gould League. It was arguably south-eastern Australia's favourite guide to birds for much of the last century, and was certainly one of the first with colour plates that also fitted in a knapsack or daypack. Cayley was a good observer, and a fine artist. A young ornithologist was proud to own a Cayley. *What Bird is That?* went on to define and shape interested people's growing love of birds, and what birds they continued to notice into adulthood.

Bill Middleton joined the Royal Australasian Ornithologists' Union (RAOU)[1] in 1941 at the age of fifteen, he told me proudly in an interview fifty-seven years later. He remembered the Gould League warmly. It was a club for children established in 1909 with a mission to discourage them from collecting birds' eggs, and it was Bill's first contact with 'ornithology'. Its field guide was 'Leach' (*The Australian Bird Book*), created in 1911 by John Albert Leach, founder of the Gould League. In format, the Leach guide was smaller, cheaper and illustrated in black and white. It complemented Cayley in many ways. In later life, Bill recalled that in his youth he would ride all over the country near his home in Nhill in Victoria's Wimmera,

> with my schoolbag on my back and Cayley and Leach bird books. They were the two I started off with. Leach was the 1926 edition. I think my father must have bought that long before I became interested in birds. (I arrived on the scene in 1926.) But ... I can remember my grandfather having bought a copy [of Cayley] from Ewins in Ballarat ... I can remember very clearly him showing me this new book that he'd bought ... I would have only been five or six at the outside.[2]

Middleton finished up with many, many more bird books and even a weekly radio program on local nature for the Wimmera region. He devoted whole programs to ideas about gardening for birds. Birds brought together well and poorly educated people, young and old, and people from all sorts of backgrounds. They all loved hearing Bill on radio. They were all birdos together.

One of the few things I know about my maternal grandfather, who died when I was very young, was that he loved birds, was a member of the

RAOU and owned both *The Australian Bird Book* and *What Bird is That?*
In the tough times of war and Depression in the first half of the twentieth
century, birdwatching was an inexpensive escape. Yet ornithology was also
more than a relaxing hobby. It became an identity—slightly eccentric, but
serious and heartwarming at the same time.

A crucial facet of Cayley was that it was organised by habitats: not
by the arcane classification systems of Linnaeus but by the real Australian
places where you might see the birds—forests, open grasslands, seashores
and swamps. Cayley assumed you were out there looking at a bird in the
bush or in your backyard, and your first question was: *What bird is that?*

As I have come to write about the people who watch the birds—the
ones with the binoculars around their necks—I have noticed they turn
up in rather weird habitats. They are frequently to be found in sewage
farms, or trailing around the remotest desert with a caravan in tow, or
even on rented boats at the very pelagic edge of what counts as Australia.
Twitchers, conservationists, ecologists, gardeners and philosophers all
watch birds for different reasons. How Country (whether with a capital
letter or lower case) is understood is closely tied to how we understand
its birds. They may be ancestral beings, harbingers of seasonal change
or opportunists of remote ephemeral water events, or they may be the
intensely local inhabitants that enliven a suburban garden or park. A field
guide to Australia's bird-people is a first step towards understanding the
complex relations between people and birds in a land of extremes at
the forefront of changing climates and habitats.

This book approaches birdwatching in Australia using the conceit of a
key birdwatching tool, a 'field guide', to open up many of the stories of
how birdwatchers have gone about their craft across the years. Its stories
have come from dusty archives, from wild places at sea as well as on the
land, from restoration projects, from gardens and from urban wastelands.
They are human stories, but the birds themselves interject and interrupt
any self-important anthropocentrism. The birds trill and force themselves
into our consciousness. They educate. They counter the imperialism of
the ever-expanding economies of the new millennium, and they adapt to

and sometimes resist change. They turn up in unexpected places, giving surprise and joy.

Birdwatching is a cover for conservation, for land management, for understanding ecological connections, for relaxation and happiness, for garden philosophies. It is also a basis for international diplomacy, for understanding global interdependency. Birds lift our eyes to the skies. They make visible the changing flows of the great atmospheric ocean that supports all life on our small blue planet.

BIRDING FOR THE NATION

The birdo's birdo

The touchstone figure for ornithologists in Australia has always been John Gould (1804–81), the 'birdo's birdo'. Other great international ornithologists lacked the insights he gained from his personal early collecting work in Australia. He understood the context for the specimens he classified, the scent of the Australian bush and the varied habitats across the vast continent.

Gould's illustrated *Birds of Australia* was a crucial, pioneering publication. Dominic Louis Serventy (1904–88), one of Australia's great twentieth-century birdos, described Gould as the 'Australian Aristotle'. According to Serventy, Gould codified 'all past information and discover[ed] with his associates much that was entirely new' to scientific ornithology in the nineteenth century.[1] Still today, discussion of Australia's 'birdos' often begins with Gould. Young birdos began their bird study as children with the Gould League, an organisation established in 1909 to protect birds and their nests; it continues in the twenty-first century as an organisation of 'environmental and sustainability education' that includes all biodiversity.[2] It now recognises and celebrates both John and Elizabeth

Gould. Gould's *Birds* and his companion volume on mammals remain important into the twenty-first century.

John Gould was taxidermist to the Zoological Society of London, and his wife, Elizabeth (née Coxen, 1804–41), was an accomplished natural history artist and partner in what became *The Birds of Australia*, which was published in folios between 1840 and 1848. The folios featured beautiful and scientifically precise illustrations by Elizabeth, limerick writer Edward Lear (1812–88) and English artist Henry Constantine Richter (1821–1902), who built up finished works from Elizabeth's Australian sketches after her death. A supplement to *The Birds of Australia* in five parts appeared between 1851 and 1869, and Gould's *Handbook to the Birds of Australia* in 1865.

The Goulds' interest in Australia began with specimens collected by Elizabeth's brothers Stephen and Charles Coxen from their property 'Yarrundi' on the upper Hunter River, which were described by John in *Proceedings of the Royal Society of London* between 1833 and 1837. He published *A Synopsis of the Birds of Australia* in 1837–38. John and Elizabeth then visited the Australian colonies together, travelling with their seven-year-old son; the family was mostly based in Van Diemen's Land from 1838 to 1840, where their 'Australian' baby was born.[3] John Gilbert (?1810–45), John Gould's most important collector, accompanied the Goulds from England and stayed on in Australia after they returned home, collecting extensively in Western Australia and across the Top End.[4] On an ill-fated expedition led by Ludwig Leichhardt (1813–48), Gilbert was killed in June 1845 by an Aboriginal group resisting the unwelcome European incursion into their remote Country on the Cape York Peninsula.[5]

Many of Gould's new species were inland birds that had not been 'discovered' by the Europeans, who often travelled by ship, or near the coast. Bird specimens were commonly formally described much later and far away in London or other metropolitan centres, by curators in museums or other eminent zoologists with access to comparative skins and specimens. The vagaries of sea travel and difficulties of preserving specimens sometimes led to bizarre geographical errors. For example, early French systematist Johann Hermann (1738–1800) at the University of Strasbourg named the distinctive Australian kookaburra *Dacelo novaeguineae* based on incorrect provenance information from botanist-explorer Pierre Sonnerat (1748–1814). Sonnerat had received the kookaburra specimen from Captain James Cook's botanist, Joseph Banks (1743–1820), as part of a larger botanical collection from New Guinea. Sonnerat, who had never travelled to either New Guinea or Australia, was based at the time in Cape Town, South Africa, an important reprovisioning post for ships travelling from East Asia in the eighteenth century. Sonnerat and Banks were both more focused on plants than birds, and the place where the kookaburra was collected became lost in the long chain of transfer.

The Australasian Ornithologists' Union (AOU) was the first national ornithological club in the Southern Hemisphere, launched in 1901, the year of the Federation of Australia. John Gould's prominent ornithological legacy shaped early thinking as the local ornithologists gathered to build on his work. In just four decades he had added more species to the Australian bird-list than anyone before or since. He had collected about thirty of the 'type specimens' himself, while Gilbert contributed about fifty. These bird-skins were the crucial reference skins for new names and were typically held in a major museum, or a private collection accessible to future workers in the field. It was very unusual for the specialist who assigned the name to be the collector. Before Gould, the Australian ornithological material described in the international literature was patchy, as the kookaburra story shows. Gould was more systematic because he understood the habitat and behaviour of the birds, having seen them in the wild for himself. The scientific illustrations in his folio publications included contextual cues that made them much more valuable than just a description of a museum bird-skin.[6] Gould described his last Australian species (the Eyrean grasswren, *Amytornis goyderi*) in 1875. Zoologist John Calaby (1922–98) commented that 'only about forty breeding birds' had been 'added to the Australian fauna' by the time he was writing 125 years later.[7]

Local beginnings

How did the prospective members of the Australasian Ornithologists' Union hope to build on Gould's legacy?

> The Objects of the Society are the advancement and popularization of the Science of Ornithology, the protection of useful and ornamental avifauna, and the publication of a magazine called The Emu … Thus bird students will be kept in touch with one another, original study will be aided, and an Australasian want supplied.[8]

The new bird network would be national (including New Zealand) and enable the exchange of news from around the country, scientific research papers and popular education. It would protect birds from threats through its authority as the peak national body and would introduce the next generation to birds and birding, and to conservation of habitats. Its scientific credentials would enable an authoritative and practical bird-list that worked for all the former colonies and would be recognised internationally.

Emu was established as a magazine of nature study, reports on collecting expeditions, and debates about bird protection and vernacular names. It united birdos of all sorts across the continent, and kept them in touch with the world. *Emu* is still published today, now with the subtitle *Austral Ornithology*, although since 2017 it has been an online scientific journal. Its formal base is with the Australian society, now called BirdLife Australia, but the production is undertaken in partnership with a major international scientific publisher.[9] Its historically more popular elements have moved into other magazines and online and broadcast media to meet new audiences.

The foundation editor of *Emu*, Archibald J Campbell (1853–1929), was an experienced journalist and pioneering bird photographer already well-known for his *Nests and Eggs of Australian Birds* (two versions, 1883 and 1900) and for popular weekly articles on birds in *The Australasian*, often illustrated with his own photos. He was a talented communicator, enthusing people about birds, and nature more broadly, on excursions and in the field. He was also the leading promoter of a national 'Wattle Day'. Campbell instigated a meeting in 1896 of the group that became the kernel of the national birding association. As a scientific oologist (egg collector), he was concerned about protecting nesting habitats. He was also keen to develop an official bird-list that would be rigorous, national and internationally accepted. He wanted better consistency in vernacular names to assist amateur bird lovers to exchange accurate information. National discoveries, expeditions, nature study and the questions of how Australian birds fitted into international systems were the concerns of the new organisation, and dominated its early decades.

Dinner with Archibald J Campbell

On the evening of Saturday 15 August 1896, Campbell invited seventeen naturalists, all men, to dinner at Britannia House in South Yarra. Rather than traditional formal toasts, Campbell gave a talk, illustrated by lantern slides, celebrating his experiences as a field naturalist and sharing his detailed observations of a bell miner (*Manorina melanophrys*, also called a bellbird) with his friends. Golden wattles and pink and white heath decorated the table, symbolising, respectively, the 'Australian' and the 'Victorian' spirit of the era. Birds, however, were the central business of the night. The table's centrepiece was the moss nest of the elusive mountain thrush (now *Zoothera lunulata*, Bassian thrush) with eggs 'fresh from the scrub'. Discussion focused on the gentlemanly passion of oology—a formal, quasi-scientific name for egg collecting. Many of those present had pursued egg and nest collection since boyhood, developing a lifelong urge to protect birds and a fascination with 'nidification' (nest-making).

Campbell's stories of his excursions in country Victoria triggered reminiscences in his fellow naturalists that raised the idea to form an Australian ornithologists' union 'on similar lines to the British and American Ornithological Unions'.[10] Three subsequent 'ornithological reunions' were held at the Victoria Coffee Palace in Little Collins Street, Melbourne, in August 1897, September 1899 and November 1900.

In addition to AJ Campbell, the group included the physician Charles S Ryan (1853–1926) and his cousin Dudley Le Souef (1856–1923), director of the Melbourne Zoological Gardens. Ryan and Le Souef were third-generation naturalists, sons of two of the five formidable Cotton sisters, who all married ornithologists. Their grandfather John Cotton (1802–49) had published a very early list of the birds of Port Phillip in 1848.[11]

At the 1900 meeting, hosted by Le Souef, the group established a provisional (first) committee of the AOU, comprising many of the prominent members of the Field Naturalists' Club of Victoria (established in 1884). The FNCV is still a lively organisation and publishes one of the oldest continuous scientific journals in Australia (the *Victorian Naturalist*). Robert Hall (1867–1949), a museum collector and author of *The Insectivorous Birds of Victoria* (1900), was another important member of the group.[12] While metropolitan Melbourne was central to organisation, the idea of a national union received support from interstate and regional ornithologists, several of whom attended the meeting; others sent apologies. Its first duties would include 'the proper protection of useful and ornamental native birds' and the publication of ornithological papers.

Le Souef, the honorary secretary, issued a printed notice soliciting support for a national body from those 'interested in the bird life of the continent'. 'As it is now the beginning of a new Century', he wrote,

> and the various Australian States have also Federated under one Governor-General, it seems that the time has arrived … Would you allow your name to be recorded as a member? It is proposed that the subscription be 15s per annum, which will be used for the publication of the papers sent into the Union, and which members will, of course, obtain free. For the guidance of the provisional committee, perhaps you would kindly state whether you will guarantee your annual subscription for one, two or three years, so as to place the Union on a sound basis.[13]

The distinguished British ornithologist Philip Sclater (1829–1913), Fellow of the Royal Society and chairman of the first meeting of the

British Ornithologists' Union, endorsed the initiative, and the committee enlisted the Duke and Duchess of Cornwall and York as patrons, a shrewd move that laid the groundwork for the Australasian Ornithologists' Union to become 'Royal' when the duke succeeded to the British throne in 1910.[14] The union also welcomed its US connections. In 1894, William McIlwraith of Rockhampton had independently written to the American Ornithologists' Union requesting information about its pamphlets and activities. John Hall Sage (1847–1925), the secretary of the American union, replied in November 1894 expressing delight 'that an effort is being made to establish a Society in Australia'. While nothing came of McIlwraith's initiative, the letter from Sage was carefully preserved, folded inside the union's first council minute book.[15] Perhaps McIlwraith sent it to the union when he joined.

The ornithological initiative was particularly welcomed across the Tasman. New Zealand later established its own 'Native Bird Protection Society', in 1923 (now known as Forest & Bird or, more formally, the Royal Forest and Bird Protection Society of New Zealand), but for the first quarter of the twentieth century New Zealanders were active members of the Australasian initiative.

Although the new union was designed by a group of 'gentlemen', it was never that sort of club.[16] Science and bird-protection were its priorities, and all classes of people were included, particularly if they could share practical knowledge about birds. In that era, there were strong reasons to include women in bird-protection initiatives; this was something the club promoted, including publicising a 1903 campaign in the London *Times* in *Emu*: 'The demands of murderous millinery and fashion will continue until a knowledge of nature comes ... Can we not enlist more ladies in our cause?' *The Times* then proposed that the new Australasian Ornithologists' Union should follow the American example and admit ladies 'at nominal subscription', apparently unaware that women were already full members and contributors to the union's journal.[17]

First meeting in Adelaide

This was a national association, and it wanted to avoid being seen as a 'Melbourne' club. Le Souef approached South Australia, home of the South Australian Ornithological Association (SAOA; established 1899), to host the national union's first general meeting. The Adelaide meeting, held on 1 November 1901, elected nationally representative office-bearers, including the first president, Colonel W Vincent Legge (1841–1914), from Tasmania, and Amandus HC Zietz (1840–1921) of the South Australian Museum as one of the vice-presidents. The practical tasks of secretary (Le Souef), treasurer (Hall) and editors (AJ Campbell and bush poet Henry Kendall) were centralised in Melbourne, where council meetings were held in Ryan's home and medical rooms at 37 Collins Street.

Foundation New Zealanders included EP Sealy (1839–1903), an explorer and internationally distinguished glacier photographer who had surveyed the rugged Tasman and Hooker glaciers carrying an old-fashioned camera with gear weighing 'at least half a hundredweight'. His photography had won him a gold medal at an exhibition in Vienna.[18] Other New Zealanders included Captain Frederick Wollaston Hutton (1836–1905), president of the Australasian Association for the Advancement of Science in 1902, who became the union's second president, and Tom Iredale, based in New Zealand in the early years and later in Australia, who freelanced for the British Museum. Iredale later collaborated with Gregory Macalister Mathews (1876–1949) on his twelve-volume magnum opus, *The Birds of Australia* (London, 1910–27).

The new national union's most intriguing supporters were far-flung individual naturalists and ornithologists with no access to metropolitan field naturalists' clubs or even the regular society of fellow ornithologists. These talented field observers and collectors were crucial to the scientific endeavours of the union. The Barnard family of 'Coomooboolaroo' in central-western Queensland came to the attention of the distinguished Norwegian zoologist Carl Lumholtz (1851–1922), who described the 'Barnard boys' in 1889 as:

the most skilful collectors I have ever met ... They climbed the trees as easily as any black man. When they had their tomahawks in their hands no tree was too high for them ... They cut niches in the bark for the support of their toes ... They were always barefooted, in order to get about more easily ... Their keen faculty of observation astonished me again and again. They studied the life and habits of animals and gave me much valuable information, for they knew the fauna of the locality perfectly.[19]

Other skilled naturalists who made their living from birds found that membership of the union put their remote and lonely work on a national and international stage. Tom Carter (1863–1931) collected for Lord Rothschild (1868–1937) in Britain and for Mathews. Sidney Jackson (1873–1946) and Fred (Frederick Charles) Morse (1874–1924) collected for Belltrees station grazier Henry Luke White (1860–1927) from New South Wales. White curated one of Australia's most significant egg collections, which after his death went to the National Museum of Victoria.[20]

After Gould, others had continued work to interest the public in birds in the last quarter of the nineteenth century and had built up both private and public collections. Brisbane-based Silvester Diggles (1817–80) published his *Ornithology of Australia* in twenty-one parts between 1866 and 1870.[21] Gracius Joseph Broinowski (1837–1913), another early member of the Australasian Ornithologists' Union, published an illustrated *Birds of Australia* between 1887 and 1891 that gave a descriptive account of more than 700 species. Broinowski's six-volume set was more affordable and accessible than the works of Gould or Diggles.[22] The Queensland Museum and Australian Museum (Sydney) were prominent in this period in Australian ornithology, with Charles de Vis (1829–1915), zoologist-clergyman and museum director in Queensland, and Edward Pierson Ramsay (1862–1914), zoologist and Australian Museum curator, describing eleven new species between them.[23] De Vis, a foundation member of the union, also established the first investigations in palaeo-ornithology, painting 'the first pictures of the fossil birds of Central Australia, most of which were of Quaternary age'.[24]

One distinguished early New Zealand ornithologist, Walter Buller (1838–1906), specialised in migratory birds. Buller recorded migrations and the arrival of vagrants, most notably the first arrival of the grey-backed silvereye (*Zosterops lateralis*) in 1856, in his prize-winning 'Essay on the Ornithology of New Zealand' (1865).[25] He subsequently published *A History of the Birds of New Zealand* in 1875, with a two-volume supplement in 1905. Buller was bilingual in English and Māori and was involved extensively in Māori affairs, including working as judge of the Native Land Court.[26] His records up to 1905 were included in the important later publication *New Zealand Birds*, published in 1930 by Walter Reginald Brook Oliver (1883–1957).

Photographs by ornithological collectors reveal that Aboriginal people were integral to work in Australia, but they were seldom named and there was no major ornithologist fluent in any Indigenous language as Buller was in New Zealand. Snippets of Aboriginal knowledge of birds and photographic plates of traditional Aboriginal rock art occasionally appeared in *Emu*, but there was nothing systematic.

Collection, particularly aviculture (the collection of living birds for aviaries), was sometimes a prime motivation for bird enthusiasts. The SAOA, which had begun in Adelaide just before the AOU, initially comprised seven serious aviculturalists. Their meetings included 'show and tell' sessions with their aviary birds, and debates about captive breeding, feeding and other concerns quite unlike those discussed by the national group.[27]

Not all those who supported the 'protection' of birds were collectors, but many were. Taxonomy and systematics (naming and classifying) were evolving sciences, and skins and eggs were the only reliable basis for identification. Museum workers were still naming new species and subspecies of birds in this period, though systematics later expanded to include evolutionary biology, cladistics and other taxonomies of the relationships between birds (see Chapter 7).

Hunters, too, were often keen conservationists. The Society for the Preservation of the Wild Fauna of the Empire (now Flora & Fauna International) was established in London in 1903 and had complex aspirations, like the Australian bird enthusiasts of this era. The Fauna

Society's 75-year history was called *The Penitent Butchers*. The change in sensibilities over the twentieth century forced the 'penitence' as guns shifted towards cameras with technological advances and redefined the concept of 'trophies' from specimens to photographs.[28] Right from the start, however, the killing of birds was never taken lightly, and sometimes had to be done discreetly to maintain the not-always-genteel politics of early birding associations such as the SAOA and AOU, and the Bird Observers' Club (BOC) established in Melbourne in 1905.

Emu

By October 1901, the committee had gathered enough subscribers to publish the first issue of *Emu*, 'a recognized means of intercommunication between all interested in ornithology'.[29] Launching the journal provided a symbolic reason for the union's inaugural general meeting and a way to include those, including international members, who could not travel to Adelaide. The British had their *Ibis* and the Americans their *Auk*, so a short, distinctive bird name put the new journal in good company. Emus were distributed across all parts of the Australian mainland, and a distinct form had been in Tasmania. The fact that the new Commonwealth coat of arms included an emu was important to the choice. The bird was big and recognisable and had beautiful large blue-green eggs attractive to carving artists. Carved eggs were prized design features. 'Ordinary bird lovers as well as scientific ornithologists and oologists' were welcome to subscribe and contribute to the magazine.[30]

The Australians wanted a society with the same kind of prestige as the American Ornithologists' Union, but chose a different sort of style and emphasis.[31] The American organisation was a highly professional group that had come together primarily to resolve debates about nomenclature.[32] Australia did not have the numbers for such a focus. One of the country's leading cataloguers of nests and eggs, Alfred J North (1855–1917), ornithological assistant at the Australian Museum in Sydney, resisted joining the Australian union (although he was a member of both the

American and British ones) because he did not want to work with his long-time rival AJ Campbell. Despite their mutual antipathy, North and Campbell both rejected trinomials, the preferred system of the American Ornithologists' Union at the time.[33]

Instead, the fledgling journal included the geographical distribution of species, a particular interest of the British Ornithologists' Union and its journal, *Ibis*, and focused closely on its own region. 'We cannot hope to extend our sphere of observation throughout the same geographical areas as the contributors to *The Ibis*,' Colonel Vincent Legge commented in his first presidential address. *Emu* should, however, embrace Australia, the Malay Archipelago, New Guinea and Oceania, 'including Fiji and New Caledonia and New Zealand'.[34] Here he described what we now call Wallacea, the region beyond Alfred Russel Wallace's 1859 line that indicated the 'south-eastern limits' of the Indian region. The line ran between the islands of Bali and Lombok, Celebes (now Sulawesi) and Borneo, and the Moluccas (Maluku Islands) and the Philippines. It was based on the distributions of significant birds: 'Barbets reach Bali, but not Lombok; *Cacatua* [cockatoos] and *Tropidorhynchus* [friarbirds] reach Lombok, but not Bali.'[35]

In fact, the material in *Emu* proved to be strongly biased towards Australia and New Zealand and largely ignored their neighbouring regions. Geographical distribution was a subject of fascination, but on a continental scale rather than the global or imperial scale expounded by Legge. Early articles included descriptions of birds new to science, either at species or subspecies level, new and undescribed eggs, and lists of birds from the little-known regions of 'our great Island continent'. The 'regions' of concern to Australasian ornithologists were generally the biological shades within the continent—what Baldwin Spencer (1860–1929), Professor of Zoology at the University of Melbourne, called Bassian (temperate), Eyrean (desert) and Torresian (tropical). The special populations of breeding shorebirds on small offshore islands were also a favoured subject for discussion.

'Cabinet naturalists' as well as field ornithologists read *Emu*. Egg collectors had a passion for plugging gaps in their collections. They also treated their craft as scientific, and distinguished their adult collections from the enthusiastic egg collecting of their youth. Lists 'from the already well worked districts of the various States' were valued for migration studies, 'the time of year that the observations are made being always an important factor in determining the movements of species'.[36] Since 1789, when the English parson-naturalist Gilbert White (1720–93) had written lyrically about the coming and going of swallows in *The Natural History of Selborne*, British ornithologists had been fascinated with seasonal migration. The Gilbert White model, however, transferred uneasily to a land with tropical latitudes and variable seasons. Referring to Le Souef's description of eggs from Port Darwin, Legge described the breeding season for raptorial birds as chiefly 'the Southern winter', a quaint turn of phrase intended to describe the tropical dry season (May–September).[37]

Emu kept collectors in touch with each other. Morse's short papers on the birds and eggs of Garah, near Moree in New South Wales, appeared in the journal between 1919 and 1922, often illustrated with photographs, and prompted both private and public responses. His private correspondence, now held at Museums Victoria, reveals how *Emu* developed far-flung ornithological networks. A 1922 paper by him, for example, provided the 'most northerly record of *Acanthiza pyrrhopygia*' (the chestnut-rumped thornbill, now *A. uropygialis*) and raised new questions about the range of the inland thornbill (then *A. albiventris*, now *A. apicalis*). Archibald G Campbell (1880–1954, son of Archibald J) asked to borrow skins from Morse 'for examination for checklist purposes'.[38] Campbell senior wrote separately praising Morse's photography: 'Your egret pictures are as grand as they are rare. With your assistance and advice, the RAOU should get a cinametograph [cinematograph] in those some seasons. A film or two of such pictures would make the union famous!'[39]

International egg collectors also read *Emu* for information to enhance their private collections. EJ Court of Washington, DC, for example, wanted Morse to provide 'two sets (5 each) of the Black Swan this September. I am especially desirous always to have *full* clutches. [In the] *Anatidae* I am pretty strong but desire all of the Australian kinds.'[40] North Americans paid their collectors well, as did some locals. JA Ross of Melbourne sought glossy-ibis eggs and included his collecting credentials in his correspondence with Morse: 'my collection contains well over 500 species, but there are a great many gaps that I hope to fill sooner or later'.[41] HL White of Belltrees was a regular correspondent, excited by Morse's exceptional finds:

> By Jove! You are in luck finding that big heronry: what a wonderful breeding ground. Yes, glossy ibis eggs are very good and should make excellent exchanges. I'd much like a set of ibis and each of the egrets and will make the value up to you later. the type clutch of plumed egret … eggs was taken in Riverina by A. H. Mattingley in 1906. I purchased the clutch eventually … I'll mention your 1/5 glossy ibis in an article I am preparing for *Emu* under the heading Abnormal Clutches.[42]

Collectors appreciated the opportunity to communicate with each other—to compare, to swap and to discuss the problems of collections, whether they were skins, mounted specimens, or, most commonly, eggs. The really serious collectors were highly competitive about their collections.[43]

In 1906 Charles Ryan observed that *Emu* was, if anything, still 'too popular'—that is, more local than international—but he argued that the organisation 'had to walk before it could run'.[44] The magazine kept the Australian audience in touch with the activities of international organisations. The first International Ornithological Congress had been held in 1884, and subsequent congresses were held about every four years in faraway Europe. Only one or two Australians managed to attend and represent the union.[45] The regular section 'From Magazines &c' reported on Australasian matters covered by *Ibis*, the *Bulletin of the British Ornithologists' Club* and equivalent publications in North America and Europe. It also recorded such events as the first issue of the *Journal of the South African Ornithologists' Union*: 'The Southern Union is to be congratulated upon its ability to publish such a first-class journal locally.'[46] Not all 'international' happenings were strictly scientific. In 1905, *Emu* reported with pride that in January an Australian bird, the varied lorikeet (*Ptilosclera versicolor*, now *Psitteuteles versicolor*), had won the Parakeet section of the Crystal Palace Bird Show in London.[47] *Emu*'s informal columns provided a varied 'window on the rest of the world' for Australasian ornithologists who might otherwise have only understood their science in a local context.

The collector: HL White

There were many private collectors, but Henry Luke White's private collection was important to the public, too. It became the foundation for decisions about naming within the RAOU and ultimately for the National Museum of Victoria's ornithological collection. White's property, Belltrees, was 'an ideal home for a naturalist'—not just because of the birds, as Dudley Le Souef argued, but also because of its birding history: 'It was in that neighbourhood that Gould worked for some time and got so many of his type specimens of birds.'[48]

'HL', who lived in the district all his life (1860–1927), started his egg collection as a schoolboy in 1875. It was, in his own estimation, 'rather a good lot, but all end-blown'.[49] In the first decade of the twentieth century, he turned again to his eggs and to his Gouldian responsibilities and began meticulously to build a major collection. He still kept his early collection, 'carefully preserved in a special case', alongside the expanding (more professionally 'side-blown') collection amassed through commissioned expeditions and judicious purchases. In parallel, he built a major collection of bird-skins. He kept records meticulously, with the ultimate view of making the collection available to the public for posterity. As Le Souef wrote in 1909, 'The data-book or catalogue is quite a monumental work. Not only is full data given of each clutch of eggs, but also the measurements of each egg.'[50] When Le Souef and Archibald Campbell senior visited Belltrees that year, arrangements were made for Le Souef's own significant collection to become one of HL's judicious purchases.

Though he weighed 110 kilograms, Sid Jackson, another of the great collectors, was surprisingly agile, climbing trees and moving silently and successfully in the bush in search of shy nesting birds. White purchased Jackson's collections in 1907 and paid for the publication of 'a handsome quarto volume containing Mr Jackson's catalogue and notes on the collection'.[51] Jackson earned the sobriquet 'The Professor' (or just 'Pro') from HL, who persuaded him to become a curator and to gather further additions to the collections.[52]

White wanted to present his collections to 'some Australian museum' when they had grown sufficiently, notionally after he 'reached 800' skins. Which museum remained an open question. White had fallen out with Alfred North, the relevant curator at the Australian Museum in Sydney, which would have been the logical place for a New South Wales collection. He had found North and others 'narrow minded and jealous' and ungenerous with their time for him: 'They've absolutely refused to give me any further help in identifying species.'[53] By the time of North's death in 1917, the collection had grown to 5000 bird-skins. White's collecting team was led by Jackson but also included F Lawson Whitlock (1860–1953), ED Frizelle, HG Barnard (1869–1966), William McLennan (1882–1935) and JP Rogers, as well as Captain SA White.[54] HL gifted both eggs and skins to the National Museum of Victoria in Melbourne, with a proviso that they never leave Victoria. Thus he ensured that Australian Museum staff would forever have to travel to use his collections. Jackson handled the transfer of skins in 1917. 'Jackson loves publicity and attention. I hate both,' HL wrote to AJ Campbell. 'If the RAOU thinks it owes me any little civility, SWJ will be on hand to receive it. The union will never get hold of me.'[55] White held on to his egg and nest collection as it was the basis for a lively correspondence with oologists and collectors from all over Australia. The eggs and nests joined the skins after HL's death in 1927.[56]

The HL White collections were valuable not only in themselves but also because they came with research tools such as journals and reference books. *Emu* of January 1916 recorded an anonymous donation of £1000 'for the purpose of procuring a central room where members of the RAOU may meet, work and discuss ornithological problems'.[57] The money was invested in the War Loan, and the interest funded the rent and furnishing of 2 Temple Court, off Collins Street, Melbourne, near where the union had met in the home of Charles Ryan. Its monthly council meetings moved to meet near the resource material, which included a reference library, and what became the RAOU collections, housed in cabinets provided by White. White presented a copy of Gould's *Birds of Australia* (valued then at £300) and a bookcase to house the volumes.[58] The following Christmas, he donated the first six volumes of Mathews' *Birds of Australia*.[59] He was also a great supporter of *Emu*, recognising its importance as the international face of Australasian ornithology. A good *Emu* meant a strong reference library, as *Ibis*, *Auk* and other key journals came to the RAOU gratis because *Emu* was a worthwhile exchange.

No doubt the strong wool prices associated with the war had boosted Belltrees' profits at the time, but White's personal generosity was great. The RAOU purchased more than 2000 bird-skins from his duplicate skins (over and above the collection that went to the museum), but he donated 365 duplicate sets of eggs. By the end of 1918, the union could boast 700 sets 'all side blown … containing about 500 species'.[60] Dubbo pastoralist Thomas Phillips Austin (1872–1937), author of *The Birds of the Cobbora District*, had donated 212 sets of eggs not represented in the HL White gift, and smaller sets were presented by JH Bettington (30), AC Stone (20), FE Howe (10) and JA (Ada) Fletcher (6). AJ Campbell was appointed curator, assisted by FE Wilson and ED Brooke Nicholls (1877–1937).[61] With headquarters, a library and collections, the union emerged from the war an authoritative leader in ornithological research.

Field excursions

Samuel White (1870–1954) was a pioneering South Australian ornithologist, unrelated to HL, who distinguished himself from the other White with his honorific 'Captain' (earned during the South African War). Captain White chronicled an official expedition to the Bass Strait islands in November 1908, following the congress of the AOU in Melbourne. The team of twenty-five chartered the SS *Manawatu* and set off into the treacherous waters of the famous 'roaring forties', which had caused many shipwrecks and where rapid changes in the weather are common. Arthur Mattingley (1870–1950), a keen bird photographer, led the group. Ethel White, Captain White's wife, was the only woman. Among the twenty-four men, there were two notable nature writers—Donald Macdonald (1859–1932) from *The Argus* and Charles Barrett (1879–1959) from the Melbourne *Herald*—and the Sydney-based United States consul, Harrison Baker (1830–1913).[62]

The party had barely boarded the ship at Storehouse Island, just east of Flinders Island, when they struck heavy weather:

> The wind went around and came upon us with a sudden burst. The water around, which was like glass during part of the afternoon, was, within an incredibly short time, lashed into foam, and began to tumble in great white masses upon the treacherous rocks that surrounded us ... We lay the remainder of the night under the lee of Babel Island.[63]

The risks of the trip were rewarded by the chance to see breeding seabirds on the remnants of the former land bridge between mainland Australia and Tasmania.[64] The highlight of Bass Strait for Captain White was the Cat Island gannet rookery, 'an acre [4000 square metres] of living nesting birds, each sitting on a little raised mound of earth ... just out of range of its neighbour's bill'.

Seabirds were not the only targets of the trip. White reported collecting four scrubwren (*Sericornis*) specimens at Deal Island.[65] Mattingley used his cumbersome cinematograph to record a colony of five or six hundred seals at Western Port, including 'old lions show[ing] fierce displeasure at being disturbed'.[66] One of the 'products' of the expedition was a slim book of his photographs.[67] Although the expedition was officially 'ornithological', JA Kershaw (1866–1946) from the National Museum of Victoria joined it to collect a Flinders Island wombat, which he (correctly) believed to be different from the mainland variety.[68] White recorded the 'primitive and peaceful community' of two or three hundred Aboriginal (palawa/pakana) mutton-birders based at Cape Barren Island, where they lived for the annual mutton-bird (moon bird) season in March every year. These women had escaped from mainland Tasmania in the genocide years between 1830 and 1834 and had married whalers and sealers. At the time of White's expedition, they and their families had extracted a living from their extremely bleak environment for eight decades; they continue to do so today. The mutton-birders' poverty in 1908 was striking to White. He noted that they had run out of salted meat from the last season by November, when the expedition arrived, and were living off limpets and other shellfish. The several doctors of the expedition spent time with the sick 'and did what they could to alleviate suffering'.[69] In his narrative, White appealed to the Tasmanian Government to do more for these people, and also sought protection for Cape Barren geese in all the islands. The AOU returned to Flinders Island for another campout in 1912.

For those for whom a fortnight's cruise in Bass Strait was 'inconvenient' (or too expensive at £8–10), AJ Campbell led a week's campout to his favourite Phillip Island rookeries at Cape Woolamai at the same time; the participants watched the *Manawatu* pass by on its expedition. Mutton-bird egging was a regular Melbourne holiday treat. In illustrated articles in *The Australasian* in 1897, Campbell wrote of '12 or 13 boats arriving with egging parties' over the Christmas period. He was an enthusiastic egger, visiting the rookeries equipped with a 'crook'—a melaleuca (tea-tree) stick with a hook—that he used to prod in the burrow and secure the prized egg:

> If the bird is at home it will rap the end of the crook with its bill: Then you commence to fence the bird and feel for its egg, till by practice you soon learn by a turn of the wrist to hook the egg and gently withdraw it to the surface. So on from hole to hole.[70]

Although most serious egg collectors were men, women also enjoyed egging with a crook.[71] The Brisbane congress in 1910 heard a full report on the Bass Strait trip from JA Leach, while AJ Campbell spoke on mutton birds and Dudley Le Souef on albatrosses. Le Souef also showed cine-matograph films of the expedition.[72]

The fascination with seabird rookeries on islands was inherited from Britain. The naval tradition of the British Empire built a particular interest in bird-migration, especially the birds that live at sea and migrate to remote places to breed. Seasonal migrations had been popularised by another White, parson-naturalist Gilbert White, whose book *The Natural History of Selborne* (1789) was a touchstone volume for birdos. For example, Margaret Wigan (1876–1970), one of the very few female ornithologists portrayed in Mathews' collection of 'portraits of 200 ornithologists', spoke at a BOC meeting in Melbourne in 1930 about her visit to Gilbert White's village, Selborne, in England.[73]

The early *Emu* also recorded serious collecting in remote parts of Australia, many items of which were destined for the skin and egg collections of the wealthy Mathews. His collections were the basis for his twentieth-century version of Gould's *Birds of Australia*. Mathews not only sponsored individual collectors through purchasing bird-skins, but financially underwrote government and museum expeditions. C Price Conigrave (1882–1961) led the 1911 Kimberley Exploring Expedition, making collections of flora and fauna for the Western Australian Museum and mapping the remote Pentecost River region from Cambridge Gulf to Napier Broome Bay. The important Aboriginal collectors who joined at Wyndham remained unnamed in official reports, in the tradition of the day. Conigrave's photographs of Aboriginal art in the region were published in contemporary newspapers. The opportunity to document Aboriginal knowledge of birds at this time was largely missed. However, Tom Carter, who had lived at Point Cloates (near present-day Ningaloo) from 1889 until 1902 while collecting for Lord Rothschild, recorded some of the Aboriginal names for birds in his field notes, 'as far as I can remember them'.[74]

Perhaps it was analysing the skins of Palaearctic shorebirds sent to him by collector JP Rogers in Derby that inspired Robert Hall to undertake one of the major ornithological international expeditions of the early twentieth century.[75] With a young companion, Ernie Trebilcock (1880–1976) from the Geelong Field Naturalists' Club, Hall set off north 'across Wallace's line' and travelled all the way to Siberia, right up into the Arctic tundra of Larix Island at the mouth of the Lena River, 72°N and '3,000 miles [4800 kilometres] from the nearest railway station'.[76] They used river barges and walked in to follow the migratory waders (now usually called shorebirds) to their breeding grounds in June–July 1903. It took them five months to get there and the same to get home (via England). 'The birds would be there [in Australia] before us,' Hall commented wryly. Because of the vagaries of Siberian shipping, he and Trebilcock had only two hours to collect at 72°N, but they still managed to gather twelve species in that time. Hall noted the overwhelming preponderance of shorebirds: 'here all were Limicoline, excepting a Lapland finch'.[77]

Hall and Trebilcock took this adventurous side-trip in order to collect specimens for the British Museum. Their limited finances made it inevitable that the collections would go to Britain rather than any impoverished Australian museum. The final 'Hall collection' was augmented in Korea because of an unexpected delay due to storms. There, local collectors and expatriate Australians brought them important specimens from the area.[78] But even so, the £230 they received for their collection barely covered their travel costs. Trebilcock wrote to his fiancée, Hessie Tymms: 'My expenses ... were just double what I expected. This was because I did not intend to go so far north. Travelling expenses in that part of the world are not what you would call cheap.'[79]

Travel was a diplomatic nightmare. Hall and Trebilcock spent five days hosted by the Chief of Police at Yakútsk, a port on the Lena River in Siberia. They were feared to be spies. Trebilcock, exhausted from sleeping out without tents in near-freezing conditions on a fruitless and mosquito-ridden trip in marshes near Yakútsk (he wrote it as 'Jarkutsk') (62°N), was rather grateful for the hospitality. Even the Russian black bread, 'which upset my stomach at first', appeared in a different light after four days without 'proper food'.[80] But it was with heavy hearts that they realised they needed to go another 1200 miles (1930 kilometres) further north to collect specimens of the birds they knew from Australia in the full breeding plumage that would make them valuable to the British Museum, home of all the important naming decisions for the fauna of the British Empire.

2

NIGHT PARROT

The night parrot (*Pezoporus occidentalis*) is arguably Australia's most elusive bird. Nocturnal, seasonally unpredictable, and a denizen of the remotest, most inaccessible desert country, it has always attracted birdos in search of a challenge. Its disappearance for most of the twentieth century gave it mythical significance. Some have called it the holy grail of birding. The Smithsonian Institution in the United States went further, hailing it in 2015 as 'the world's most mysterious bird'.[1] There was always a 'hopeful possibility' of sighting it, or of hearing its long mournful notes deep in the spinifex at dusk.

John McDouall Stuart (1815–66) was the first European to collect a night parrot, in 1845, somewhere north of Cooper Creek. But this bird did not become the 'type' specimen. The type, a bird shot by Kenneth Brown in 1854 on the Robert Austin surveying expedition to the interior of Western Australia, came from the remote Great Victoria Desert. The specimen was carefully preserved by William Ayshford Sanford (1818–1902), the Western Australian colonial secretary, who sent it on to John Gould in England for identification. In 1861 Gould described it as a new species, *Geopsittacus occidentalis* ('western ground parrot').[2] But it seems there was a mix-up there, too, as the description was not quite right, and the correction was made later. The type specimen (of the correct bird from the Austin expedition) finally came to rest in the collection of Gould's benefactor Lord Derby, now part of the collections of the National Museums Liverpool.[3]

Most of the specimens held in museums today were collected in the nineteenth century, including two birds, a male and a female, that were remarkably transported live to the London Zoo in 1867 and 1873. Neither survived long once they arrived there. Luckily Gould managed to see the 1867 bird alive and updated his description accordingly.[4] The London Zoo skins are now held in the British Museum collection.

Frederick William Andrews (1824?–84), who was employed as a taxidermist and collector for the South Australian Museum in the 1860s and 1870s, was responsible for collecting at least seventeen of the specimens of the bird, mostly from the Gawler Ranges in South Australia.[5] Natural history writer and ecologist Penny Olsen (1949–) has suggested that the director of the South Australian Museum pressed Andrews for as many skins as possible of this valuable bird as he could then swap them with international museums for other rarities, thus strongly biasing the world collections to South Australian birds.[6] Andrews was the unparalleled authority on the night parrot, finally publishing about it himself in 1883.[7] A year later he was dead, drowned in a waterhole near Mount Jagged, one of the few temperate parts of South Australia. An inquest found that he 'came to his death by falling into a waterhole while suffering the effects of sunstroke'.[8] Olsen comments that Andrews was nearly as mysterious as the bird he so famously collected—even his age at death, 'about 60',[9] was a guess, and he had no known family in the colony.

Night parrot sightings continued in the twentieth century, widely scattered across what Baldwin Spencer called 'Eyrean Australia' and ecologists today call the arid zone.[10] Ethel White was one of those who sought this elusive bird. She 'would sooner sight the tail of a night parakeet among the reeds, than have a tame ostrich eat out of her hand'.[11] She endured great hardships in outback South Australia, travelling on camels with her husband, Captain Samuel White, but like many outback enthusiasts since, they never saw a night parrot.

The birds were never common, and their behaviour is cryptic. Theories have abounded about whether their preferred habitats were spinifex (*Triodia* spp.) or the chenopod (saltbush) and samphire shrublands associated with gibber plains. Even in Andrews' day, sheep were overrunning their known territories in the Gawler Plains north of Adelaide, and by the early twentieth century pastoral degradation and droughts had changed their range irrevocably. In 1915 Archibald J Campbell described the bird as 'missing' (presumed 'exterminated'). His great regret was that 'Few skins remain of this remarkable species, while there is not an egg in any collection'.[12]

But such pronouncements became a challenge, and wave after wave of searching followed, with several sightings, and even a specimen collected and lost again in Western Australia by Martin A Bourgoin, a surveyor from the Public Works Department who was working inland on the Canning Stock Route and recorded his close encounters between 1920 and 1935. At Ned's Creek he sighted eight birds—two adults and six young, in the mouth of a cave—and described their call as 'a long-drawn-out mournful whistle'.[13]

Evening watches at waterholes are the favoured method for night parrot aficionados, although luck seems the only guide to confirmed sightings. Many a watch has been maintained on a bore, a dam or a pond—day and night—in the hope of a squeak, a 'fluttering' wing-beat, a squatting run close to the ground, or a slow two-note whistle. This overweight short-tailed budgie—or undersized kakapo, depending on your point of view—is the subject of many bizarre ornithological stories, the equivalent of fishing legends about 'the one that got away'.

The elusiveness of the night parrot inspired entrepreneur Dick Smith, the founder of *Australian Geographic* magazine, to offer $50,000 in 1989 for 'proof' that the bird still existed. Smith was not the first to offer financial incentives to find night parrots. In 1923 HL White commissioned the hardy Lawson Whitlock to undertake an expedition to chase up a report of a bird that was consistent with the description of a night parrot. 'I confess I hesitated somewhat,' Whitlock wrote, 'but I realised that, if Mr White was willing to risk the financial burden of the expedition, it was "up to me" to do my part."[14]

Whitlock had an unpleasant trip. He developed no affection for his camel, an ill-smelling beast that blew half-chewed cud at him and would not 'go straight forward even with his head pulled around at right angles to his body'.[15] To reach Henbury station, just over the border into the Northern Territory, the scene of the reported sightings, he travelled north for twelve-and-a-half days, covering the 480 kilometres from Oodnadatta. By the time he finally arrived, the station manager greeted him with the disappointing news that big bushfires had since swept through the country in question. Seeding dry spinifex is very flammable.

Undaunted, Whitlock struck out further north and travelled on for more than six months around Central Australia. His list of birds seen and collected is particularly valuable because he recorded their Arrernte names. These were mostly from the totem names recorded by the Hermannsburg missionary Carl Strehlow (1871–1922), but modified 'to comply with English pronunciation'. Whitlock heard the pronunciations himself as he was helped in his fieldwork by Arrernte people in Hermannsburg/ Ntaria. He travelled there following a report in July 1923 that 'some local children had fired the spinifex, flushing a parrot that dived into an isolated clump, from which they had caught and cooked it feathers and all'.[16] Whitlock went out and found bird prints in the sandy spinifex country near what he described as 'a small lair, not unlike the nest of the western ground parrot'.[17] He and his companions brushed away the prints. They returned the next day to find fresh footprints but, alas, no bird. Whitlock never found the fugitive night parrot but remained convinced it was still alive 'in small numbers', probably 'in country not stocked with cattle or horses'.[18]

All the historical specimens of this bird were from South Australia and Western Australia, yet sightings were reported from all mainland colonies until the late nineteenth century.[19] The next century of confirmed night parrot sightings did not take long to record, but there were just enough unauthenticated reports from all states of mainland Australia and the Northern Territory to hold out hope for the rare bird of the desert.

Sightings were reported in every decade of the second half of the twentieth century, yet the number of specimens in museums is vanishingly small.

Truth is, of course, stranger than fiction. Dal Stivens' 1970 novel *A Horse of Air*, about a fictitious search for the night parrot, the 'Craddock and Drake expedition' of 1967, explored the competitive rivalries that rare birds bring out in birdos. Amateur ornithologist Harry Craddock, the fifty-year-old son of a newspaper tycoon, teams up with a much younger professional zoologist, Tom Drake, in an extended quest that takes them all over Central Australia and tests the limits of their ability to cooperate with each other. 'Ornithologists can be as territory-minded as the creatures they study,' Joanna, Harry's estranged third wife, expostulates.[20] Luck rather than expertise seems to dictate who sights the bird. Harry's journal captures the friction when the 'expert' Tom gets to decide where to go next and ignores Harry's intuitions: 'He's a career ornithologist and I'm not—I'm a bloody amateur!'[21] Yet Harry is not 'just' an amateur: he is obsessed. He has converted the ballroom of the family mansion into a perfect habitat for a flock of Bourke's parrots, another rare outback species. He also lives with bipolar disorder. The novel itself is allegedly based on an autobiography Stevens had been required to write as 'therapy' for his own mental illness. It is hard to tell who is mad and who is sane out in the rugged Gibson Desert (named for the man who died on the expedition led by Ernest Giles in 1872). The quest ends with the pair finding the parrots but being unable to trap them because of a suspicious spinifex fire. Tom (the probable arsonist) mounts another expedition and brings in a dead specimen. Meanwhile Harry continues his search alone, wanting live birds to study, not just a specimen to show they are not extinct. Through misadventure he loses his car and wanders for eight days in the bush without water. He is rescued by what is, perhaps, the ghost of Gibson's horse—a 'horse of air'.

A bird of mystery is attractive to poets, novelists and twitchers alike, but a sighting without proof can pose a real problem for a professional ornithologist. The South Australian Museum's curator of birds, Shane Parker (1943–92), was confronted with exactly this situation on a tourist camel trip with Rex Ellis (1942–) in 1979. 'He was frozen on the rear

camel, one arm pointing, and his face looking whiter than his pith helmet,'
Ellis recorded. He ran back to Parker, who seemed 'in a temporary state
of shock'.

> When I asked him what the matter was, he replied in a shaking voice,
> 'I have just seen a night parrot!' Shane was normally a very articulate
> person, but he was having considerable difficulty in that department
> right now. As the walkers ran up to see what the excitement was
> about, I had mixed emotions. My initial one was of disbelief, because
> to find a night parrot had always seemed an unattainable dream ...
> [But] my disbelief was only momentary, for the sight of Shane's face
> and his incoherency could leave no doubt in anyone's mind that he
> had seen a night parrot.[22]

Ellis continued for many years to offer birdos camel-tours in search of
night parrots, using the 'professional authentication' of the Parker sighting
in his advertising.

The tallest and best stories about night parrots are often the 'maybes'.
In Alice Springs, the locals have become exhausted with talking to
hopeful tourist-birdos about night parrots. There are many other rare
treasures of their area, including another nocturnal parrot, Bourke's parrot
(*Neopsephotus bourkii*), and the delicately coloured and elegant princess
parrot (*Polytelis alexandrae*), which is also 'rare, highly nomadic: irregular'.[23]
There are no organised bird groups in this remote town, but enthusiastic
atlassing by both locals and visitors has meant the area has been well
surveyed. Locals resent newcomers who arrive and expect to find night
parrots that same evening.

Some locals have their own tales. Dick Kimber (1939–) is one of
Alice Springs' long-term residents, a schoolteacher, footballer and well-
known expert on Central Australian human and natural history. On 1 May
1980, he visited the then nearly inaccessible Kalipinypa claypan west of
Alice Springs with eight Pintupi men, guided by Johnny Warangkula
Tjupurrula (1925–2001), the senior traditional owner of the site. The
group had travelled for a full day west from Papunya, the nearest homeland

community, across spinifex-dominated sandhill country, when they reached a traditional well. Kimber described what happened the next morning:

> Although it had substantially collapsed over the decades since its last regular use, dingoes had kept it open at the base. This also allowed birds to obtain a drink. Early in the morning the oldest man present, Ray Tjampitjinpa, set fire to dense spinifex at the base of the nearby southern sandhill. This kind of firing is conventional, but in this instance, and to everyone's surprise, it flushed a parrot from the spinifex … [M]y immediate thought was: 'Night parrot!' Ever since my grandfather had given my brothers and me a copy of *What Bird is That?* as a Christmas present in 1948, I had dreamed of seeing this bird.
>
> The parrot flew up over the crest of the sandhill and, as its flight was low and it seemed to have landed, I hastily grabbed my camera from the vehicle, ran to the sandhill crest, then carefully approached the point at which the bird was likely to be. Yes, there it was, walking about in amongst the spinifex tussocks on the sandhill. In case it was about to fly away I took a photograph from thirty metres away, then found that it was the last 'shot' in my film …

Kimber replaced the film and explained to the Pintupi men that he thought it was a very unusual parrot. He asked that they remain quiet while he tried to photograph it. For the next hour he stalked the bird, 'creeping and crawling about'. At one stage one of the men said, 'Why don't you shoot it?' Kimber was appalled: 'Shoot the first night parrot definitely seen for ninety years? Shoot perhaps the last night parrot on earth? I did not need to think for long to reject this very practical solution to the problems I was having.'

While attempting to photograph the bird, Kimber also tried to observe it, recalling everything he knew about night parrots. The habitat was definitely suitable. It was early morning and overcast, and the bird's generally low flight and apparent preference to walk about on the ground were also 'right'.

But should the bird have landed in a tree? I recalled a discussion with Shane Parker … and he had said that there was no known record of them landing in trees. Furthermore, it gave every indication of being a young bird, and when it flew there appeared to be deep blue beneath the wings and the under-part of the tail. That didn't seem correct, but did the colours of a night parrot change over time? … The size? I could not recall the dimensions of a night parrot, but I had the feeling that it was a bit like an extended portly version of a budgerigar. The size of this parrot was probably a bit small, the shape was perhaps a little slender and the tail a little long.

Kimber went home and had the slides developed. They were not very good, but he chose the largest and clearest image of the bird, spent 'a small fortune' having a large print made, and sent it to the RAOU, which in turn sent it to the night parrot expert Shane Parker. Parker replied along the following lines: 'Your photograph is of a blue-winged parrot, *Neophema chrysostoma*. It is an immature bird, but if you consider it very closely you can see a fine blue line immediately above the beak. It must have been a vagrant, perhaps blown off course by storms.'

Kimber was 'crushed'. He recalled the suggestion 'Why don't you shoot it?' It did not seem to have been such a bad idea after all.[24] His sighting of the blue-winged parrot, far to the north-west of any other known sighting, was recorded by a lonely little circle on page 287 of the first edition of the *Atlas of Australian Birds*. But this is no comfort to Kimber. He still dreams of seeing a night parrot out bush.

Sightings of night parrots are so rare that they are doubly difficult to 'prove'. Many professionals would not even attempt a search. Consultant biologist Ian McAllan, a night parrot enthusiast who maintains a database of more than 100 reported sightings of the species, commented, 'I wouldn't go looking for it myself, because finding it would be pure luck.'[25]

In September 1987, however, the RAOU did attempt a search. The country around Lake Disappointment (now known as Kumpupintil Lake) in Western Australia, a mosaic of spinifex and samphire, had been recently inundated through three cyclones in succession. Its claypans had filled, generating a massive crop of spinifex seed. Stephen Davies (1935–2020) seized the opportunity. Led by a navigation control party from the Australian Survey Office, eight four-wheel-drive vehicles set out into the area. The party traversed the spinifex and samphire on foot in a long line abreast, holding a rope between walkers. They listened at dawn and dusk for any calling and went spotlighting at night. They searched for nests and analysed them for feathers. The *RAOU Newsletter*'s banner headline said it all: 'Princess—But No Night'.[26] 'We still have not made first base,' Davies summed up. 'We still do not know how to find the bird.'

Then, on 17 October 1990, Walter Boles and Wayne Longmore, curators of ornithology at the Australian Museum and the Queensland Museum respectively, were driving home from a six-week Australian Museum expedition to central and northern Australia. They stopped briefly just outside Boulia in north-central Queensland because the overseas visitors in the other vehicle had requested a break. 'It was stinking hot and we just wanted to go home. We didn't even want to get out of the car,' Boles recalled.[27] Imagine his amazement when he looked out the window and spotted a desiccated 'fat budgie' lying beside the road. It had apparently been hit by a truck, possibly some distance away, and carried to the spot. Even though its head was nearly falling off, Boles and Longmore immediately recognised it as a night parrot. They were well aware that Dick Smith's reward had not been claimed. Was this sufficient 'proof' that the night parrot still lived?

Smith honoured his promise. The Australian Museum (as sponsor of the expedition) received the $50,000, which it immediately promised to use for 'the study and conservation of the night parrot'.[28] The specimen, because of where it was found, was deposited with the Queensland Museum.

Despite the inevitable 'dead parrot' jokes, serious efforts to find the bird resumed. There were seven sightings in north-central Queensland over an eighteen-month period in 1992–93, and another concerted search in the Mount Isa uplands during June 1993. Although night parrots were not recorded, the plants and general habitat of the sites concerned were closely observed. Ecologists Stephen Garnett and Gabriel Crowley did record rare spinifex pigeons (*Geophaps plumifera*) and rufous-crowned emu-wrens (*Stipiturus ruficeps*) around the sites. They recommended night parrot conservation measures such as 'mosaic burning of the properties' even without photographs or specimens, as unburnt spinifex designed for night parrots would also help spinifex pigeons and rufous-crowned emu-wrens. Night parrots, for them, became a charismatic hook, a basis for good ecological practices.[29] A bird that is 'seldom seen', 'terrestrial, nocturnal and secretive' makes for interest, if not for detail, in designing threatened species management plans.[30]

A decade later, Birds Australia appealed for funds to buy Newhaven station in the Northern Territory. The appeal brochure featured a picture of night parrots and a note that in 1996 a pair had landed 3 metres from trained observers at Newhaven. The sighting had been kept secret until the station went on the market. The appeal attracted 4000 donations and the money was raised in just three months. Newhaven station, renamed Newhaven Wildlife Sanctuary, is now managed by the Australian Wildlife Conservancy. This was not the last conservation purchase for night parrots. In 2016, Bush Heritage Australia acquired Pullen Pullen, a property not too far from where Boles and Longmore had found the dead bird over two decades earlier.[31]

The new century has seen a wave of sightings, including another dead bird in 2007. 'Shorty', a western Queensland grader driver, found a decapitated bird that had flown into a fence; its head had been sliced off. ABC Science reporter Ann Jones tells how this story sent naturalist John Young looking again.[32] 'He thought it could be a juvenile, which would mean that there were other birds—its parents—still alive in the area,' she explains. 'He set out to search. An old-style yarn-spinning bushie, Mr Young knows how to build the incredulity of the situation into his narrative.' In 2013 he captured a photograph, which shook the bird world and inspired the Pullen Pullen purchase. By 2016 others had also observed the birds and recorded their voice in central Queensland, and even taken black-and-white film footage (taken at night). Then in 2017, on the other side of the country, a group of four birdwatchers from Broome photographed Australia's most mysterious bird in Martu Country in inland Western Australia, not far from the site of the RAOU search thirty years before.

Night parrots continue to represent the hopeful edge of the possible, something that some private donors are keen to support. The birds are classic 'boom and bust' species, like many of the inland's inhabitants. Penny Olsen argues that if 'the night parrot must capitalise on the good times and survive the bad … like the budgerigar *Melopsittacus undulatus*, zebra finch *Taeniopygia guttata*, letter-winged kite *Elanus scriptus* and black-tailed native-hen *Tribonyx ventralis*', then conservation plans to protect them have to be focused on times of 'explosive breeding'. And what happens 'when conditions are severe, as they are many more years than not'? Does the night parrot 'stay put and tough it out'? Perhaps, rather, it travels extraordinary distances, 'guided by some mysterious force, to where food plants are seeding?'[33]

The night parrot remains unpredictable and very, very vulnerable. Its habitat is still being cleared and destroyed, now more by mineral and gas exploration than pastoral expansion. Perhaps the biggest danger of all is in renewed hope itself. Conservation managers now have to contend with obsessive birdos, desperate to see this rare bird for their life list. Worse, these birdos might fancy themselves a latter-day Frederick Andrews and shoot a specimen to prove they saw it.

The night parrot Quest is a 'whitefella thing', writer and artist Kim Mahood notes. She observes that Martu people say 'it is not our place to find the bird'. And perhaps Mahood herself is forging a new way to follow the birds, as she explores the Martu Country of her childhood and writes of her 'wanderings with intent' in what is now 'night parrot' country.[34] More important than a 'bird in the hand' is protecting their habitat. As she wanders, seeking understanding, she is also caring for the elusive birds.

3

NATURE STUDY AND NAMES

Filling the idle hours

Nature study was part of the primary school curriculum in most states in the first decade after Federation.[1] It focused on the protection of plants, birds and other animals, and on developing basic skills of identification. Nature study was deemed to 'improve' the schoolchildren by gainfully filling what journalist, nature study enthusiast and ornithologist Alexander Hugh Chisholm (1890–1977) liked to call 'idle hours'. Indeed, the phrase so captured Chisholm's spirit that Russell McGregor titled his 2019 biography of Chisholm *Idling in Green Places*.[2]

Walter W Froggatt (1858–1937), a well-known Sydney-based writer and government entomologist, argued in 1906 that introducing nature study into schools should ensure that 'school children will take an intelligent interest in the many wonderful and beautiful things they come in daily contact with, and a bird will not be simply a thing to throw a stone at'. To 'learn one little fact about any common thing', he said, was to 'invest it with new interest' and thereby to 'open up new fields to thousands of bush children, and fill what might otherwise be dull hours with brightness'.[3] He urged naturalists to recruit country and metropolitan schoolmasters so that field naturalists' societies could become de facto 'training grounds for good teachers'. The clubs could also provide specialist support for classroom questions. Nature study, in short, gave a purpose to field naturalists' endeavours, and the expertise and energy of their clubs could breathe new life into the school curriculum, either directly or through the teaching staff.

One of the earliest and longest-lasting ventures into nature education and the reform of popular values was the Gould League. The first pledge of its members was 'I hereby promise that I will protect native birds and will not collect their eggs'.[4] It was established in 1909 by John Albert Leach (1870–1929), whom we have already met as the author of *An Australian Bird Book*, first published in 1911.[5] That book's inexpensive small format was only part of what made it so suitable for teachers of nature study. Leach's day job was Supervisor of Nature Study for the Victorian Education Department, and he was a qualified scientist, with a Master of Science in biology from the University of Melbourne at the time the first edition was published, and a Doctor of Science in 1912 for a thesis that included a major revision of the 'myology and classification of *Strepera* (currawongs)'. He was a teacher of teachers as much as a teacher of children, and his bird guide reflects this. As McGregor has commented, this was not a 'field guide' in the sense of the American guides made famous by Roger Tory Peterson (1908–96), but more in the British mould of a natural history book. The original guide was only partly about identifying birds, as McGregor observed:

> the book contained two adjacent but distinct texts. One text, usually placed at the top of each page, comprised descriptive notes to aid identification. The other, which ran as a cohesive passage of prose from the beginning of the book to its end and was usually placed in the lower half of each page, was a dissertation on the natural history of birds. Leach called it, aptly, 'A lecture'.[6]

The 'natural history exposition' created what we might call teachers' notes, to accompany the identification kit for young birdos. Leach edited *Emu* for over a decade from 1914 and was president of the RAOU in

1923 and 1924. He believed in the scientific training of teachers, and that this training should include background in broader natural history developments from the nineteenth century and earlier. His lengthy description of the biogeographical and evolutionary work of Alfred Russel Wallace (1823–1913), for example, was important to setting the scene for an 'Australian' bird book whose scope was birds that are found to the east of Wallace's line, most of which were first described in the nineteenth century. Leach's very practical guide was regularly revised and still in print in the 1970s. The final (ninth) edition appeared in 1958, long after his death in 1929. It still carried the lecture; the notes for teachers were what gave the volume enduring appeal.

The suggestion for an educational league focusing on birds came from another teacher, Jessie McMichael, who wrote that 'the thoughtless destruction of bird life would lead to an increase in numbers of insects, which would if left unchecked take a disastrous toll on crops of all kinds'.[7] Supporting farmers was very important in schools in 1909, with strong agricultural education (especially for boys) and, in some cases, practical horticultural skills developed through school gardens (see Chapter 12).

Bird Day

The AOU put forward the idea of a Bird Day as 'a corollary to Arbor Day', which was already well established in schools. The first Bird Day was held in Victoria on 29 October 1909, with the launch of the Gould League. Dr HW Bryant, an ornithologist and medical doctor, suggested the name 'The Gould League of Bird Lovers'.[8] Within a year the movement had caught the eye of teachers in New South Wales, South Australia and Tasmania.[9] Mr Walter Finigan, a nature study teacher in the New South Wales country town of Wellington, learned about the Gould League from McMichael and contacted his headmaster, Edward Webster (1866–1928). Webster knew of the work of the Junior Audubon Society in the United States and liked the idea of an Australian version honouring Gould. He enlisted the crucial support of Chief Inspector of Education James

Dawson. The Gould League of Bird Lovers in New South Wales started in October 1910 and built quickly to 10,000 members by 1917 and over 130,000 by the 1930s.[10] Western Australia, which later had one of the most active Gould League groups in the country, was the last to begin. A Western Australian league was first mooted in 1920, but it was not until 1939 that the idea was picked up by the director of education, Charles Hadley, and a Gould League of Bird Lovers of Western Australia was finally established.[11]

Back in Victoria, McMichael provided generous donations and an endowment for 'competitions and prizes'[12] and the prime minister, Alfred Deakin, consented to be the Gould League of Victoria's inaugural president. The enterprise was built on the idea of 'progressive conservation'—the moral improvement of people through caring for nature. The warm support of directors of education such as Dawson in New South Wales, Frank Tate (1864–1939) in Victoria and, later, Hadley in Western Australia was essential to making nature study part of the curriculum, and to celebrating initiatives like Bird Day in schools.

Tate was a strong supporter of all forms of nature study. He viewed the school as an 'efficient unit of organisation' and a way of reaching into nearly every household in the state. Birds and gardens created opportunities for schoolwork to be taken home.[13] The Victorian Education Department *Gazette* of Tate's era addressed itself not only to teachers and students, but also to families and school communities. In New South Wales, the *Public Instruction Gazette* had a similar purpose. Sydney Teachers' College lecturer AG Hamilton (1852–1941) advocated that 'School bird study should begin with the birds of the playground, and gradually extend to wider fields'. Bird-spotting became a training ground for scientific observation: 'Children should record the birds seen and their observations on them in their note-books, and in a wall chart, such as that published in the "Gazette" for June 1911 … The local name and, if possible, the scientific name of the birds should be recorded.'[14]

Tate's introduction to the 1911 edition of Leach's *Australian Bird Book* extolled the idea of familiarity with Australian nature. Birds should be part of mainstream culture and literature, he argued: 'It is time we Australians fought against the generally received opinion that the dominant note of our scenery is weird melancholy.'[15] He blamed awkward scientific names for the paucity of Australian birds in poetry, quoting a clumsy 'romantic' poem published in *The Argus* to make his point:

> Dear, all the secret's ours. The Sharp-tailed Stint
> Spied, but he will not tell—though you and I
> Paid Cupid's debts from Love's own golden mint,
> While yellow-bellied shrike-tits fluttered nigh.[16]

The Gould League became a way to bring honour to the nation through birds. Leach immediately changed the 'white-throated thickhead' to the golden whistler and the 'white-winged caterpillar eater' to the white-winged triller, but such name changes were not always welcome. Hamilton did not see a particular problem in the fact that there were thirty local names for the babbler or chatterer (*Pomatostomus temporalis*) around just Wellington. Although he advocated inventing names where no local name was known, he did not see why 'peewit, blue wren and jacky winter should be altered to magpie lark, superb warbler and brown fly-catcher' (the Victorian names for the same birds).[17] Hamilton focused on using birds to develop a sense of *local* place and pride among the children of a district, rather than a national consistency. The RAOU, whose first interest was the birds, not the children, was much more concerned about the need to communicate reliably between districts, and to develop a common bird vocabulary. Tensions arose most sharply where Leach and others advocated the national adoption of the dominant Victorian names.

From 1910, Queensland joined the other states in producing a special 'Bird Day' issue of the *School Paper* (the name of the magazine issued regularly to schools by the state governments), although it was 1916 before Queensland had a Gould League and associated Bird Day.[18] The journalist Alexander (Alec) Chisholm, then a journalist for Brisbane's *Daily Mail*, was an important leader in the Queensland Gould League. When he left the state in 1922, he received a charming letter signed by 106 students from Southport State School, which is preserved in his papers:

Dear Sir,

We the pupils of the Southport SS regret that you are leaving this State. Many of us, largely through your influence, have become members of the Gould League of Bird Lovers.

We wish to thank you for the many interesting articles and photographs which you have given us from time to time in the Queensland School Papers. Your writings have taught us much about birds, to love them more, and to understand more clearly how worthy they are of protection.[19]

The New South Wales Gould League, strongly endorsed by the active Ornithological Section of the Royal Zoological Society of New South Wales (RZSNSW), published *Gould League Notes* and sponsored a variety of field camps, exhibitions and bird-call competitions. At the end of each bird-call competition, the imitators would cooperate to produce a dawn chorus—'as each child seeks to out-whistle or out-call the other, the result is a terrific hullabaloo', Chisholm recorded.[20] The league also sponsored a badge for 'any boy or girl who can induce a native wild bird to alight on his or her person'. In four years an astonishing 500 children received the award.[21]

Not all Bird Day activities were good for the birds. Chisholm recalled an early Bird Day in central Victoria where the school party was walking through the bush with a teacher

'leading' in the fashion of a Zoo-visiting father—well in the rear— while the kiddies rambled along with an aimless noisy heartiness calculated to scare every undomesticated creature in the neighbour- hood. Presently one bright boy spied the nest of a yellow-tufted honeyeater. He yelled gleefully, made a hurried grab, and within the next minute was triumphantly presenting the dainty cradle, with its trio of hapless baby birds, to the accredited leader of the expedition.[22]

Chisholm commented that in later years there was a better distinction made between bird-nesting and bird-observing. Bird study became a favourite in schools. With the slingshot banned, wild birds were coming into schoolyards at lunchtime. 'I have seen wild birds catching flies from the hats of children and eating crumbs at their feet,' wrote the director of nature study in South Australia.[23] Chisholm's estimate in the early 1920s was that more than 200,000 children had joined 'nature leagues'; many more have joined since. Although nature study is no longer formally part of the primary curriculum, organisations such as the Hawthorn Junior Field Naturalists in Melbourne continue to offer young nature enthusiasts field excursions and other opportunities in partnership with its parent group, the Field Naturalists Club of Victoria.

'Improving' and ethics

The 'improvement' of young people through scientific training was a recognised part of the work of bird associations in the interwar years. Most birdos had become enthused as children. Intergenerational conversations in the field delighted older and younger people alike. Oliver Fuller, later a medical doctor, recalled that he joined the SAOA to be a proper 'birder', not just 'a boy who collected eggs'. In an era when the only field guide was *What Bird is That?*, his own field notes were exemplary. When he was sixteen, he prepared careful notes with good drawings, known information about species and informal notes on calls. Of the eastern shrike-tit (now known as the crested shrike-tit, *Falcunculus frontatus*) he wrote: 'Its call is knock-at-the-door.'[24] Fuller consciously educated himself with his ornithological diarising.

The details of what constituted 'improving' activities for children, for adults and for the nation were sometimes contested. Sometimes 'improvement' was used to justify the dubious activities of 'grown-up boys'. 'Lads and lasses would be much better men and women' if they spent their early life working as naturalists, South Australian businessman Edwin Ashby (1861–1941) declared in his 1927 presidential address to the RAOU. The training of 'a real ornithologist' made 'an all-round man':

He must be a collector; he must go through the drudgery of making
skins after a day of long toil in the bush ... The work of collecting,
as well as observing with the aid of a field-glass and photographing
birds in 'real life', develops qualities in the growing mind of youth as
well as in that of adults, that cannot otherwise be developed. Under
our present methods of issuing permits I have had on numberless
occasions to refuse to instruct young fellows in the art of skinning,
though they would have been keen to learn. My refusal has not been
because it would not be good for the lad to collect, and not because
his collecting would be harmful to the survival of any native bird, but
because our law-makers have never understood the *educational* value
of collecting. Our laws as framed do not effectually save our birds, but
they do effectually prevent the development of young ornithologists ...
[I]f we could effectively insist that every person who shot a native bird
should make a skin of it, we should probably have all the protection
that was needed ...[25]

The privilege of collecting must be reserved for those who are prepared
to undertake the improving drudgery of real science, Ashby suggested.
This fine distinction, neither practical nor legally enforceable, became
a real problem for an ornithological union with a mission to protect
birds. Chisholm counter-argued that Ashby's views were at odds with
RAOU policy and 'not in accord with the experience and opinions of most
members of the union'. There was no longer, in Chisholm's opinion, any
'justification for promiscuous collecting ... nor will any national purpose
be served by teaching boys to slaughter birds so that they may "go through
the drudgery of making skins" ... to be followed by stowing lifeless bodies
in a cabinet.'[26] Birds, in Chisholm's view, belonged not to collectors but
to 'the nation'. It was much more 'improving' to observe them alive, to
cultivate a 'mateship with birds', the title of one of his best-known books.
    Arthur Chenery (1869–1948) used his 1932 RAOU presidential
address to extol the 'improving' values of field ornithology. By focusing
on health (he was a medical doctor), he neatly sidestepped the awkward
question of collecting. Fieldwork, he said,

takes us of necessity into the open air. It will cultivate our powers of observation and our patience ... [W]e moderns [suffer] wear and tear on the nerves due to the strain imposed by our business or profession ... I wish to stress the benefits to the general health and well-being of those who wander in the open, sometimes for many miles, intent on probing a problem set them by the behaviour of our feathered friends.[27]

For the young, it offered 'a hobby apart from athletics ... the best of anti-dotes for demoralising idleness'. Chenery's fieldwork improved mental health, not cabinets of curiosity.

The question of local names

Collecting was most commonly justified by those keen to find birds unknown to science, to add their rarities to the list of 'Birds of Australia'. Being first was a competition between humans, not a relationship with a bird. Vernacular names, the 'pet names' of local observers, served a very different purpose. These were the names children were taught and new birdos most frequently chose to use. They were often cues to behaviour or colour. But in Australia many of them were borrowed from English names, so were not appropriate to Australian conditions. The challenge for the RAOU was to develop popular names that fitted into scientific systems and yet included the nostalgic favourites of the birdos' own journeys into birding.

Ornithological names reflect the rules of taxonomy, the science of classification; they also reflect history, for the rule of priority gives prefer-ence to the 'first' name given to a bird. Unfortunately, both taxonomy and history have the potential to be controversial, and questions of whether 'priority' or 'simplicity' should take priority had the potential to disunite the still-young union. The arcane rules alienated juniors and amateurs, as well as creating competitive anxieties among the 'serious' ornithologists. In fact, the classification of birds in Australia was peculiarly difficult as Europeans 'discovering' Australian birds in Australia were required to fit them into an already near-complete system designed for the natural history of the Northern Hemisphere.

The 'type specimens' on which the species-naming depended had to be compared and contrasted with other 'types'. For most Australian fieldworkers, type specimens were too far away to inspect; for the leading taxonomists of Empire, the living birds of Australia, and their distinguishing habitats and behavioural and physiological features, were also impossibly far away. The study of the biology of variation, based on observing living specimens or taking blood or tissue samples from live birds, was not available to the RAOU in the 1920s as they sought to review and determine the scientific and vernacular bird names for the Australasian region. Was it the nest of a ground thrush or a mountain thrush on the table at that first dinner? There was some awkwardness in the report in the first *Emu*, which gave two names for the one bird.[28]

One of the problems immediately confronting the national organisation was the lack of an agreed 'checklist'. Bird names have generated more dialect distinctions between Australian states than almost any other group of words in English. Mostly, foreigners marvel at the uniformity of Australian accents from Perth to Sydney and from Darwin to Hobart. But if you want to find out a birdo's state of origin, ask them what they call the *Grallina cyanoleuca*. The official vernacular name is the magpie lark, but in New South Wales it is still often a peewee, in Victoria a mudlark and in South Australia a Murray magpie. The galah (*Cacatua roseicapilla*) is a galah in the east but a 'pink-and-grey' in the west. There was no national 'convention' or regularity of vernacular names to help the RAOU with its national list, nor for the schoolteachers enthusing their pupils about birds in the grounds of schools.

Vincent Legge, author of *Birds of Ceylon* (1880), who later became the union's first president, attempted a national list of vernacular names in Australia in the 1890s. He felt the lack of a 'list of suitable and applicable English names' for the 'collectors, field naturalists, sportsmen and others taking an interest in the birds of this continent'. At the Hobart meeting of the Australasian Association for the Advancement of Science (AAAS) in 1892, he argued that 'The best popular names are applied in an old and well-worked region, like England, for example, as a result of the custom of generations ... The names are ... good; for they are based on habits and well-known and recognised characteristics.'[29] Although John Gould had done 'a marvellous amount of work in a short period' in bestowing vernacular names, he 'did not evidently trouble himself about English names that would be suitable to the coming Australian naturalist or sportsman'.[30] The AAAS could see the value of a common list, particularly for protecting native birds, but Legge felt too far away in Tasmania to take on this task alone. A series of committees developed a list, with varying support from the different colonies. The final list was edited by Legge and AJ Campbell and presented at the Sydney AAAS meeting in 1898.[31] The 'Yellow Book', as it was called, immediately sparked controversy in South Australia, where the new SAOA set out to develop a better checklist:

> This Society is of the opinion that the classification and list of vernacular names for Australian birds as presented to the A. A. for A. Science and adopted at the Sydney congress in 1898 is most confusing, and likely to lead to many blunders being made in ornithology and oology, and therefore not such as to lead to the advancement of science.[32]

AHC Zietz, a curator at the South Australian Museum, read letters from various ornithologists in New South Wales and Victoria 'upholding the decision of the SAOA in discarding the "Yellow Book"'. AJ North from the Australian Museum was, unsurprisingly, among the objectors. He took the opportunity to ask SAOA members 'to communicate any knowledge of our native birds to him to be recorded in his work on ornithology'.[33] Campbell defended his work on the AAAS list, citing its 'nearness to Gould's names'. He then diplomatically offered to 'entertain members of the SAOA with a lecture on birds with lantern slides' at the next SAOA meeting. As 'Mr Campbell tried to reconcile members to the "Yellow Book"', local members pushed back, suggesting various alterations to its vernacular names.[34] Campbell agreed to some of these, but not all. Rather, he proposed that a national body—an 'Australian Ornithological Union'—take up the challenge to develop 'an up-to-date list of Australian birds for general use in Australia'.

In 1903, the first national checklist committee was formed, convened by Robert Hall with representatives from each of the states except Queensland: the members were Archibald J Campbell (Victoria), Alfred North (New South Wales), Vincent Legge (Tasmania), Alex Milligan (Western Australia) and John Mellor (South Australia).[35] The combination of Campbell and North on the committee proved fatal. North never publicly contradicted Campbell; rather, he studiously ignored him and any committee that included him. North's *Nests and Eggs of Australian Birds Found Breeding in Australia and Tasmania*, published between 1901 and 1914, was 'world-class', except for the fact that it systematically omitted any species described by Campbell and his associates.[36] The committee had long-running battles about states' rights to their own vernacular names, and Hall and others lost faith in it. Meanwhile, Archibald G Campbell (Campbell junior) prepared a sixty-page *Dichotomous Key to Australian Birds* in 1905, based on Lamarck's system of selecting two contrasting characteristics, a bit like a modern flow chart. He acknowledged earlier work and the British Museum's *Catalogue of Birds*, but because his *Key* was independent of the checklist committee, it raised little reaction from *Emu*'s readership.

In Gould's footsteps

Gregory Macalister Mathews moved to England from Australia in 1902 with his new wife, Marion Cecil (formerly Wynne, née White), a cousin of HL White. Marion was more than ten years older than Gregory and travelled to England to educate the two children from her first marriage, a practice common among rich Australians at the time. Matthews grew up on the land in New South Wales and moved to Queensland to manage a cattle station about 130 kilometres from Charters Towers, where his father had 'obtained an interest for me'. He and his wife were independently wealthy. He found himself in London, based near the British Museum, with no need to earn a living and little interest in debutante balls and the London 'season', and turned to his passion for Australian ornithology, deciding to become a latter-day Gould of sorts.

Mathews wanted to start by commissioning a set of coloured plates of the birds of Australia. Richard Bowdler Sharpe (1847–1909), the British Museum's curator of ornithology, was worried that Mathews was just a rich dilettante and suggested he draft a 'down to date' list of Australian birds, 'there being no such guide in existence'[37] (Sharpe thereby completely dismissed the Yellow Book). Before Mathews rushed out to employ the distinguished artist JG Keulemans (1842–1912), known for his regular and beautiful plates published in *Ibis*, Sharpe wanted to test his persistence.

Mathews took up the challenge, and Sharpe respected this. Mathews' *Handlist of Birds of Australasia* (with an introductory letter by Sharpe) appeared in 1908 as a supplement to *Emu*. It was conservative and dealt exclusively with scientific names, thus avoiding the interstate rivalries and acrimony sparked by vernacular names back home. Mathews listed the birds of Australia alone, 'Australasia' for him meaning the mainland plus Tasmania, rather than the region including New Zealand.[38] His *Handlist* was drawn up 'to invoke the criticism and co-operation of ornithologists, in order to enhance the value of my larger undertaking', he wrote in the preface.[39]

Mathews continued his ongoing work on bird specimens in the British Museum (Natural History) and the Australian bird collections of the Hon. Walter Rothschild at Tring. Rothschild's collections were managed by his German-trained curator, Dr Ernst Hartert (1859–1933), who was seventeen years Mathews' senior. Mathews' next task was to build his own collections to support his bigger project; he began in South Australia with Captain SA White, who was recommended to him as a collector through the SAOA's founding president, Alexander Matheson 'Mat' Morgan (1867–1934), who travelled to England in 1908.[40] Although Mathews was added to the RAOU's checklist committee in name, he was far away and did not get on particularly well with Campbell senior, so his work progressed largely independent of the national list. He bought specimens from London dealers and sent collectors (including Captain White) into ornithologically unknown districts of Australia to develop his collection. He also puchased any published works that had reference to the taxonomy or nomenclature of Australian birds, resulting in a world-class collection of 5000 books that he ultimately donated to the National Library of Australia in Canberra.[41]

Mathews' major oeuvre, *The Birds of Australia*, was published in London between 1910 and 1927 by HF Witherby (1873–1943) in twelve volumes with five supplements, totalling some 7000 pages (including 600 coloured plates). The work demanded enormous resources, including the inspection of over 100,000 bird-skins. Mathews' passion became an obsession, but even he struggled to keep up with his task. From 1911 until 1923, he employed Tom Iredale (1880–1972) as his 'secretary'. The well-travelled Iredale went on to be curator of conchology at the Australian Museum from 1924 to 1944, and an honorary associate until his death. Iredale, who had spent much of the previous decade collecting not only birds but also marine animals in New Zealand and Australia, in fact wrote much of the text credited to Mathews.

In his historical review of Australian ornithology, John Calaby described Gregory M Mathews as 'the most important figure in Australian systematic ornithology' in the twentieth century: 'He introduced more scientific names, mostly of new subspecies, to the literature than any other person at any time.'[42] Introducing more names, however, was not necessarily helpful to Australian birdos. Dom Serventy remarked wryly: 'the confusion resulting from the creation of many worthless sub-species by Mathews led to a marked disinterest in taxonomical research within Australia for many years'.[43] Indeed, even with the reinvigoration of taxonomy by DNA and other technologies since the 1980s, the task of sorting out the 'Mathews mess' continues.[44] Mathews' work did demand trinomials (three-part names that recognised geographic variation), which forced Australian ornithology into systems used by the rest of the world—something that might otherwise have taken even longer. He was a prolific checklist writer. In addition to his 1908 *Handlist*, his *Birds of Australia* work led to six more checklists, published in 1912, 1913, 1920–24, 1927, 1931 and 1946.[45]

Mathews' collection eventually amounted to more than 40,000 skins,[46] but he ran into financial difficulties and had to sell them to Lord Rothschild in the late 1920s. Parting with them was a wrench, but the bitterest blow came in 1931 when Rothschild, himself under financial pressure, sold the whole Mathews collection along with his own to the American Museum of Natural History in New York. Not even the Australian Government could afford to buy such a bird-skin collection, especially after the financial crash of 1929. Mathews was not the only one upset: Rothschild's recently retired curator, Hartert, who was living in Berlin, 'broke down and wept when he received the letter' telling of the sale.[47] Only the Mathews book collection made it back to Australia, and that was because it was a donation.

While international scientific decisions about species were often pedantic, vernacular names accepted by national lists were just as competitive, stimulating a different sort of passionate discussion. Democracy and literary euphony could weigh into these disputes. Alec Chisholm had very strong views on literary sensibility and 'elegance'. He was committed to engaging and enthusing young bird observers. In 1921 he wrote about *Atrichornis rufescens jacksoni* and *Pachycephala olivacea macphersonianus*, calling them 'mystery birds of the jungle'. Behind 'these technical names are two of the most winsome creatures in Australia', the rufous scrub-bird and the olive whistler, 'birds possessing voices to put their unmusical titles to scorn'.[48] Leach agreed that many vernacular names were 'vulgar, discordant, and unsuitable', especially for use in schools.[49] Chisholm chaired the RAOU Vernacular Names Committee for nearly half a century and enthused people about birds all his life. The RAOU was a scientific organisation, but its outreach to children and to bird enthusiasts who were not interested in the finer points of names was always at the forefront of his mind.

An *RAOU Checklist* was finally agreed in 1926. After many drafts and disputes, it became an anchor point. The numbering system it adopted remained in use for decades, because it was practical and soon familiar (although there were ongoing tweaks to the checklist's contents). It was important, in the end, to stop arguing and just enjoy birds again after a quarter-century of squabbling about names. The distinguished Sydney ornithologist Keith Hindwood (1904–71) used the 1926 checklist order to arrange his filing cabinet. He had one folder for every bird numbered, and into these he placed correspondence about rare sightings, discussions about synonymy, fragments of letters and newspaper cuttings, mostly about the birds around the Sydney region. The system was so logical that when Hindwood died suddenly in 1971, Ern Hoskin (1914–2009), his great friend and bird artist, continued to maintain the files at his own home for a further three decades and used them to update Hindwood's *Birds of Sydney* in 1989. The collection of bird files and cards eventually went to the Mitchell Library with the rest of the Hindwood papers; they are still useful as historical references because of the logic of the 1926 *Checklist*.[50]

The checklist committee continued to revise and refine the '1926' list until 1968. At this point, the president, Dr Alan Lendon (1903–73), and the chair of the committee, Herbert Condon (1912–78), arranged for the South Australian State Library to publish a facsimile reprint of the 1926 list including all the amendments and updates agreed since. Debates about taxonomy and systematics shifted under the new ornithology of the 1970s, and structural changes to the list began in 1975, with Condon's *Checklist of the Birds of Australia (Part 1: Non-passerines)* and Richard Schodde's *Interim List of the Australian Songbirds*, published by the RAOU the same year.

Birdos working in the field needed easy-to-use guides to what they were seeing. Leach's *Australian Bird Book* (1911) and Neville Cayley's illustrated *What Bird is That? A Guide to the Birds of Australia* (first edition 1931) were the preferred choices throughout the life of the 1926 *Checklist*.[51] The 1970s brought new checklists and, alongside these, very different practical field guides, beginning with those written and illustrated by naturalist, artist and photographer Peter Slater (1932–2020). The first 'Slater' appeared in 1970, and it was updated several times in the 1980s.[52]

CAMPOUTS AND CAMERAS

Norman Wettenhall (1915–2000) and his wife, Joan (1925–2019), were serious amateur birdos of the generation when campouts, fieldwork, family holidays and science all worked together. When I interviewed Norman in 1998 about the key moments in a century of ornithology, the '1935 Marlo incident' was the first story he told me. It still rankled and divided birdos decades later.

The Marlo incident

George Mack (1899–1963) was a regular RAOU member who was also a regular speaker for the BOC, but he identified as a scientist, not a 'birdo'. He was an authorised collector for the National Museum of Victoria and brought his gun, along with his museum permits to shoot, to the 1935 RAOU campout at Marlo, near the Gippsland Lakes. The museum records that after the campout Mack deposited twenty-six specimens from Marlo—nineteen species, none of them rare.[1] The species are documented in the museum's register. Significantly, there was no scarlet robin in Mack's 1935 Marlo collection, yet a scarlet robin was at the heart of one of the biggest rifts in a century of birding.

The RAOU faithfuls—as usual, a 'delegation' from each state and a larger local group—met up at a campground at Marlo, chosen for its varied bird habitats. Near the end of the camping area, a nesting scarlet robin delighted them all. Everybody enjoyed the proximity of this pretty little bird attending its nest, unafraid, feeding its young. Then, one morning at breakfast-time, Mack went over and shot the bird in front of everybody.

The whole New South Wales contingent was horrified by the incident. All ten delegates, led by journalist and nature writer Michael Sharland (1899–1987), immediately left the camp in disgust.[2] Although this mass exodus was not recorded in the RAOU report of the camp, accounts of the incident appeared in the *Sydney Morning Herald*, *The Argus*, the Sydney *Sun* and the Melbourne *Herald*, a testament to Sharland's independent publishing connections.[3] The first-class row that followed resulted in the Victorian Fisheries and Game Department raiding and seizing a number of private collections, to the great embarrassment of the RAOU.[4]

The scarlet robin is not a rare bird, and the museum was not short of specimens of it. George Mack was testing the 'professionalism' of the RAOU. Why was there no scarlet robin in the museum's register of bird-skins collected at Marlo? Perhaps the bird was destroyed by the shot, as frequently happened with small, delicate birds. A bird collected in vain, 'a wasted bird', would have aggravated the outrage. Or perhaps the museum was distancing itself from the politics of the action. It certainly did not wish to be officially associated with its impetuous collector. The director of the museum, Daniel James Mahony (1878–1944), was present at the campout. He would have feared that all museum collecting permits might be cancelled by this foolish action. At a time when scientific funding was very tight, exchanges were often the only way museum collections could be expanded, and there is a possibility that this specimen was sent in an exchange to Europe or North America without being registered.[5]

The atmosphere at the 1935 congress, held in Melbourne straight after the Marlo campout, was electric. A whole afternoon was devoted to a resolution to ban collecting at campouts, including a motion that 'any member disregarding the rule be not permitted to remain in camp'. Mack, predictably, spoke against the motion, pointing out that he had a permit and pleading historical precedent, but his wilful flouting of the spirit of his permit pushed the RAOU to take a hard line. Finally it decided that 'no collection be permitted at Camps-out except in case of supposedly new birds or eggs and then only with the approval of a committee of camp members'.[6] Alec Chisholm and Neville Cayley moved that the RAOU Council formally review collecting practices.[7] Chisholm, another prickly character, felt Mack's slight personally. Chisholm's charming photograph of two young boys admiring a robin's nest, captioned 'Mateship with Mother Robin', in his 1922 book promoting the work of the Gould League, seemed to be directly in the sights of Mack's gun.[8]

Chisholm chaired the RAOU committee 'Appointed to Consider Collecting'; its other members were Charles Bryant and two well-known egg collectors—lawyer John Alexander Ross (1868–1957) and Frank Ernest Howe (1878–1955), a tailor and specialist in Mallee birds and their eggs. The committee reported back in 1936 that it was prepared 'to allow that a certain amount of collecting is necessary' and that it supported the government policy of 'allowing collections which have been built up legally (under permit) to be continued'. But it was sharply divided on the subject of 'new' collections. 'Nearly one hundred years after the time of John Gould, the day of the individual collector has passed', the report records. The two private collectors on the committee were unconvinced. Ross 'reserved judgement' on the resolution. The only strong conclusion reached was that members who collected without a permit should be expelled.

The embarrassment about collecting continued, and campouts and fieldwork were largely suspended until the late 1940s, at least partly because of the war. The RAOU Council was very afraid of alienating members at this time, as 'membership of the union has fallen away considerably in recent years' and 'special efforts' were needed to enrol new members.[9] There is no evidence that anyone was ever actually expelled for collecting, but the recommendation that 'all collections shall ultimately be donated to the public' ensured that collectors could not (legally) sell their collections, especially to the lucrative American market.[10]

Field guides as life guides

Before World War II there were just six universities in Australia, one in each state. Anyone who wanted to undertake doctoral studies had to go abroad. Most, like Dom Serventy in the early 1930s, went to Britain and studied at Cambridge or Oxford because the scholarships there were generous and that was where their professors had studied.[11]

By the 1960s Australia had more than doubled its number of universities. It became more common to undertake postgraduate studies (including PhDs) in Australia, and to work on Australian subjects.[12] One of the pioneering professors in Australian zoology was Jock (AJ) Marshall (1911–67), appointed in 1960 to the foundation Chair of Biology at the new Monash University. He had taken two doctorates from Oxford himself (DPhil, 1949; DSc, 1956), but had returned home passionately committed to 'all things Australian'. As a mature senior zoologist, he was most concerned about habitat loss and the extinctions of Australian birds and mammals. He wrote the popular and impatient book *The Great Extermination: A Guide to Anglo-Australian Cupidity, Wickedness and Waste* in 1966, when he knew he was dying of cancer. But his backstory begins with a local field guide.

Marshall was an amateur who deliberately and self-consciously 'went professional' in later life. He had left school without matriculating, partly because of a shooting accident that cost him his left arm, but mainly because he was not very interested in study. One schoolmaster described him as 'totally undisciplined, though gifted at English'[13] (Marshall wrote all his life, and his talent with words stood his later work in good stead). His mother was worried about her fifteen-year-old who was cut adrift from school, had only one arm, and seemed to have no particular aspirations. The one thing that Marshall was positive about was birdwatching and spending time in the bush. His mother contacted Sydney birdo, writer and illustrator Neville Cayley (1886–1950; later author of *What Bird is That?*) and Cayley showed her letter to Alec Chisholm, then editor of the Sydney *Daily Telegraph*. Chisholm introduced the young Marshall to contacts at the Australian Museum and the Ornithological Section of the RZSNSW, and also offered him introductions to the world of journalism, which came to fund his love of birds.

Marshall joined the RZSNSW in 1929 and was soon visiting the 'bird cabin' in the National Park (later Royal National Park) with Chisholm and other ornithologists. During the economic crisis of 1929–30 he began collecting birds for the museum in an honorary capacity. He had to live on a shoestring. He travelled free for thousands of kilometres in Queensland by 'jumping the rattlers'—riding the freight trains—along with many others who were out of work and penniless. This was a dangerous and illegal way to travel. You had to jump on the train on its 'blind' side just as it was pulling out of a station, and hang on while clambering into a freight truck—no mean feat for someone with two arms, but for a one-armed man it must have taken exceptional balance and determination. Determination was not a problem for Jock Marshall: anything a two-armed man could do, he could do better. He even trained himself to use a gun and to skin birds with five fingers, pins, his knees and anything else at hand.

Marshall's collecting was well received by the museum, and he was made an honorary fellow in 1934. In the same year, he was given an unexpected opportunity to participate in an Oxford University expedition to Espiritu Santo in the New Hebrides (now Vanuatu) with John Baker (1900–84) and Tom Harrisson (1911–76).[14] Professor WJ Dakin (1883–1950) at the University of Sydney had been asked to suggest a third-year Zoology student for the Oxford expedition. When the student he first nominated declined to go, Dakin nominated Marshall, confident that he would cope well with the rough conditions in the bush. Marshall mainly worked with the feisty Harrisson, who had an infectious interest in the breeding cycles of birds. Much of Marshall's most important subsequent work in physiology and ornithology built on his early collecting of birds' sex organs in Espiritu Santo. Baker later supervised Marshall's DPhil, which was based on the cytology of the testes of fulmars gathered in the opposite end of the world in 1948, at the remote and desolate island of Jan Mayen (71°N).[15]

Marshall loved exploration and tolerated hardships cheerfully. He and Harrisson soon planned another Oxford ornithological expedition, this time to Dutch New Guinea (now West Papua) in 1936. It was on this trip that Marshall discovered the connections between his writing and his scientific ambitions: '[N]o scientist could ever spend a dull day in the hot belt. In my own case, even after the most strenuous soaking day, a biological conscience never let me escape from the evening ritual of writing up my diary.'[16]

Marshall's field diaries placed him in the Humboldtian tradition of travelling scientists. He was fascinated by Charles Darwin, whom he saw as a hero and role model. He wrote a book, *Darwin and Huxley in Australia*, that was published posthumously in 1970. Yet at this stage, while he was definitely an explorer, he was less clearly a scientist. His only professional qualifications were diplomas in tropical medicine and hygiene, although he had also undertaken Zoology 1 at Sydney University as a non-degree student. Marshall finally enrolled at Sydney, where he funded his 'mature-age' Bachelor of Science by tutoring, journalism and other writing. He worked more than full-time all the time he studied.

Then the war broke out in the Pacific. Marshall immediately volunteered, offering his knowledge of New Guinea to the cause. After much discussion about whether a one-armed man was fit for combat, the army posted him to a fighting unit. In the Wewak campaign, early in 1945, Marshall captained the 'Jockforce' patrol, an AIF contingent who found their way through remote parts of the west of the country where there were no maps.[17] Ornithology, with a little help from his discerning mother and her friends, turned this particular boy with a disability and no sense of his future into a senior scientist and a war hero.

Campouts and fieldwork

Most expeditions were not as rugged and logistically challenging as Harrisson and Marshall's New Guinea ventures, but the adventure of being in the bush was important to amateur birdos of all ages. Regular 'campouts' associated with rotating annual meetings were key opportunities for the RAOU in interstate collaboration and visiting new bird haunts, building a national sense of ornithology—a science that until the twentieth century had been very much centred on the colonial museums. A trip to Western Australia in 1920 was a major venture for those who travelled from afar, and the national organisation's visit also suggested new institutions for the west. John Leach from Victoria commented, 'There is no reason why a "Bird Day" should not be as necessary here as it is in the Eastern states.'[18]

The RAOU met again in Perth in 1927 and arranged a campout at Nornalup in the south-west corner of the state, in country with 'big timber (including the giant karri and tingle-tingle), swamps, plains and the many miles of inland waterways' that are the 'haunt of many rare and vanishing species of the Australian avifauna'.[19] The campout attracted eleven visitors from interstate, including RAOU president Edwin Ashby, who was excited by the 'absolutely virgin' site where 'settlement has not penetrated'.[20] In this case, the behaviour of nationally accredited ornithologists became an embarrassment to local birdos. Serventy, who organised the Nornalup campout, remarked many years later on the 'orgy of egg collecting' at campouts, which were timed to coincide with the spring breeding season each year: 'In the evening one heard continuous gurgling noises while eggs of waterfowl were being blown. Every now and then an oologist would stagger out of a tent to discard a bucketful of yolk and water.'[21] The last of the big collecting campouts was at Moree in 1933, when Queenslander Frederic Louis Berney (1865–1949), another important egg collector, was president of the RAOU.

Changing sensibilities about conservation and the sheer cost of such expeditions, particularly in the 1930s Depression, shifted the nature of campouts to a focus on fun for all, whatever their means. Local day or weekend trips, often arranged by regional field naturalist groups or bird observers' clubs, became much more important. These were inclusive of enthusiastic young birdos, who sometimes attended with their families. Being with birds in the field was the key to enthusing new ornithologists and creating a sense of community and focused early conservation initiatives. The Melbourne Bird Observers' Club, for example, campaigned for a bird and animal sanctuary in Monbulk State Forest, where members met regularly for day excursions, bird-observing and photography.[22]

Nature reserves and sanctuaries

While nature could 'improve' a young birdo, older birdos often found themselves opposing the 'improvement' of nature. Soldier settlement and other schemes for expanding agriculture and pastoralism demanded 'improvements', particularly clearing the beloved habitats of bush birds. Ornithologists and field naturalists tried hard, but it was difficult to get a hearing for nature reserves and bird sanctuaries in the interwar years, overshadowed by the financial crash of 1929. The global impetus was to 'feed the world', a phrase promoted by the (British) Empire Marketing Board that persisted throughout the 1940s and into the expansive postwar years of the 1950s (and still has echoes in terms such as 'global food security').

Throughout the twentieth century, the RAOU was active on broader conservation issues. Habitat protection was a more unifying task than the direct protection of birds, which put the shooters at odds with the non-shooters. Habitat protection also encouraged partnerships with field naturalists' clubs and other like-minded bodies and enabled the national organisation to contribute to local and regional initiatives, where conservation projects were often most effective.

The (Royal) National Park, just 36 kilometres from the centre of Sydney, was described as a 'green lung', a defence against the miasmas of the city.[23] Once the railway arrived in 1886, Waterfall became a favourite destination for birdos; as we have already seen, this was the place where the young Jock Marshall first developed his bird networks. In South Australia, Belair National Park was established in 1894 and served a similar purpose for Adelaide's birdos.[24] Victorians had Sherbrooke Forest near Monbulk, not far from a city trainline; it became a mecca for the BOC in the 1930s. Victoria also had earlier reserved two important large tracts of land remote from Melbourne: Wilsons Promontory in 1908 and Wyperfeld (the latter renowned for malleefowl) in 1909.[25]

Queensland's earliest bird preservation movement focused largely on island sanctuaries.[26] The distinctive avifauna of the remarkable high country around Green Mountains in Queensland also attracted birdos, who stayed at O'Reilly's family guesthouse from which they explored Lamington National Park, declared in 1915.[27] Lamington National Park became the centre of the pioneering National Parks Association of Queensland, formed in April 1930. Engineer and timber merchant Romeo Lahey (1887–1968), an outspoken campaigner for national parks, established Binna Burra in 1932 in partnership with Arthur Groom (1904–53), a well-known nature writer and conservationist. Binna Burra is the other great lodge in the Lamington area; much of it survived in its original form until the Black Summer fires of 2019–20.[28]

Other states developed national parks and conservation organisations later than this, but in the mid-1930s the task of conservation, particularly protecting birds and their habitats, was often led, nationally and locally, by bird clubs.

Conservation and ornithology

The Gould League had a mission to re-educate children about egg collecting, to make them understand that their hobby was a threat to birds. By the end of the 1930s *Emu* reported 'visible results': the public was 'definitely becoming "nature minded"', and 'egg collecting by children [had been] reduced to a minimum'.[29] Much of the leadership in this work came from the BOC, which was established in 1905 'to study bird life in the field'. It was disbanded during World War I. When it was revived in 1927, it distanced itself from the RAOU and took a firm position against egg collectors—yet it continued to tolerate 'sporting shooters'. The BOC and RAOU worked together with sporting shooters to introduce 'close seasons', to protect breeding birds. They also lobbied for gun licence fees that would help support conservation measures and stronger game protection laws for 'game birds'. The BOC focused its efforts on Victoria, launching a 'Save Woolamai' campaign to revoke grazing leases held over their beloved mutton-bird rookeries at Phillip Island.[30] But there were crucial differences in the spirit of the two big birding organisations. These came to a head in 1935.

Charles Bryant (1902–60) and his wife, Dulcie, were enthusiastic supporters of both the BOC and the RAOU, and they loved campouts and field excursions. Charles' day job was as a Melbourne city lawyer, but he defined himself by his passion for birds. He was a nature writer under various *noms de plume*, including Wanderer, Vagans and Halcyon. He was also a serious taxonomist and edited *Emu* for over thirty years, from 1929 until his death. Bryant was typical of the serious amateurs of the RAOU, as Norman Wettenhall was later, who were passionate about observing birds in the field, like the BOC people. He was president of the RAOU in 1955–57; Wettenhall served in the same role a generation later, in 1978–83.

Charles and Dulcie were friendly with all. Norman Wettenhall recalled the welcome they gave him and Joan when they had 'thrown in their lot' with the Bryants and other (unknown) ornithologists and joined the RAOU for the 1953 campout at the exotic Lake Barrine in Queensland: 'Lake Barrine was absolutely wonderful. It was pristine. There was nothing there but an old house. The birds used to come and eat from the breakfast table with you. You could walk round the periphery and you might bump into a cassowary.' Wettenhall credited this camp for getting him 'hooked' on birds. At the Bryants' invitation, he and Joan joined a small contingent at the end of the formal campout and went on to Dunk Island. They both described it as their best holiday ever, far from the stresses of Norman's specialist medical practice and their young children at home in Melbourne.[31]

Norman Wettenhall began with campouts, but increasingly his birding was limited by other pressures and he became an armchair traveller through the literature of Australian birds. His library supported major philanthropy, bird conservation, bird science and, in the late twentieth century, the *Handbook of Australian Birds* project (see Chapter 9). His collecting impulse was not defined by bird-skins or eggs or even photographs, but by historical bird-literature that sustained him in his later years when campouts became physically difficult. Norman's astonishing natural history library, including full sets of major ornithological journals, Gould's *Birds of Australia* and other treasures, was something he willingly shared with historical researchers such as myself, and with those working on the *Handbook*. The collection was sold complete after his death to fund an ongoing foundation, now known as the Wettenhall Environment Trust.[32]

Professionals and amateurs

For some, the Marlo incident underlined the disadvantages of including 'sentimental' amateurs in the RAOU. For others, it exposed an irresponsible element in the scientific community that offended the principles of bird lovers. Ornithological science benefited enormously from its relationship with birdos who had no formal scientific training. Most museum collectors were 'honorary' rather than paid, so the line between professionals and others was blurred. *Emu*'s column 'Stray Feathers' encouraged short, informal communications from birdos who would never have thought to write a formal scientific article. Such observations have historical significance and value a century later.

In an era before talkback radio, the question-and-answer column was another form of popular participation in birdwatching, if not formal science. Journalist and nature writer Donald Macdonald maintained 'Nature Notes and Queries' and 'Notes for Boys' in the Melbourne *Argus* over decades, and became the first president of the BOC.[33] Other nature writer-journalists such as Charles Barrett, Alec Chisholm, Crosbie Morrison (1900–58) and Michael Sharland, all RAOU members, were enthusiastic exponents of the sort of writing that bridged the gap between popular and scientific observation.

A curious example of this was the practice of 'anting'. A twelve-year-old Melbourne boy reported seeing European starlings 'picking up sugar-ants and putting them under their wings and then flying away'. Chisholm matched this story with a similar one from an adult observer in Sydney, and pursued the matter with the local entomological society. In an essay called 'Queer Relations of Birds and Insects' in *Bird Wonders of Australia*, first published in 1934, Chisholm formally reported this behaviour; he updated the story in later editions.[34] Eminent German ornithologist Erwin Stresemann (1889–1972) from Berlin read *Bird Wonders* and drew Chisholm's attention to a German bird journal that had published a similar observation in 1929 with respect to crows. That observer had put forward the idea that the formic acid of the ants might be effective in removing parasites. In 1935, Stresemann and Chisholm together coined the term 'anting' (*einemsen* in German) and combed the international literature, turning up a few more obscure references. Before long, reports appeared from Salim Ali (1896–1987) in India and Axel Adlersparre in Sweden referring to anting. In the United States, WL McAtee (1883–1962) published a review on the subject, finding literature references going back to 1876. Chisholm then found earlier ones—from 1830 and 1847.[35] By 1943, four professional articles on the issue had appeared in American and Canadian journals. Theories about the behaviour varied: some explained it as skin cleansing, others as odour attraction or the carriage of food.

Chisholm was interested in the phenomenon but also noted the value of keen young birdos and set out to make them feel proud to be part of science, to feel that they had 'started something'. The observant amateur, watching birds for pleasure, was integral to the future of ornithology. *Emu* of the 1920s and 1930s captured the spirit of this 'crossover' period when the most technical and the most amateur observations supported each other. The alliance was to flourish much later (see Epilogue).

Wildlife on the home front

Amateurs and professionals alike were affected by the outbreak of World War II. Congresses, annual meetings and campouts were all suspended.[36] In 1943, the RAOU's premises at 170 La Trobe Street, Melbourne, were commandeered by military authorities, forcing a hasty move of skins, egg collections and the wonderful library donated by HL White. Much of this material was placed in the museum and in private homes for safekeeping because it could not be accommodated in the new, smaller office. By the time the RAOU resumed operations after the war, the research resources were dispersed and the camaraderie of the La Trobe Street rooms, with easy access to the museum and the HL White ornithological collections, had been replaced by 'temporary' accommodation at 386 Flinders Lane. This became headquarters for both the union and the BOC for the next quarter-century. With the loss of a 'scientific centre', the RAOU's emphasis shifted towards the popular and the local. Technical matters retreated to the museum's bailiwick.

Chisholm was concerned about the RAOU's diminishing professional profile and its strained finances. He wrote in 1941 to Keith Hindwood, Sydney's most prominent ornithologist who was also an associate of the Australian Museum:

> Things in RAOU are in a lousy state financially ... [A] huge bill has come in from the printer (CB [Charles Bryant] made the last *Emu* 16 pp too large) and there is no money to meet it because subs are not coming in ... if we don't take a grip of Chas he will ruin the show financially ... As matters are, CB and the treasr are barely playing speaks.[37]

Aubrey Stubbing Chalk (1883–1957), a bank manager and field ornithologist, was the treasurer in question. He was a longstanding executive member (1941–50) and advocated a more popular *Emu* that would bring in more paying memberships. He was particularly critical of Bryant who, as well as overspending on production, was, in Chalk's view, alienating the 'general reader' with arcane content.

Broadcaster Crosbie Morrison, who was a master of both scientific and popular writing, defended *Emu*, arguing that 'there was no other journal in Australia where [scientific articles] could be published' but there were alternatives for nature writing.[38] Bryant battled on, trying to strike a middle course between the scientific and the popular. He argues for his approach to *Emu* in a letter to Barrett:

> It is not as easy as you might think to make a general article that keeps away from nomenclature, the historical aspect, and, above all, too

detailed references to individual species ... With over twenty years of
trying to keep *Emu* a judicious blend of academic and popular, I feel I
know something of the matter ... [E]ven though a book is popular and
required to be popular by the publishers, due allowance must be made
for [more knowledge of] ... the subject than [the article can fit].[39]

Morrison was a marine biologist, ornithologist and journalist and he
understood the complexity of Bryant's dilemmas with *Emu* as a fellow
editor. In 1938, on the brink of the war, he had established *Wild Life*, a
magazine and radio program that celebrated Australian nature. The magazine was published in the offices of the Melbourne *Herald* with the strong
support of its proprietor, Keith Murdoch. Murdoch had chosen Morrison
as an experienced scientific journalist with a flair for natural history.
Morrison began his journalism with Murdoch by supporting the elderly
Donald Macdonald, co-writing 'Nature Notes and Queries' and 'Notes for
Boys' (later 'Notes for Boys and Girls') when Macdonald was ill. He took
over both columns in the hiatus between Macdonald's death in 1932 and
the appointment of Chisholm as his successor early in 1933, and again
when Chisholm became editor of *The Argus* in 1937.[40] By the time *Wild
Life* was launched, Morrison was already an accomplished popular science
and nature history journalist; *Wild Life* made him a household name.

Macdonald had begun his early columns with questions from the
public: what did they want to know about nature? He was impatient with
the earnest writings and nomenclature debates of AJ Campbell and Gregory
Mathews. They didn't interest him and he (rightly) believed that others
were also bored by them. He positively flaunted his amateur credentials,
describing himself as 'nothing more than a bush loafer, with the time and
mood occasionally to give an eye and an ear to Nature ... and not within a
hundred miles of being a scientist'.[41] But he was an excellent communicator
and built up a very personal following through the Q&A format.

Morrison, a generation younger, was far more sympathetic to science
but equally impatient with arcane discussions that put people off birds and
enjoying nature. Perhaps because he was confident of his own education
as a scientist, Morrison was a good listener, and under less pressure to be

scientistic than many who contributed to *Emu*. A good number of the early *Emu* authors would type 'RAOU' after their name (or 'FRAOU'—that is, Fellow of the RAOU) because they lacked other formal ornithological qualifications. Morrison's qualifications were formal (an undergraduate and a master's degree in biology), but his professionalism was in writing and journalism. He was also deeply respectful of the amateur traditions of the Macdonald generation. As a young man he had learned much when he worked closely with the self-taught Charles Hedley (1862–1926), the Australian Museum malacologist, documenting shells and other biota on the Great Barrier Reef on an official museum expedition in 1925.

The *Wild Life* project was launched at a time when scientific collectors and bird observers were at loggerheads. The question of what the RAOU stood for and how campouts should be conducted was central, and the Marlo incident was a live flashpoint. The birdos loved their campouts and excursions but were ashamed of what had happened. The incident eerily echoed the lyrics of the old nursery rhyme 'Who Killed Cock Robin?' Some birdos felt that 'All the birds of the air / Fell a-sighing and a-sobbing, / When they heard the bell toll / For poor Cock Robin'.[42] Perhaps they felt complicit in supporting George Mack's 'scientific' collecting. They certainly wept for the little nestlings they had watched become orphans. Dry descriptions of bird-skins in a museum completely missed the thrill of watching the birds alive. Increasingly, the bird club realised that prospective members were much more attracted to being *in* nature than to storing it in institutional cabinets.

'Along the Track', Morrison's editorial page in the magazine, travelled with his readers' interests, answering queries and sharing observations. *Wild Life* became the hub of a lively new sort of 'nature club', a sort of armchair fieldwork, very different from campouts and flexible enough to survive the war years when travel was severely curtailed. Murdoch was keen to promote the new magazine and arranged for 3DB to carry a radio program of the same name 'to publicise it for a few weeks'. The program became extraordinarily popular, outstripping the magazine in reach, and ran live to air on Sunday nights for sixteen years from 1938 until 1954.[43] Morrison proved to be a brilliant speaker and presenter.

He embraced the weekly commitment and made it his own, and his audiences sent him far more questions than he could answer, even with both the magazine and the radio program. At one stage, *Wild Life* drew 75 per cent of Melbourne's listening audience to the 6 p.m. Sunday slot. In this time before television, radio broadcasts were social events. Typically, young naturalists sat around the wireless with their whole family. It was a weekly highlight. Morrison was soon broadcasting nationally, and later to New Zealand and South Africa.[44]

On the back of the *Wild Life* initiatives, Morrison launched a junior nature club in 1943 near his home in Melbourne's eastern suburbs, as part of the Field Naturalists' Club of Victoria (established in 1880). The Hawthorn Junior Field Naturalists still host meetings and field trips suited to younger naturalists and their families.

Morrison complemented his natural history knowledge with passionate pleas for conservation. 'The birds and the beasts and wildflowers have no votes, and therefore they don't interest the politician,' he declared in 1946.[45] By establishing a 'voice' for nature and putting the interests of nature before the eyes and ears of the voting public, he also shifted the emphasis of birding clubs to the task of conserving birds.

Morrison promoted the contemplation of nature as a healing craft for wartime stress: '*Wild Life* commends to its readers the release from cares which contact with nature can bring.' To contemplate nature was 'a duty to the nation', he wrote, in the language of the day.[46] Morrison's writing and broadcasting sponsored a personal responsibility to nature and a very different sort of collecting. He collected stories and took excellent photographs. He was also a pioneering amateur filmmaker, and travelled his films around natural history societies and social clubs such as Rotary and the JayCees, bringing the joy of nature study and the task of conservation to broader audiences.

These new conservation initiatives, which were often led by amateur birdos, soothed tensions within the ornithological fraternity. Morrison promoted what we now call 'citizen science' and nature writing as integral to the progress of science. A bird-observation scheme sponsored jointly by *Wild Life* and the RAOU created 200 observation stations throughout the Commonwealth in 1949.[47] This was not unique at the time: similar schemes were being run by the Tasmanian Field Naturalists' Club and the SAOA. Observation stations were a new trend for birding in the postwar era, inclusive of professional and amateur alike.

Camera craft

Light-hearted writing, a renewed commitment to conservation and good pictures (including films) enlisted new support for ornithology. The excitement and skill of bird photography had motivated many to take up ornithology from the earliest years of *Emu*. An early photograph of gannets by Dudley Le Souef foreshadowed a long trend: most volumes in the first fifty years carried 'state-of-the-art' photographic illustrations. AJ Campbell, *Emu*'s first editor, was a pioneering bird photographer who is credited with Australia's earliest published native bird picture, 'Lesser Noddies Nesting', taken on 23 December 1889 in the Abrolhos Islands in Western Australia.[48] Seabirds were commonly photographed in the early years because they sat still in bright light. When flash photography meant explosions of magnesium powder, strong sunlight was a boon.

Not all bird photographs were charming. Arthur Mattingley famously took a series of horrifying photographs of bloodied egrets shot in a rookery in 1907. They were 'plundered for their plumes', he wrote, a message that was reproduced in 1909 by the Royal Society for the Protection of Birds in Britain. *The Story of the Egret* was an important pamphlet for James Buckland's eventually successful campaign to close the world's major plumage markets in New York and London.[49]

Claude Kinane (1879–1927), whose bird photographs were published in Australian magazines from as early as 1905, was another campaigner for replacing the gun with the camera. His intimate photographs of small brown birds feeding their nestlings championed the challenge of technical difficulty. Rather than shocking the viewer as the Mattingley egrets had done, Kinane's artistic portraits created another way of seeing birds and celebrating their place in the natural world.

Ina Watson (1909–92), one of very few female photographers at the time, used images to complement her nature writing, particularly for children. She was an enthusiastic supporter of other photographers and curated a major 'Jubilee' photographic exhibition in 1951 to celebrate fifty years of the RAOU. It showcased entries from all around the country and included a surprisingly large number of entries of small bush birds, such as pardalotes, fairy-wrens and honeyeaters. Because they were so challenging to photograph in their dark habitats and with their constant movement, particularly in a time before telephoto lenses and colour film, these pictures displayed the latest achievements in photography.[50] As photographic equipment became less cumbersome and more readily available, RAOU presidential addresses talked about 'camera craft' and *Emu* featured detailed technical notes on exposures and equipment. In 1956, it carried a full review by Norman Chaffer (1899–1992) of the history of Australian bird photography.[51]

There was a strong alliance between photography and conservation, and educating the public about birds for the purposes of conservation. Another well-known photographer, Ray Littlejohns, argued that 'illustrations in a lighter or popular vein' were a way to create 'a national sentiment for native wildlife'.[52] By 1948, there had been official pressure within the RAOU to see the gun altogether replaced by the camera, and there was also strong feeling that professional egg collectors should no longer be part of the union's official campouts and field trips:

> Nothing should be done to disabuse the public in its regard for the union as the upholder of bird protection. There should be nothing that might give the public the impression that, after all, there were a few strings attached to this business of conservation.[53]

In 1949 the RAOU took the major decision to sell its egg collection (and the cabinets in which it was housed). This decision was officially attributed to 'limited space' in the new rooms. More importantly, shifting the egg collection out of sight worked to clean up the union's image with the general public. The remaining minority of serious oologists in the ranks of the union no longer talked publicly about egg-collecting efforts in *Emu* and other records of union activities.[54] The National Museum of Victoria paid the RAOU £50 for the collections, a small amount for such major collections but a useful sum for the financially stretched club at the time. The scarlet robin of Marlo hadn't died in vain.

5

LYREBIRD

In my family, ornithology meant lyrebirds. Not long before I started school we moved to the market town of Croydon, then just beyond the fringes of suburban Melbourne. The Dandenong Ranges were our backyard—too close when bushfires swept through in the summer of 1962 and my father joined the firefighters and came home late, blackened, with his eyebrows singed. In late autumn and early winter, however, the mountains were cool, friendly and at peace. Dad and I would rise at 5 a.m., long before dawn, and creep around a chilly and dripping Sherbrooke Forest with sticky black soil clinging to our hands and knees.

Ornithology meant being quiet, listening, searching for 'Spotty'. I could never quite work out how my father knew which of the birds we heard was Spotty, except that we seemed to follow the loudest and clearest calls. Usually we would find him in a clearing, foraging in deep leaf-mould with his long feet. Sometimes, if we were really lucky, he would throw his long tail over his head and dance.

My father, like so many enthusiasts before and since, never tired of the antics of the lyrebird *Menura novaehollandae*. He never noticed if the day was cold or wet. Much has been written about the beauty of the lyrebird's tail, but the fascination of this bird for him was its almost-human personality. With large bright eyes adapted for dark forest life, and teasing calls, a master of mimicry and ventriloquism, Spotty lured *us* into thinking like a bird. If we could wriggle into a position where we could watch for a sustained period, we could observe the tricks of his trade. He would be here—but his call was over there. Whose call? My favourite was his eastern whipbird imitation, but it could equally be a bell miner or one of the many scratchy little calls of as-yet-unidentified 'little brown jobs'. Spotty was an ornithological schoolmaster. As he worked through his mellow repertoire, Dad would whisper to me the names of the birds Spotty was imitating. The sounds were not all bird calls. He did a splendid breaking twig, too— possibly the noise he associated with us.

Learning to live with people

The lyrebird is secretive, but not always shy. It takes the trouble to bury its discarded feathers and drop the faecal sacs of its young in streams to be washed away. Yet its bold encounters with the human species have given it a special place in the popular imagination. A mutual fascination for lyrebirds and people emerges from many of the curious lyrebird anecdotes recorded in the 'Stray Feathers' columns of early *Emus*. A gang of men building a road into Walhalla, east of Melbourne, in 1907 were favoured with a regular 'building inspector'—a male lyrebird who capitalised on the grubs and worms disturbed by the works. The *Emu* reported:

> On Friday morning last it paid no fewer than ten visits to the scene of operations. The bird whistles beautifully, sitting on the bank near, and seems to have no fear of his friends. He has several dancing- beds in the vicinity, and is a beautiful bird, with a tail about 2 feet [60 centimetres] or over in length.[1]

Many early reports expressed concern about the lyrebird's habit of nesting so close to the ground. 'In Southern Gippsland foxes have become so numerous that all ground nesting birds are in a fair way to extinction', the *Australian Naturalist* reported in 1906. 'It is to be hoped that before the last of [the lyrebirds] fall victims to Mr Reynard, they will learn to build out of reach.' LC Cook at Poowong in South Gippsland recorded that indeed lyrebirds did learn: they built their nests higher and higher when fox numbers increased.[2] HV Edwards described the lyrebird nesting habits as 'erratic'; in 1919 he reported a nest in the fork of a tree more than 18 feet (5.5 metres) above the ground.[3]

The idea that this bird could 'learn' where to place a nest was supported by its ability to learn sounds. It was well known traditionally for its double calls. Many of the Aboriginal words for lyrebird pick up on the double call, including *golgol* in the Newcastle area and *buln buln* in West Gippsland (after which a small town is named). The lyrebird was a quick learner of new sounds. There were anecdotal reports of it imitating knapping (chipping stone), chainsaws and even the three blasts of a timber-mill whistle. One bird caused havoc when it imitated the mill's three-whistle sequence in its own 'double' format, inadvertently ringing out the six-blast signal that was reserved for reporting a fatality.[4]

The lyrebird's curiosity about human activities made it possible to domesticate if caught when very young. Jack (1885–1905), a tame friend of S McNeilly, grew up on a farm at Drouin in Gippsland. Jack's life history and antics were closely monitored. At the age of six or seven he developed his magnificent tail, which he shed in an annual moult. He fed on grubs, worms and the occasional bit of meat. He loved his bath and preened his feathers for some time afterwards. He was so interested in people that he was constantly getting in the way: his favourite saying was 'Look out, Jack!' He could mimic the noise of a horse and dray, dogs howling and chains rattling, a range of musical instruments (including violin, piano and cornet), and useful sayings such as 'Gee up, Bess!' People so often said to him 'Poor Jack' that he learned to reply, 'Not poor Jack, fat Jack.' His death on 18 April 1905 was recorded in *Emu*, the only obituary of an individual bird in a journal with hundreds of obituaries of birdos over the years.[5]

Tom Tregellas (1864–1938) was one of the earliest ornithologists to make a specialist study of the lyrebird. He sought everything he could about its life-patterns and behaviour. For seventeen years Tregellas camped regularly in a large, boarded-up hollow log he called 'Menura' in Sherbrooke Forest, observing and photographing the superb lyrebirds after whom his home-away-from-home was named. About 1913, he started using identifying bands of his own making—one of the earliest instances of banding birds in Australia. He banded every nestling he could find, but never saw any of his banded birds as adults. It is possible that the bands were worn off by the lyrebirds' energetic foraging on the forest floor.[6]

Tregellas' passion enthused a younger photographer, Ray Littlejohns (1893–1961), who in the 1920s was responsible for the first moving footage of the bird. Littlejohns recalled that his introduction to lyrebird technology had been 'one of the most harrowing experiences of my life'. He had volunteered to assist Tregellas with a lecture on the lyrebird, operating 'a lantern of ancient design, illuminated by an intricate carbon-arc system. My failure to coax more than a flickering glimmer of light from the infernal engine wrecked the visual aspect of the lecture.' Nonetheless, the dismal lecture kindled enthusiasm for lyrebirds in the assistant's heart. Twenty years later, in 1943, Littlejohns wrote *Lyrebirds Calling from Australia*, a small book illustrated with his own photographs that he produced to cheer up the troops at war. 'Australians are more than a little proud of the lyrebird', he wrote.[7]

Littlejohns credited Tregellas with changing Australian attitudes to lyrebirds. The collector-turned-observer certainly crusaded for lyrebird protection with all the zeal of a late convert. And lyrebirds needed protection. In the Federation era, lyrebird tails had been used as decorations in a misplaced gesture of patriotism. The taste for the tails as parlour decorations was deplored by Dr Spencer Roberts (1882–1939) from Toowoomba in Queensland: 'numerous tails adorned, *horribile dictu* [dreadful to say], the houses of many of my patients'.[8] John Leach observed one in a woman's hat on the corner of Collins and Spring streets in Melbourne.[9] Sid Jackson, HL White's most significant collector, reported on horrific lyrebird drives in northern New South Wales when hundreds of male lyrebirds were slaughtered 'to supply globe-trotting curio-hunters with the unique tail feathers'.[10] The practice was common in Gippsland, too, where male birds were disappearing at an alarming rate. In 1915 LC Cook reported stories of female lyrebirds 'deprived of their consorts'. One lone female had chosen to live with the domestic hens on a farm at Glen Alvie, and became a brilliant mimic of her new companions' clucking.[11]

Littlejohns was wrong when he credited Tregellas with creating a connection between lyrebirds and nationalism: the birds adorned colonial and national postage stamps, furniture and coats of arms long before Tregellas took up their cause.[12] Lyrebird motifs were prominent, for example, on an arch erected by the German-Australian community to commemorate the opening of the first federal parliament in Melbourne in May 1901.[13] Tregellas did, however, redirect destructive patriotic fervour towards lyrebird protection and observation rather than trophy-hunting. He made his trips to Sherbrooke Forest as visits to a sacred place, something he undertook with respect, on hands and knees.

More than any other bird, the lyrebird challenged the technology of every era, particularly sound technologies. When Littlejohns took up its cause, he felt the need to show the bird singing and dancing. Filming birds in the 1920s was a major enterprise, and *Emu* published some frames from his 1925 film.[14] Littlejohns was behind early live broadcasts on the wireless and the first live gramophone recording, *The Song of the Lyrebird*, in 1931.[15]

Lyrebird enthusiasts have often become serious photographers. As well as the Campbells, LG Chandler (1888–1980) and AH Chisholm were keen lyrebird photographers. Chisholm, author of *The Romance of the Lyrebird*, researched the history of lyrebird discovery as well as studying the birds in the field.[16] Michael Sharland, who watched over the lyrebird's introduction to Tasmania in the period from 1934 to 1945, was also an outstanding photographer, as was Ralph F Kenyon, who started the first Sherbrooke Lyrebird Survey Group in 1958 with chemist Leonard Hart Smith (1910–2004), who later became the second director of the National Parks Authority of Victoria. Smith wrote two major books about lyrebirds, illustrated with his photography.[17] He also recorded lyrebird song and mimicry. Moving photography advanced with the century: Laszlo and Jenny Erdos's 1986 video, *The Kingdom of the Lyrebird*, included a spectacular sequence capturing the birds dancing, courting and mating in the wild.[18]

New films are still being made. Elmar Akhmetov won the 2022 Portfolio prize in the BirdLife Photography Awards for his stunning series of portraits of 'Pretender', created while he was working with this star lyrebird for a documentary film.[19]

What sort of bird is a lyrebird?

Lyrebirds challenged science as well as technology. Because of the patient studies of Tregellas, who thought nothing of waiting 'from dewy morn to dusky eve' to photograph and observe the birds, we know much about its habits and its habitat, its antics and breeding behaviours.[20] We even know from Charles Stone's observations that its eggs are porous: 'during the process of blowing beads of water exuded over the whole surface'.[21] But in spite of such extraordinary details, for many years we seemed no closer to understanding how the lyrebird fitted into the systematic classification of birds. Here was a bird who could sing like a dream but could barely fly. It had distinctive big feet, adapted for scratching the forest floor. Its failure to fit known categories is reflected in the diversity of its names: in the eighteenth and nineteenth centuries some called it a 'mountain pheasant'; others thought its tail demanded that it belong with the birds of paradise, while still others referred it as the 'wren as big as a peacock'.[22] By the beginning of the twentieth century, lyrebirds were in an order by themselves, adjacent to but not part of the 'perching bird' order.[23]

The twentieth century saw passerines transformed from 'perching birds' to 'singing birds'. 'Singing' birds were then divided into oscine (*Passeri*) and suboscine (*Tyranni*) according to the structure of their syrinx (the syrinx, named for the nymph chased by Pan who became the reed of the pan-pipes, is the voice-producing organ of birds). The *Passeri* have the most advanced and complex syrinx, and most Australian passerine families are in this class.[24] The lyrebird's grouping among the *Corvida*, a largely southern branch (parvorder) of the *Passeri*, was built on established knowledge of the lyrebird and on new studies of its close relative, the scrub-bird (see Chapter 8). Its superfamily, Menuroidea, also includes bowerbirds and treecreepers.

The other very Australasian superfamilies included in the corvine assemblage are *Meliphagoidea* (mound-building birds such as the malleefowl) and *Corvoidea* (the 'classic' corvids—crows and ravens; see Chapter 11).

In the history of birdsong recordings in the Australasian region, the lyrebird, master of mimicry, was first, and has remained very significant. The Sherbrooke lyrebird was the subject of the first-ever Australian broadcast of a wild bird on 'A'-class radio in Melbourne (3AR and 3LO), on 5 July 1931. The recording, undertaken by the Australian Broadcasting Company (a precursor to the Australian Broadcasting Commission established a year later) included commentary from Tregellas and Sharland.[25]

When the CSIRO Division of Wildlife established a laboratory for the study of animal sounds in the 1960s, the lyrebird was again the first species recorded. (Frank) Norman Robinson (1911–97), who led the lab, was a pioneer in the field of sound recording and analysis for specialist scientific workers.[26] The scientific study of birdsong has contributed significantly to understanding territorial behaviours and evolutionary histories. Among many bird species of the north temperate regions, only males sing, but in the Australasian region and elsewhere, females sing, too, sometimes in a cooperative display called 'duetting'.[27]

Regional variation and even lyrebird history have been inscribed in its song. In a remarkable study spanning more than thirty years, Robinson and Syd Curtis (1928–2015), a Queensland lyrebird enthusiast, analysed the territorial songs of lyrebirds by region. The song of Tasmanian lyrebirds, which had been introduced from Toolangi in Victoria, astonishingly, still resembled that of their counterparts north of Bass Strait: more than fifty years later they had maintained a 'Gippsland dialect' over generations.[28]

Working for lyrebirds

Lyrebirds provide an excellent motivation for ornithological excursions, at least in the eastern states, because they are active in late autumn and winter, a time of year when other birds tend to be at their least interesting. Sydney, Melbourne, Brisbane and Canberra all have lyrebirds within an easy drive of the city and the (introduced) superb lyrebird is an attraction of Mount Field National Park, near Hobart.[29] They are not found in South Australia, the Northern Territory or Western Australia. Attempts to introduce them to the karri forests of south-western Australia in the 1920s, something discussed at length during the RAOU campout at Nornalup in 1927, came to nothing.

Lyrebird habitat conservation has been a particular concern because of the birds' proximity to large and sprawling cities. Isobel and Harold Bradley and other members of the Sherbrooke Lyrebird Survey Group are some of the many voluntary enthusiasts who have supported conservation work through banding and observing over the years. In 1998 the Sherbrooke group, with a dozen or so members, spent 1000 hours surveying lyrebirds and their habitat in 377 visits to the forest; they produced 233 written reports of sightings, all located with compass bearings.[30] This group continues to be 'the eyes and ears of the forest' for Parks Victoria. After many years of decline, lyrebird numbers are at least stabilising through predator-control programs directed at foxes and feral cats. Indeed, when the Sherbrooke Lyrebird Survey Group celebrated sixty years of action for lyrebirds in 2018 (and an astonishing annual total of 2575 volunteer hours, including dawn-survey volunteers over 316 days), the signs were promising, with increasing chick-survival rates.[31] The group continues its vigilance as major storms have affected the area since, and the effects of climate change are still unfolding.

The people of Brisbane must drive to the forests in the mountain country on the southern border of the city and search a little harder to see the rare, rich-chestnut Albert's lyrebird (*Menura alberti*), which is a little smaller than the superb. Albert's is now the only other species of *Menura*; Gregory Mathews distinguished it from *M. novaehollandiae* because its tail lacked 'the long curved out rectrix'.[32] Queensland's Albert River was part of its home territory, but echoes of its royal name also appear in the historical subspecies the Victoria lyrebird (*M. novaehollandiae victoriae*), a darker superb.

Albert's lyrebird is much less studied and more threatened than the superb. It is more secretive and less inclined to mimic. With a very limited range and precise habitat needs (forest floor with thick leaf-litter and deep soil, in high-rainfall areas), it has been described as 'near threatened', with only 3500 breeding birds and one of the smallest distributional ranges of any bird on the continent. Knowledge of the optimal habitat needs of Albert's lyrebird came from a major doctoral study conducted by Sandy Gilmore between 1996 and 1998. Gilmore found that, all things being equal, the birds prefer eucalypt rather than 'rainforest' habitat.[33] Unfortunately, eucalypts growing in deep soil in high-rainfall areas are very productive and attractive to the timber industry, especially if they are accessible. The March 2000 Regional Forest Agreement, for example, resulted in logging concessions being granted in Whian Whian forest in the Nightcap Range, New South Wales, in exactly the place that Gilmore's study showed was the best remaining habitat for the bird.[34] In 2019–20, the Black Summer fires broke open the forest canopy right through most of the Albert's lyrebird haunts. Expanding cities and changing climates constantly dice with the future of these evolutionarily distinctive and much-loved birds.

Spotty (1942–64)

Spotty was not just Spotty for my family—he was a Melbourne institution from the 1940s to the 1960s, famous well beyond the local Sherbrooke Lyrebird Survey Group. His dates are recorded: 1942–64. Like his predecessor, Timmy (1927–53), he was a reason to visit Sherbrooke Forest for generations of parents and children.[35] Spotty starred in a television documentary, *Dancing Orpheus*, in 1963.[36] He was one of many 'famous', personally named lyrebirds.

The proximity of his haunts to a growing city made him famous, but also vulnerable. In 1964, Spotty disappeared. Although he was very old, there were suspicious circumstances: my father murmured about vandals and shots being heard in the area. Along with much of Melbourne, our family went into mourning on learning of his disappearance. I was seven years old when I heard of the tragedy. His death marked the end of an era.

6

SCIENTISTS AND CITIZENS

'S' for science

The late 1940s was a time of postwar reconstruction all over the world. Scientists had crucial expertise to support industry. They brought with their expertise a 'world-mindedness' that also gave them diplomatic authority. The United Nations Educational, Scientific and Cultural Organization (UNESCO) was established in 1945 with Julian Huxley, an ecologist and ornithologist, at the helm. The original plan was for a United Nations Educational and Cultural Organization to build peace. Huxley added an 'S'—for science.[1]

Scientists were the pre-eminent experts in the postwar reconstruction of Australia. The old Council for Scientific and Industrial Research (CSIR), established in 1926 to support the international efforts of the Empire Marketing Board to promote science 'to feed the world', was restructured and massively expanded as CSIRO (Commonwealth Scientific and Industrial Research Organisation) in 1949. This brought an influx of international scientists to Australia.

Postwar reconstruction included building up independent local manufacturing and food security for Australia and the world. There were also development opportunities supporting returning soldiers (soldier settlement schemes) and a building boom to go with the baby boom. New migrants displaced by the war became crucial to grand national projects such as the (first) Snowy Mountains hydro-electric scheme. Sir William Hudson (1896–1978) famously welcomed Eastern Europeans with experience in mountainous environments to this megaproject with the words: 'You will no longer be "Balts and Slavs" but "Men of the Snowy".'[2]

By far the largest group of immigrants, however, were from Britain. The White Australia policy lingered on. Severe food and other rationing continued into the 1950s in Britain, and its people sought better opportunities elsewhere. Australia was an attractive option as successive governments invested heavily in British immigration. From the point of view of ornithology this was important, as new birdos favoured British models for bird projects. The term 'birdo', the peculiarly Australian variant of 'birder', became popular in the 1950s, possibly because so many birdos were keen to discover their new country, adopting its birds as part of their identity. Birdo, with its Australian flavour, was inclusive of newcomers. You just had to love birds and document their behaviour with precision to feel useful and 'at home' in your new country.

Many of the initiatives in postwar birding in Australia were led by British-born birdos who had grown up with the parson-naturalist Gilbert White's famous *Natural History of Selborne* (first published in 1789 and continuously in print since). White meticulously recorded the spring migrations of swallows in Hampshire and inspired generations to mark individual birds and record their recovery. Seasons and migratory birds figured strongly in their thinking. A nationwide British 'bird-ringing' scheme was inaugurated in 1909 in association with the popular magazine *British Birds*.[3] Australians had followed these developments closely and made some tentative steps, but in the postwar era, after the bombing of Darwin, there was a new urgency: so much of the continent was underexplored zoologically and far from the centres where most birdos were based.

Internationally, the concept of 'the environment' came of age in this period. More than just 'nature', the environment encompassed soils, the atmosphere, fresh water and the oceans. The environment was more scientific in emphasis, where the older 'nature' had a romantic and literary ring to it. Bird behaviours were often a clue to environmental problems, whether on land, at sea or in the air. The postwar years brought together scientists trained in physics, chemistry, geology and biology to work together on environmental projects. Earth sciences came to the fore in the International Geophysical Year (IGY) of 1957–58, and by 1962 some people had begun to use the term *environmental scientists*.[4] In the 1970s, the international biological project Man and the Biosphere (MAB) was highly influential in Australian ornithology as it required precision mapping of ecological niches; birds were often key indicators because they had been more closely studied historically than other animals, and because of the meticulous historical records maintained by birdos in *Emu* and elsewhere.

CSIR and CSIRO

In Australia until this time, most scientific policy leadership had come from the states, particularly from departments of forestry, agriculture, fisheries and game, and, from the 1930s, soil science. The small CSIR was the national science employer tasked with developing primary industries and manufacturing. Its headquarters, built in 1927, was one of Canberra's first public buildings (alongside the first Parliament House). There were other specialist groups such as the Commonwealth Solar Observatory, established in 1924 (employer of astronomers), and the much earlier Bureau of Meteorology, established in 1906, which remained headquartered in Melbourne with stations all over the continent.

The CSIR employed biologists, particularly entomologists, to work on the problems of agriculture. Economic entomologists took a particular interest in what birds ate, especially the birds that ate agricultural pests. The CSIR first expressed a formal interest in ornithology in 1936, when its Standing Committee of Agriculture reviewed the question of the impact on agriculture of the straw-necked ibis (*Threskiornis spinicollis*), cousin of the Australian white ibis (*T. mollucus*, the bird disparagingly known today as the 'bin chicken'). John Burton Cleland (1878–1971), then president of the RAOU and Professor of Physiology at Adelaide University, wrote to David Rivett (1885–1961), the chief executive officer of CSIR, suggesting that the RAOU might be consulted in bird-related matters, an offer that was gratefully accepted. Spencer Roberts of Toowoomba convened an RAOU 'Standing Committee to Co-operate with CSIR' in the 'study of the ecology of birds'.[5] It was hoped that CSIR, with its national jurisdiction, might be in a position to make recommendations for action on the basis of RAOU research findings. This early collaboration never quite came to fruition as the war intervened.

International ecologists were prominent among the early staff of CSIR. Francis Ratcliffe (1904–70) came to Australia twice to undertake specific projects, first on the grey-headed flying fox, which was a problem for fruit growers, and then again, several years later, when he returned from the University of Aberdeen to assess the problems of the dust storms of the 'dirty thirties'. Ratcliffe stayed on in Australia and wrote the popular book *Flying Fox and Drifting Sand: The Adventures of a Biologist in Australia*, which became part of the curriculum in Australian schools.

The pressures of postwar reconstruction, particularly in agriculture ('feeding the world') and manufacturing (making Australia self-sufficient in building and other materials for a fast-growing population), led to a major reorganisation and expansion of CSIR in 1949. As CSIRO, it became a major employer with activities around the country. It was a significant employer in the small city of Canberra, where a new Wildlife Survey Section was based. Ratcliffe was appointed officer-in-charge. The section was modelled on the Oxford Bureau of Animal Population, where Ratcliffe had trained. It favoured projects of 'economic significance' and was a new and very different hub for ornithological projects. Ratcliffe had studied under Charles Elton, whose acerbic lectures on 'ecological explosions' are still remembered today. South African ecologist David Richardson (1958–) regards Elton as the 'father' of invasion ecology.[6] A war on problem animals appealed to the nation-building rhetoric of the time but was quietly resisted by many wildlife scientists. Ratcliffe had a much broader view of what 'national' science entailed:

It seems to me that a living interest in the bush and its animal inhabitants is a manifestation of one of the most desirable and decent traits in human beings; and it should be an obligation on the part of the government of a civilised country to do something positive to foster and encourage it.[7]

CSIRO wildlife scientists and their technical support staff were generally enthusiastic and competent fieldworkers, not just theorists. They were keen for Australia to improve its global status in wildlife protection. At a time when so little of the nation's wildlife was even described, they were frustrated that their time was devoted to the ecology of 'problem animals', most of which were non-native. Nonetheless, they found inventive ways around the CSIRO constraints. The Wildlife Survey Section aspired to accommodate the applied problems set out by its charter, but if it were also to advance scientific knowledge for a 'civilised country', a 'quiet' solution was to devote Fridays to CDK ('Chief Doesn't Know') projects. Ratcliffe and his successor, Harry Frith (1921–82), certainly *did* know. They applied an informal rule of thumb that one day a week should be set aside for 'pure' science. Thus, 'unfundable' projects, such as the study of native birds, generally came out of personal time. One day a week was insufficient alone, but a significant number of bird projects blossomed with the help of weekends, evenings and other fieldwork travel. Sometimes family members gave free assistance, too.

The public service required that all scientific projects should be published by CSIRO.[8] This made little sense in the case of bird projects, especially where work was carried out in private time. In 1955 Ratcliffe wrote an impassioned plea to CSIRO's Executive to allow his staff to publish more widely, where appropriate:

Many of my staff publish, or want to publish, a lot of unofficial stuff; and sometimes the line between the official and the unofficial is quite impossible to draw. Sometimes work which started as a purely hobby interest, done in a man's spare time and at weekends, may develop into a piece of official research—the best example of this is Harry Frith's interest in the mallee fowl, and the physics of its egg incubation ... Dom Serventy presents an even more difficult case. As far as I can make out he spends his whole waking life being an ornithologist, at times acting and thinking as an officer of CSIRO and at times as a private individual.[9]

Exercising 'discretion' in making such distinctions was a constant source of stress for the anxious Ratcliffe. In fact, a committee that reviewed the section's work in 1960 was very impressed with its bird work and its national banding program, but offered no guidance as to how it could continue this work alongside 'the applied side—our responsibilities to the taxpayer and the land-holder you might say'.[10]

Ratcliffe bemoaned the constant pressure to focus on rabbit eradication at the expense of knowing anything about all the Australian native animals the rabbit had replaced already throughout the country, especially in the arid zone. A small ecological unit was based in Alice Springs from 1953, and CSIRO's arid-zone research was internationally well-connected throughout the UNESCO Arid Zone Research Programme. The Australian *Arid Zone Newsletter* connected scientists from all over the world working in desert landscapes, including prominent Israeli scientist Immanuel Noy Meir, who came to Australia to do a PhD at the Australian National University (ANU) and went on to revolutionise international arid-zone ecology using Australian field studies.[11]

Harry Frith was reluctant to take up the management of the expanded Division of Wildlife in 1961, when he was appointed to succeed Ratcliffe. He loved fieldwork and pure science, and was not excited at the prospect of an office job where he would be inundated with paperwork. As chief of a big division, he travelled a lot but seldom had time for fieldwork. He demanded that CSIRO provide an aviary outside his office at Gungahlin as a condition of his appointment. Thus, he solved his dilemma by maintaining his own CDK project (and his sanity) with observations of the pigeons and doves of Australia, the group of birds least perturbed by life in a cage. This behavioural project reminded him every time he looked out his window that he was a scientist, not an administrator. In 1982, Frith published Australia's first 'definitive' book on these birds.[12]

A national bird-banding scheme

The idea of banding or marking migratory birds started early in Australia. In 1913 members of the Bird Observers' Club placed aluminium rings labelled 'Inform BOC Melbourne' on fifty-one 'mutton birds' (short-tailed shearwaters, *Puffinus tenuirostris*) at Phillip Island and began to survey their breeding behaviours. By 1917, the Victorian Fisheries and Game Department had assumed responsibility for the rookeries at Phillip Island, protecting both mutton birds and their eggs from overenthusiastic visitors.[13] Banding work was more often related to documenting seasonal arrivals and departures. Much later, in the postwar years, the international importance of protecting the 'feeding stations' along the pathways of migratory birds became recognised.

Australia's longest-running records of individual migratory banding projects, on mutton birds in Bass Strait, were maintained systematically by Dom Serventy for over four decades and have continued since, with others taking up the task. Serventy began work in 1947, when materials were scarce, but he persuaded the Tasmanian Fauna Board to provide copper rings for the first three years because it was a population study of a commercial bird rather than 'just' a migration study.[14] Serventy's day job in the CSIR Fisheries Division gave him the right Tasmanian contacts for the project, but the work was maintained in his own time (as his later boss Ratcliffe was well aware). Serventy appealed in *Emu* for recoveries throughout eastern Australia and New Zealand.[15] By 1957, when he wrote a long formal report on the work, over 18,000 birds had been banded. Serventy was quickly able to establish that the birds' instinct for 'homing' was very precise, with most returning to the island of their birth, often to the same burrow.[16] He was still introducing newcomers to the project at Fisher Island in the 1970s.

Serventy had long been interested in bird movements. He was just eighteen when he wrote to the BOC from his home in Maddington, Western Australia, in 1922 seeking practical advice about suitable materials and techniques (including trapping) for banding 'passerine species', particularly the woodland birds (including introduced song thrushes) in his rural agricultural area. He had seen manufactured metal bands and homemade rings made out of tin, 'but neither of us [Serventy and a schoolfriend] knew how to affix them to the birds' legs'.[17] Les Chandler, a jeweller by trade and the leader of BOC banding, wrote a long, helpful letter in reply, recommending aluminium for the rings, but he was unable to help with trapping methods as his own work was all done with mutton birds in nesting burrows.[18] Since bands were expensive, Serventy suggested that the RAOU might support a more systematic scheme; however, this was too expensive for the club, so banding operations were left to the few who could afford them, and to specialist museum expeditions with government resources.

Not all individual bird studies demanded bands. Western Australian farmer Angus Robinson (1907–73) recognised individual magpies (and magpie larks) by their markings. When he returned from difficult military service, including three-and-a-half years as a prisoner of war in Malaya, he turned to studying birdsong and the way individual birds sang to defend their territories on his property at Coolup, south of Perth. In 1949, he suggested that western magpies (*Gymnorhina tibicen dorsalis*) defended territory in groups rather than pairs, an important insight that pre-dated the term 'cooperative breeding' that is now widely used. [19]

When petrol rationing ended in 1949, ornithologists seized the chance to get out in the field with friends and scientific colleagues. Small bird-banding projects sprang up simultaneously in a number of places, sometimes with support from government agencies and sometimes without. There was a growing concern that there should be some 'national' coordination of banding activities in the interests of protecting the birds from injury and because birds moved around beyond state boundaries. The Australian National Antarctic Research Expeditions (ANARE) included banding at Heard Island from 1949 and Macquarie Island from the next summer.[20] Bird-banding has continued to be an important dimension of scientific work in Antarctica.

Salt fields were the site of banding operations in South Australia. Oliver Fuller recalled visits in the 1950s to the ICI (now Penrice) salt fields and the growing interest in migratory waders fostered by beach counts and some of the earliest mist-netting.[21] SAOA trips in this period, like those of the BOC, recorded abundance figures. Fuller's notes from 1953 recorded netting more than 300 birds of eleven species in one afternoon. There was a growing interest in rarities and vagrants.

The question of a postwar national banding scheme was first raised in 1946 with the RAOU by the Gould League. The RAOU referred the matter to CSIR, where it languished for three years. The new Wildlife Survey Section, established in 1949 when CSIR became CSIRO, revived the possibility, but Ratcliffe, rather overwhelmed by other pressures, felt the best CSIRO could do would be to be a 'wholesaler' of rings, rather than run an active banding program.

The expansion of CSIRO carried new expectations that scientists would provide expertise to solve a wide range of policy and postwar dilemmas. The question of who to run the national banding scheme resulted in awkward relations between the RAOU and CSIRO, possibly because neither was convinced that administering a national banding scheme was *scientific* business. Many CSIRO Wildlife scientists were very good bird observers and loved birds. They would gladly have worked on birds rather than 'national economic' priorities. Yet the rabbit problem was always pressing for an organisation focused on primary industry.

Where agricultural issues involved birds, such as the clash between magpie geese (*Anseranas semipalmata*) and rice-farming at Humpty Doo in the Northern Territory, the case for CSIRO intervention was easy. Indeed, the work undertaken at the Fogg Dam experimental rice farm in the 1950s and 1960s by Harry Frith and Stephen Davies proved internationally significant. Their ecological work on magpie geese resulted in a taxonomic breakthrough. These birds are the only living species of the ancient family of Anseranatidae. The ornithological world became very interested in their ecology for reasons that had nothing to do with rice crops. In 1974, Frith chose the magpie goose as the symbol for the International Ornithological Congress to represent the distinctiveness of Australian ornithology (see Chapter 7). Later, anthropologists realised that the magpie goose was a prized traditional food for Indigenous people, and worked with local people to understand its irruptive behaviours. Meanwhile, the Fogg

Dam experimental station, which outlasted the rice, was converted to study the spread of cane toads when they invaded in 2004.[22] Humpty Doo became the heart of the ecological work by prize-winning scientist Rick Shine that has saved many rare birds—and mammals and reptiles—in the Top End.[23] Many worthwhile ornithological studies languished, however, because there were no official resources for 'curiosity-driven' research, even where there was a genuine scientific problem and the curiosity and talent to work on it.

By 1953, four years after the CSIRO Wildlife Survey Section had been launched, support was found for the Australian Bird Banding Scheme (ABBS), possibly because it would attract the free labour of excellent fieldworkers. National schemes for bird-banding were becoming widespread, with the United States, Canada, Britain, India, Egypt, South Africa, Japan, New Zealand, the Soviet Union and most of Europe all ahead of Australia.[24] The United States was banding 500,000 birds a year, the British 17,000 and the Russians had a target of 150,000.[25] To match such international growth, Australia needed a single national scheme, not a series of little schemes with confusing bands. The fact that migratory birds (and sometimes others) were recovered all over the world underscored a need for consistency. In the 1950s, a common tern banded in Sweden and an Arctic tern with a Moscow band had washed up in Perth, and a southern giant petrel (*Macronectes giganteus*) banded in the Falkland Islands was found at Encounter Bay in South Australia. Meanwhile, bands from two of Serventy's Fisher Island short-tailed shearwaters were recovered in Japan.[26]

Scottish zoologist and experienced bird 'ringer' Robert Carrick (?–1988) arrived at the CSIRO Wildlife Section in 1953. By this time, Ratcliffe had returned to the idea of a national bird-banding scheme as the myxomatosis revolution had moved rabbits off the priority list. Since Carrick had just the right experience to manage a bird-banding initiative, his first role at Wildlife was to establish and coordinate the ABBS. It was to be closely modelled on the British Trust for Ornithology scheme, running since 1937 and familiar to both Ratcliffe and Carrick. Carrick started assessing the scope of the task from his first arrival in the port of

Fremantle en route to Canberra. In Coolup, Western Australia, Angus Robinson introduced him to his magpie studies, which were done through identifying individual magpies by their markings.[27] Theories of territory were of mutual interest, and were a basis for intriguing practical fieldwork. Both Carrick and Robinson knew and respected Eliot Howard's *Territory in Bird Life* (1920). The latest edition (1948) carried a new introduction by Julian Huxley (1887–1975) and James Fisher (1912–70), Britain's most popular natural history broadcaster. Carrick's first Australian study of territorial behaviour, onsite at the CSIRO Wildlife Survey Section headquarters at Gungahlin, was inspired by Robinson's work. Canberra's convenient and famously territorial magpies were an obvious choice. Thus, the first bird recorded as marked with a CSIRO band was a nestling black-backed magpie.[28]

Carrick remained officer-in-charge of the scheme until 1960, when he moved to the Mawson Institute for Antarctic Research in Adelaide and Frith took over formal responsibility for the national banding scheme. However, from 1957 much of the work of the ABBS was delegated to its secretary, Warren Hitchcock (1919–84), another CSIRO officer, who had moved back to Canberra after a horrific car accident in the Northern Territory. Unlike Carrick, Hitchcock got on well with people, including local amateurs, many of whom he knew from his previous work at the National Museum of Victoria and time spent with various BOC banding projects.[29] Hitchcock was also secretary of the RAOU in 1951–52, its president in 1962–63 and editor of *Emu* from 1962 to 1965. These activities provided him with important networks outside CSIRO and helped to knit together the work of scientists and volunteers.

Hitchcock introduced the concept of 'state regional organisers', encouraging local groups to share the administrative load and enable on-the-spot checking of bands and training of new banders. He visited the organisers in person when he could, but mostly gave encouragement to good local volunteer leaders. South Australian banders joined the national scheme in 1955, led by the enthusiastic regional organiser Max Waterman, whose cormorant studies were important in the early years. In 1962 the Altona Survey Group, which had been an informal hub for Victorian

BOC banding operations, became the core of a much larger Victorian Ornithological Research Group (VORG), which, in turn, became an official ABBS regional group.[30] VORG in 1968 initiated the important Penguin Survey Group at Phillip Island led by Pauline Reilly (1918–2011), which pioneered the use of 'flipper bands' because penguins have fleshy feet, unsuitable for banding. (Reilly also wrote children's books, including several about penguins.)

In Western Australia, the shorebirds at Pelican Point on the Swan River, not far from the CSIRO laboratories in Crawley, were the subject of intensive study and banding work from the 1950s. Dom Serventy was a driving force, but there was never a 'regional organiser' for Western Australia since CSIRO had a base there. Banding work in Western Australia was official CSIRO business, and the projects were framed in terms of national and international scientific questions rather than local interests. Davies' work on emus out near the rabbit-proof fence was one prominent project and Denis Saunders' work on white-tailed black cockatoos in radiata pine forests another. Saunders (1947–) discerned a new species, Carnaby's cockatoo, named for the enthusiastic amateur birdo Ivan Carnaby (1908–74) who alerted Saunders to its behavioural differences from other white-tailed black cockies. Saunders also supervised doctoral students, including Richard Hobbs, whose ecological restoration of the Western Australian Wheatbelt continues to be important in the twenty-first century (see Chapter 11).

A Bird Banders' Association was established in New South Wales in 1962, with the ABBS regional organiser Bill (Selwyn George) Lane (1922–2000) as president. Lane had begun banding seabirds in 1956 with Keith Hindwood and Arnold McGill (1905–88) at Lion Island, near the mouth of the Hawkesbury River just north of Sydney. He set up the Sydney Group of Albatross Banders, who conducted regular surveys of the Cronulla foreshore, seeking beach-washed specimens and bands.[31] Rather than each local group working in isolation and reporting direct to Canberra headquarters, the ABBS sought to 'gather and distribute as much information as possible on the technique, results and literature of our common interest'.[32] From July 1962 the association produced *Bird Bander*, renamed *Australian Bird Bander* in 1964. When the group went national and became the Australian Bird Study Association in 1977, this journal was superseded by *Corella*, which is now a refereed journal that publishes not just banding studies but 'any field study of birds'.[33] It still actively encourages contributions from 'amateurs'.

Some of Australia's earliest mist-netting was carried out in the Brindabella mountains near Canberra. Mist-netting is particularly suited to smaller forest birds (and bats). It uses fine, nearly invisible nets (typically made of nylon or polyester mesh) suspended between two poles, resembling a volleyball net, to trap birds for research without injuring them. Steve Wilson (1912–2009) was the indefatigable bander and bird enthusiast who led the Australian Capital Territory team. From April 1961 until May 1982 he conducted 292 trips (just about every possible weekend) to banding sites in New Chums Road, an apt name for a place where 'new chum' banders, some still high school students, learned their craft. Before mist nets, cuckoos and swifts had been regarded as 'untrappable'.[34] In 1964, Wilson and Lane joined forces with John McKean from CSIRO to write a practical handbook on the use of mist nets in Australia in the hope that others would try it.[35] In 1970 the Australian Capital Territory banders became the Canberra Ornithologists Group (COG) and subsequently led much of the fieldwork for the International Ornithological Congress (see Chapter 7).[36]

While CSIRO and some universities were active in banding programs, the vast majority of banders identified with amateur bodies: BOC, VORG, SAOA, COG, RZSNSW (Ornithological Section) or the New South Wales Bird Banders Association (later the NSW Field Ornithologists Club and the Australian Bird Study Association). Because CSIRO and other groups led the banding schemes, the RAOU was seldom involved with banding in this period (the 1950s and 1960s). Serious university-student researchers such as the young Anne Kerle (1954–) in the early 1970s sought out banding groups because they simply had more to offer a practical fieldworker than just 'twitching' or a national organisation. Kerle commented thirty years later that:

the BOC were the twitchers, VORG contained the people who wanted to carry out research (penguins, waders, lyrebirds, banding etc.) and

RAOU was the national organising body but didn't seem to get its feet dirty. This is of course a gross generalisation but that was how it struck me.[37]

In the summer of 1978–79, Kerle invited Pauline Reilly to join her research team to Macquarie Island to study gentoo penguins (*Pygoscelis papua*) as part of her new postgraduate work in zoology at Monash University. While the little penguins they were familiar with were about a kilogram in weight, the big gentoos, the third-tallest of all penguins, were five times as heavy. Reilly (then aged sixty) and the considerably younger Kerle, neither large in stature, succeeded in catching those gentoos for their banding program, but the challenges were significant.[38] Kerle recalled:

> The difficulty with the gentoo was that they were so nervous of you. They'd see you coming. They were on the beach, so you had to run after them and the beaches there are not sand. They are covered in pebbles, really rounded pebbles. They're hard to run on. We used to start off by doing a flying tackle to pin them down. It was a bit hard. The flippers are very long. You'd put the bird underneath your knee and pull the flipper out, and of course the flipper would thrash against you. My thigh was always bruised. They'd bite and they'd scratch. And they'd defecate all over you, too. The only thing they didn't do was regurgitate.[39]

Real science and real fieldwork went hand in hand and many scientists needed the experience of fieldworkers in their teams, even when what counted as 'science' ended up being published in arcane journals. Birdos need both practical skills and a sense of how their observations fit into the international literature. If you didn't have the passion of an amateur, it was impossible to achieve the studies that science needed. Often professional scientists felt the need to hide their passions, but some were quietly proud of their practical skills. Ian Rowley (1926–2009), who was a CSIRO research scientist for almost four decades (1953–91), was a pioneering bander in the ABBS (no. 005). He commented on the *joy* of bird-banding: 'It's like going fishing,' he said. 'It's pitting your skills against another animal.'[40] In his 'retirement', Rowley edited *Emu* for over a decade (1990–2000).

In the 1970s, the RAOU found itself rethinking its niche: it was caught between the serious 'international' scientists of CSIRO and universities and being the 'national' ornithological body. The latter was becoming increasingly irrelevant. The membership was in decline despite birdwatching being as popular as ever. There was a new urgency to find ways to engage fieldworkers—birdos—and make them feel included in the union. It wasn't until the late 1970s that the RAOU launched a new project, the *Atlas of Australian Birds*, that turned its fortunes around. Finally, then the national organisation again began to grow significantly. Its new mission gathered birdos, whether professional or amateur. Its focus was no longer arcane science or competitive collecting (of birds, or eggs, or photographs, or tall tales), but rather practical fieldwork in service of the birds themselves.

THE REST OF THE WORLD
COMES TO AUSTRALIA

Bringing the IOC south

The decision to bring the sixteenth International Ornithological Congress (IOC) to Canberra in 1974 was not taken lightly. IOCs had begun in 1884 and had been held every four years since (except during major wars and international crises), always in Europe, except for one in upstate New York. But there was a dearth of alternative offers in 1970 when the IOC met for the fifteenth time in The Hague. Jean Dorst (1924–2001), the French president, welcomed the invitation from Harry Frith, who was Australia's IOC general secretary, 'in spite of the difficulties' of 'a Congress held far away from their home country'.[1] Such Eurocentrism was met with impatience by Frith, a veteran of past IOCs, who was quick to point out that Southern Hemisphere ornithologists had borne the expense and difficulty of attending all the previous international congresses.

Frith's first IOC was the 11th, held in Basel, Switzerland, in 1954, where he presented an impressive autecological and behavioural study of the malleefowl (*Leipoa ocellata*), developed under the influence of British ornithologist David Lack (1910–73) at the Edward Grey Institute in Oxford, where he was based that year. Frith's practical fieldwork had been undertaken near Griffith, New South Wales, when he was stationed with CSIRO Wildlife for several years. The megapode (mound-building) family, of which the malleefowl is an example, had not been studied in depth before. The idea of a bird who built an incubator and controlled the temperature of the mound by adding or removing humus was a new and exciting one (this method of incubation is unknown outside the Australian region).[2] Frith's malleefowl work firmly established his reputation as an ornithologist rather than an agricultural scientist, and the study became a first salvo in his long and determined campaign to put a Southern Hemisphere stamp on international ornithology.

The idea of a conference in Australia was first mooted at the 14th IOC in Oxford in 1966 by Dom Serventy, who was a member of the IOC's Permanent Executive Committee. Lack, the general secretary at Oxford and a doyen of the British ornithology establishment, was also keen, because of his own strong biogeographical interests and friendship with both Francis Ratcliffe and Frith.[3] Other members of the 'Committee of One Hundred'—or the 'hundred wise' as Dorst liked to call them, including Ernst Mayr (1904–2005; Agassiz Museum), Klaus Immelmann (1935–87; University of Bielefeld, West Germany), Don Farner (1915–88; Washington State University) and Charles Sibley (1917–98; Peabody Museum)—had ongoing research interests in the Australasian avifauna.

Dorst became an important supporter of the Southern Hemisphere IOC but initially needed some convincing, so having a team of senior ornithologists who already understood Australian conditions was important. Dorst and Frith differed initially on the issue of languages. Frith was very keen that the congress should attract ornithologists from the *region*, including Japanese and South-East Asian workers, so he arranged for the first circular to be translated into seven languages: English, French, German, Spanish, Russian, Japanese and Indonesian. Dorst was not happy about this:

> I strongly support the view that the official languages of the Congress should be concurrently english, french and german, which languages are officially recognize according to our rules and customs. I have the highest opinion of japonese and Malaysian ornithologists but the

lectures or discussions should be given only in the recognized languages, that is for obvious reasons english in most cases. Japonese or Malaysian have never been recognized as official languages at least in Europe and in the western hemisphere. I strongly keep to this attitude.[4]

Frith, determined to broaden the base beyond Europe, solved the issue by running an English-only congress. No simultaneous translations were made available, no doubt saving considerable cost.[5] It was to Dorst's credit that he graciously accepted this rather bloody-minded solution and worked to improve relationships between Paris and Canberra from this low point. Frith's files contain numerous charming letters from Dorst, always written in (rather French) English. Frith never used French. Dorst personally attacked 'the tyranny of distance' by coming to Australia with his wife, Éliane, in August 1971 to be part of the first meeting of the Scientific Programme Committee for the congress.[6] Frith paid a flying visit to Paris, and Serventy followed in 1973, seeking guidance from Frith about 'sensitivities' before he left. Frith replied that 'Dorst and I are in complete agreement on the detail of the Congress and there is nothing of which you need to be careful with the French'.[7] This was an impressive statement at a time when diplomatic relations between the Australian and French governments were deteriorating because of French nuclear testing in the Pacific. Dorst and Frith discussed the international difficulties quite openly. In June 1973, Dorst wrote:

> I have been informed that postal relations are interrupted between Australia and France for reasons you know better than I. I deeply regret that we are continueing the atomic test in the Pacific but I cannot do much in that aspect. I also regret that this makes a conflict between our countries and I hope the situation will be settled next year.[8]

Frith was reassuring in reply: 'There has been some talk here of Australia breaking off diplomatic relations with France. I do not think this will happen but even if it did, I could not imagine it having much effect on the Congress.'[9]

Congresses traditionally consisted of two programs: the scientific symposia and the general program. The standards and subjects of the scientific program were closely guarded by the International Ornithological Committee, while the 'general programme' was more inclusive of amateurs and encompassed any number of subjects. Dorst, who regularly dealt with the Committee of One Hundred, the vast majority of whom came from Europe, favoured an Australian-driven scientific program with a 'Southern Hemisphere' focus.[10] As well as choosing a suitable subject for his presidential address—the history of avian diversity in the 'bird continent' (South America)—he also ensured that Europeans and North Americans felt suitably consulted.[11] The subject of the congress played to the strengths of the home team.

Gondwana and other southern themes

In 1912 Alfred Wegener (1880–1930) put forward the notion that all the world's continents had once been joined but had subsequently drifted apart. This idea was refined by the South African Alexander du Toit (1878–1948) in the 1920s and 1930s, who suggested that rather than a single land mass, there had been two: Laurasia (northern lands) and Gondwana (southern lands). Interest in continental drift—the idea that the continents shifted in relation to each other—had gathered pace in the 1920s, but the theory's power was limited by its lack of a mechanism to explain the movement of continents. It attracted new interest in the early 1960s, when various theories of plate tectonics or sea-floor spreading provided the crucial mechanism whereby the continents could move. A 1965 computer map showing the remarkable 'fit' of the continents against each other, the 'Bullard Fit', was discussed and debated by geologists, geomagnetic theorists, ocean-floor specialists, sedimentologists and seismologists.[12]

In 1970, Ernst Mayr declared: 'Continental drift, a geological theory that was rather unpopular from the 1930s to the 1950s, is now highly fashionable.'[13] Mayr ran a symposium titled 'Causal Ornithogeography' at the 15th IOC in The Hague, where both Serventy and Mayr's former PhD student (James) Allen Keast (1922–2009), from the Australian Museum, spoke. The symposium focused on comparisons between Australia, South Africa and South America.[14] In 1972, Mayr and Joel Cracraft (University of Illinois Medical Center) debated the question of a southern origin for some bird families in *Emu*, laying out ideas for discussion at the IOC.[15] The critical question was whether the Australasian avifauna had island-hopped across a sea barrier from the north, or radiated from Africa and Antarctica during the break-up of Gondwana. Mayr maintained that since bird speciation postdated the breaking-up of the continents, the land bridge from South-East Asia was still the best way to account for the origins of Australasian bird families. Cracraft, better acquainted with the latest theories in plate tectonics, argued that the final fragmentation was primarily a late Cretaceous and Cainozoic event (not Triassic or Jurassic, as Mayr had argued) and there was therefore a distinct probability of a Gondwanaland element in Australian bird fauna. Gondwana was an idea whose time came just in time for the Canberra congress.

The first flyer for the congress, issued in 1972, announced the theme as 'Two Hemispheres', reminding participants that 'the world has two hemispheres wherein lie sharp differences in ecology and fauna. Each ... presents a tale half told; in each we are seekers in common of the whole story of birds.'[16] The congress sought to redress the balance of earlier congresses: 'to display Southern Hemisphere birds and discuss aspects of ornithological science that are particularly relevant to arid zones and to the Southern Hemisphere'. [17] Frith later remarked that although the theme might have been considered a little parochial, it was generally welcomed, probably because of the rise of Gondwanan thinking. The 'arid zone' emphasis, appropriate to the venue in the world's driest inhabited continent, was more explicitly Australian and reflected the two decades of CSIRO research in the arid zone as a leader in the UNESCO Arid Lands Programme. It also had a strong appeal for German ornithologists who had longstanding interests in world deserts, particularly in Namibia and Saharan Africa.

The staff of the CSIRO Division of Wildlife Research were strongly represented among the symposium organisers. Dom Serventy, Richard

Schodde (1936–), Stephen Davies, Ian Rowley and Jerry (Jonkheer Gerard Frederick) van Tets (1929–95) were responsible for five of the symposia. Stephen Marchant of the RAOU chaired the symposium 'Migration and Movements in the Southern Continents' arranged by Bunty (Mary Katherine) Rowan from the Percy FitzPatrick Institute of African Ornithology (Cape Town). (This session was dropped from the published *Proceedings* as Rowan had been unable to travel to Canberra.) Allen Keast from the Australian Museum and previous IOC president Finn Salomonsen (1909–83) from Denmark took over responsibility for the symposium that Lack had planned.[18] Most of the other symposia were arranged by North Americans. The numerically predominant European group had surprisingly little to do with the scientific program. Uncertainty about travelling to Australia perhaps limited initiatives from Europe.

The first symposium, 'Origins of Australasian Avifauna', was organised by Serventy and chaired by New Zealand's distinguished geologist Charles Fleming (1916–87). Serventy had expanded his 1970 work in a major survey paper published in JD Macdonald's *Birds of Australia* in 1973. His concern was to ensure the freshest and most important findings for the 1974 congress, not just a rehash of earlier debates, yet he needed to make suitable plans in advance. At the end of 1971, Frith approached Mayr to contribute. 'Any discussion of this subject without your participation,' he wrote, 'would be like staging *Hamlet* without the Prince of Denmark.'[19] The tactful Serventy, aware that Mayr's views were at odds with his own, wanted to make sure that the prominent Harvard evolutionary biologist was part of the congress team.

Joel Cracraft (1942–) was already known for his work on the origin of ratites—the Southern Hemisphere family that includes emus and ostriches—though he was still in the early stages of what has since become a long and distinguished career with the American Museum of Natural History. By May 1972, with Cracraft's response to Mayr in press in *Emu*, Serventy decided that Cracraft was essential to his seminar on the relations between plate tectonics and the distribution of avifauna. He added Charles Sibley, too, surprising him with the suggestion. Sibley wrote: 'I usually think of my protein data in terms of "nearest relatives" and of "natural clusters", but of course they do reflect "origins" as well. It is just a matter of the window you view them through.'[20]

Soon after, at Keast's suggestion, Serventy invited Patricia Vickers-Rich (1944–), then completing her PhD at Columbia University (also Cracraft's alma mater), to join the symposium. 'Having Mrs Rich and young Cracraft as contributors,' Serventy wrote to Frith, 'will help to counter the arguments of people like [outspoken British ornithologist] Bill Bourne that at these symposia only the older ornithologists, with crystallised ideas, rehash their older opinions.'[21] In the end, Mayr decided that he would be a 'discussant' only in this session, as he had nothing new to add to his *Emu* paper. Mayr's Australian student Keast presented his work. The other paper was from Janet Kear (1933–2004) and Ron Murton (1932–78) of England. It was a symposium where younger and female ornithologists were, for the period, uncharacteristically well-represented.

When Mayr realised that he did not want to speak about 'adaptive radiations' in the Serventy/Fleming symposium, he approached Walter Bock (1933–2022) of Columbia University and together they conceived a complementary session. The question they posed was 'Which taxonomic characters contribute what to avian classification?' What are the relative roles of gross morphology (muscles and bones), special morphological characters (intestinal tract or glottal apparatus), behaviour, immunology and other character complexes? 'The Value of Various Taxonomic Characters in Avian Classification' had particular appeal to museum workers everywhere.[22]

Schodde convened the symposium 'The Biology of Southern Hemisphere Species', which was chaired by Sir Robert Falla (1901–79) from New Zealand and Mayr. All the contributors were Australian except for Gordon Williams (1920–83; from New Zealand's Wildlife Service). This symposium was overwhelmingly 'Australasian' rather than 'Southern Hemisphere'. It was led by Davies and Keast.[23]

Davies also convened the symposium 'Breeding of Birds in Southern Continents', with speakers from Germany, Australia and South Africa. All were concerned with adaptive mechanisms that govern breeding seasons, an issue particularly relevant to the unpredictable annual cycles of southern continents, especially South Africa and Australia. Local

CSIRO ecologist Henry Nix (1937–2022) gave an important paper titled 'Environmental Control of Breeding, Post-breeding Dispersal and Migration of Australian Birds', which was still in demand a quarter of a century after its publication.[24] When it came to editing the congress proceedings, Frith and Calaby allowed Nix thirty-five pages in a volume where a twelve-page maximum was otherwise fairly strictly enforced—a latitude that indulged the promise of Nix's new, systems-based approach.[25]

The symposium 'Physiological and Behavioural Adaptations to Arid Zones' was convened by Don Farner from the United States and Klaus Immelmann from Germany. Both had worked extensively in Australia and South Africa and been key contributors to southern ornithological ideas in the 1950s and 1960s. Davies and Wayne Braithwaite (1941–2011) from CSIRO both spoke in this session, as did Gordon Maclean (1937–2008) from the University of Natal; Maclean contributed two very different papers, one comparing Southern African and South American arid-zone ornithology, the other a close study of sand grouse adaptations to aridity.[26] This symposium also effectively set up the working team for the next IOC: Farner was elected president and Immelmann general secretary of the 17th congress, to be hosted by West Germany in Berlin in 1978.

The symposia titled 'Biology of Crowned Sparrows (Zonotrichia) in Two Hemispheres' and 'Structure of Feathers' both originated in the United States. The sparrows symposium dealt largely with American material, attracting six speakers from the United States (including Farner). The 'Structure of Feathers' symposium, convened by Alan Brush (1934–) of the University of Connecticut, attracted scientists from all over the world. The two Australian papers on feather keratin, one from the University of Adelaide and the other from the CSIRO Division of Protein Chemistry, were largely biochemical, reminding participants that 'ornithology' had outliers in many other sciences.

Sibley had used biochemical studies and electrophoresis to develop a whole new systematics of Australian passerines at Yale University's Peabody Museum of Natural History. His work was so important, both to the conference theme and to the host nation, that it justified a whole seminar in its own right. Working with his new technique of comparing egg-white proteins, he was revisiting the question of 'relatedness' between birds and their families. In the early 1970s he was finding 'remarkable puzzles' among such groups as thornbills, honeyeaters, pardalotes, scrubwrens and bristlebirds, magpies and currawongs. Sibley was 'convinced that there are more complex situations among Australian passerines than in any other area of comparable size'. He continued:

> This is not to say that Australian non-passerines are lacking in inter-esting problems, but I do think their higher category allocations are closer to being understood. The passerines were messed up originally because they were crammed into the most similar European family. To sort things out will require the comparison of all genera with one another and with the 'standard' families. There are some true sylviids in Australia—but there also seem to be some convergent-sylviids that belong elsewhere. And so forth.[27]

Sibley perfectly read the mood of the Australian Scientific Advisory Committee (and Frith in particular) by pointing to where the European bias had 'messed things up' for Australian ornithology. Sensitive that the Australians may also have been wary of American imperialism, he was (uncharacteristically) modest in the throwaway remark 'I suppose that I'm as deeply involved in the higher category systematics of Australian birds as anybody these days'.[28] Because of the Australian bias of the audience, Frith argued that Sibley needed time to expound on behaviour and other aspects of passerine biology as well.[29] His work framed a high-profile forum in which the younger and 'up-and-coming' Australian systematists Keast, Schodde, John McKean (1941–96) and Julian Ford (1932–87) could offer papers. Sibley also impressed many younger and prospective professional ornithologists at the congress by representing avian family trees on a huge poster that went the full length of one wall in the public area. In an era before 'poster sessions' became a regular feature of conferences, this was an impressive way to lay out a complex theory.

The symposium 'Evolution of Island Land Birds' honoured the late David Lack, the world expert on the evolution of avian clutch sizes, who had argued that they were based on individual rather than species selection. Keast, arguably the greatest general biogeographer of the Australasian region at the time, brought together a number of island specialists from North America and Europe, including the now well-known geographer and avian physiologist and science writer Jared Diamond (1937–) of UCLA's Medical Center.

On his return to South Africa, Richard Liversidge (1926–2003) of the Percy FitzPatrick Institute of Ornithology commented that 'co-operative breeding ... was the outstanding topic of the congress for everybody'.[30] This was undoubtedly a 'Southern Hemisphere' view, but it was indicative of a growing interest in the evolutionary strategy of non-breeding adults acting as 'helpers at the nest', in the 1935 words of American naturalist Alexander Skutch (1904–2004).[31] Rowley's pioneering work with white-winged choughs and fairy-wrens in the 1960s had suggested that 'helpers at the nest' were an efficient evolutionary strategy particularly favoured in Australia, Africa and the tropics.[32] It was an area of ornithological research where Australian studies led the rest of the world. Rowley's 1974 symposium included other specialists presenting overviews of cooperative breeding in Africa, America and Eurasia. Here was an Australian theme explored in the context of northern lands.[33]

The final symposium, convened by CSIRO palaeo-ornithologist Jerry van Tets, was titled 'Seabirds: Distribution, Speciation and Ecological Diversification at Sea'. This theme showcased important Antarctic work by Australian and New Zealand scientists, as well as work from the Netherlands, northern Scotland and Nova Scotia. The Standing Committee for the Coordination of Seabird Research also met as usual as part of the administrative proceedings of the IOC. The study of seabirds, with their long migrations and minimal contact with land, demands a particularly high level of international cooperation, something long supported by successive IOCs.[34]

Conservation issues, museum collecting and international professionals

Some of the visiting museum professionals had scientific agendas of their own to pursue while in Australia, but the host nation was reluctant to offer collecting permits, particularly where specimens were to leave the country. The large North American ornithological community had diverse views on the subject. Keast, as an Australian with strong North American connections, found himself regularly trapped between the expectations of the visitors and the rules of his home country. He wrote to Frith two years before the congress:

> Because of proximity, I have fallen into the role of de facto agent with various people writing [for] suggestions and for information about where they should visit. Most embarrassing are the professionals who ask me about collecting permits. I do my best to give them the addresses to which to write and end up by saying (lest I be thought of in Australia as organising a blood bath), 'Don't mention my name'.[35]

Keast was, like Jock Marshall, a polymath with connections and networks across a range of international museums and universities. His obituary in *Auk* described him as 'an anatomist, an anthropologist, a botanist, a herpetologist, an ichthyologist, a lecturer, a lepidopterologist, a mammalogist, a morphologist, a museum curator, an ornithologist, a photographer, a physiologist, a populariser of science, a university professor, and a television producer'.[36] Like Marshall, he had come late to formal qualifications. He was a scholarship student at Harvard, completing a PhD with Mayr in 1955 titled *Bird Speciation on the Australian Continent*, when he was thirty-three, after working as a museum collector in New Britain and serving in the war in New Guinea. From 1962 he spent most of his time in Canada, having established a long-term research program on fish community ecology at Queen's University Biological Station at Lake Opinicon, north of Kingston. He remained on staff at Queen's University for the rest of his life but never lost touch with his Sydney family, visiting them and the Australian Museum in Sydney at least annually. His ongoing work in Australia was recognised by the RAOU in the 1995 award of the DL Serventy Medal honouring a distinguished ornithologist.[37]

Collecting was a hot topic at the XVI World Conference of the International Council for Bird Preservation, which met in Canberra from 19 to 25 August 1974, straight after the IOC. Dorst, the IOC president, was also a vice-president of the ICBP. Eighty delegates were present representing member organisations, along with other observers.[38] Its thirty-three resolutions addressed issues ranging from establishing an international register for the material of endangered species held in museums through to specific recommendations to individual governments.[39]

The resolutions reflected the scientific community's growing ambivalence about collecting, even for museums and public collections. The conference recommended that shooting permits should only be issued to accredited museums and scientific institutions and their agents, and mist-netting permits to 'properly qualified persons', and urged scientists to 'consider alternative ways of obtaining information'. A suggestion was made that the International Council of Museums should provide 'policies and guidelines' and 'ethical standards'. There were clearly differences between nations, as well as between individuals, on the subject of collecting. The ICBP was based in London and reflected its ethically conscious homeland.

Frith reported to Farner that the debate at the ICBP meeting was 'confused'.[40] Sibley had instigated a meeting on 'Conserving and Collecting' during the IOC itself following a heated discussion of the subject at the October 1973 meeting of the American Ornithologists' Union. Serventy chaired the meeting, which set out to address Sibley's concerns that 'unless we begin to fight for sensible regulations based upon facts rather than upon fancy we are doomed to lose all collecting rights within a few years … Collectors are already extinct in Britain and are endangered species in many other areas. Shall we try to reverse the trend?'[41]

Sibley took a tough line, reflecting the annoyance many Americans felt with British rules. Sibley himself had upset the conservation lobby not long before the conference when 'the last egg of a northern European sea eagle turned up in his collection'. The conference buzzed with rumours of illegally collected eggs of endangered species in association with egg-white protein assays.[42] British collectors were not, in fact, 'extinct': JD Macdonald had spoken out vociferously in favour of collecting throughout the British Museum's Harold Hall expeditions of the 1960s and had made a film about the first of them to explain the importance of collection to science.[43] Sibley probably asked Serventy to chair the session because of his role in the Harold Hall expeditions, and because he was neither British nor American.

In spite of all this, the IOC was able to recommend (and the ICBP endorsed) that:

> Governments allow scientific institutions to collect materials they need for research with the requirement that applying institutions, in need of material of endangered species, must ensure that such material is necessary for this research and will not threaten the existence of that population.[44]

Other conservation concerns included land-use planning and habitat protection (including feral plant and animal control and protection against oil spills). The fate of seabirds in both the Northern Hemisphere (salmon gillnet fishing) and the Southern (commercial exploitation) was the subject of several resolutions. The Australian parrot specialist Joe Forshaw (1939–) arranged a special symposium for a whole day on the biological effects of the international trade in live birds, and one ICBP resolution dealt specifically with this issue. (Parrots are still popular aviary birds and pets in the United States.)

Threats to the paths of migratory birds from East Asia to Australia were another concern. The term 'East Asian Flyway' had been coined as part of the Migratory Animal Pathological Survey (MAPS) work by the United States Army, headed by ornithologist H Elliott McClure (1910–98). As part of the 'Migration and Movements' symposium in the General Session of the IOC, McClure reported on his work banding 1.25 million birds of 1214 species from 1963 to 1971. He grouped the migration routes of the multiple species moving from north to south through Eurasia into four major distinct flyways: East Asian (including Australasia), Indo-Asian, Eastern Afro-Europe and Western Afro-Europe. 'Migration patterns of the present millennia probably reflect glacial patterns of the Pleistocene,' he hypothesised, and these patterns therefore have implications for 'current theories of continental drift'. The MAPS work also had practical implications for conservation: habitat disturbance had clearly altered flight paths and destinations during the course of the project.[45] The Australasian region was the particular focus of conservation concerns. Five separate resolutions raised concern for avifauna of the north-eastern tropical rainforests in mainland Australia, Christmas and Norfolk islands, New Caledonia and wetlands in Hong Kong (Deep Bay marshes, now Mai Po Nature Reserve managed by WWF).

Frith's Canberra team

As chief of the CSIRO Division of Wildlife Research, Frith was one of Australia's internationally best-known and most senior ornithologists, and many of his staff were also well known in IOC circles and among the museum collectors and others who stayed on in Canberra for the meeting of the ICBP. But CSIRO Wildlife could not sponsor big expensive international congresses alone, and Frith relied heavily on local and national connections. Some federal government money came via the Australian Academy of Science (AAS). The congress's location in Canberra was attractive for federal funding and its facilities were more compact and convenient than in a bigger city like Sydney or Melbourne.[46] Canberra's vibrant scientific culture was important, particularly as many of its most distinguished senior scientists were amateur birdos. The CSIRO's foundation chief executive officer, FWG (later Sir Frederick) White (1904–95), was also a foundation fellow of the AAS and an enthusiastic member of the Canberra Ornithologists Group. He retired as chairman of CSIRO in 1969, and the upcoming Australian congress became his pet retirement project.[47] As a member of the AAS council, Sir Fred rallied support from official channels. He was also the congress's number-one registrant.[48] The project to showcase Canberra's birds for the world resonated well with him and other senior figures, who gave practical help with fieldwork as well as lending authority and international distinction.

Given a choice, Frith might well have preferred to organise the IOC without help from the RAOU, but he needed more financial support than the AAS and the federal government could offer. The financial cost of air-fares for keynote speakers, most of whom were coming from Europe and North America, was vastly more than the costs for a Northern Hemisphere conference. The RAOU's promise of $10,000 in donations was essential to the Australian bid and a key to the success of the enterprise. The choice of Canberra was generally popular with the RAOU except for a comment from Western Australian Museum curator Glen Storr (1921–90), who 'shuddered to think of a conference in Canberra in August'.[49] Others generally cracked hardy about chilly weather and recognised that the internationals expected a conference in the northern summer, when they could best afford the time to travel so far. The Canberra location enabled the AAS to 'host' the enterprise and to accept 'full financial and management responsibility' for it, and its prestige greatly assisted in gaining government support. The RAOU provided a route for private, tax-deductible donations, and added scientific personnel to the organising committee.[50] The junior partner in the arrangement was Frith's own CSIRO Division of Wildlife Research, whose considerable support for the congress was given 'in-kind'. The time and energy of the whole division given to the event reflected the many closet birdos in its ranks, not just scientists but also administrative and technical officers, and the strong connections between these people and the local, very energetic Canberra Ornithologists Group.

The IOC and the RAOU

Dom Serventy met RAOU president and museum curator Allan McEvey (1919–96) in Melbourne in mid-December 1968 on his way to band shearwaters at Fisher Island in Bass Strait. It was the end of a famously revolutionary year internationally. The world of birdos had also imploded that year: just as the IOC had signed up to make its first-ever trip to the Southern Hemisphere, Australian birdos had descended into internecine warfare. The Review Committee that had been grappling with the RAOU mess had disbanded, and the union had had more resignations than new memberships. It seemed that they had no way to raise the money they had promised to contribute to the IOC. In the pub, over a beer, Serventy and McEvey decided that reform was needed and they would have to 'be' the committee, as the situation needed urgent attention. 'He came home to dinner with me and over a glass of port, he wrote out the terms of reference,' McEvey said.[51]

Serventy wrote the 'RAOU Review Report', couching it carefully in terms acceptable to his professional CSIRO colleagues, and McEvey used his presidency to sell the idea of reform to the general membership. Coming from Western Australia, Serventy had the advantage of being outside the poisonous politics of the eastern states, but his regular trips to his Fisher Island shearwater banding sites kept him abreast of the issues. He had a simple message for the membership: 'The RAOU must become a true society for the *study* of Australasian birds, or it will become useless and be replaced.'[52] The report recommended upgrading *Emu* to ensure that 'only additions to existing knowledge' were published (rather than 'stray feathers' and gossip); that the annual congress become a scientific meeting (modelled on the successful Canberra meeting of 1968); and that a 'Field Investigation Committee' be established to coordinate the scientific work of the union.[53] 'Conservation' had become a flashpoint, so the report recommended leaving that to the 'many efficient animal and habitat conservation societies [that now] exist'. The RAOU could maintain a 'watching brief', but should refocus its efforts on bird study.

Serventy realised that McEvey also needed a successor before the 1974 meeting, someone who could bring dignity to the position of RAOU president but not frighten off the amateur enthusiasts, particularly those engaged with banding and other useful citizen science initiatives. He took the experienced bander Pauline Reilly with him to work at Fisher

Island for sixteen days, and eventually convinced her to take on the task of RAOU president.

Reilly much preferred fieldwork to administration and did not feel suitably qualified to be RAOU president at a time when the rest of the world was coming to see what Australian birding might offer. Pioneering female lawyer Rosemary Balmford (1933–2017) and Harry Frith pressed her to take on the task. Instead of trying to do everything, they encouraged her to focus on the tasks that would make the international congress work, the long-unfinished *Checklist* (Balmford), a good talk for the IOC delegates (Frith) and, above all, raising substantial funding for the IOC (both).[54] The only woman to have been president of the RAOU before Reilly was the New Zealander Perrine Moncrieff (1893–1979), in 1932–33, who had been a largely absentee president because of her base on the other side of the Tasman. Reilly felt diffident taking on the role, but she found support in unexpected places. She had been a successful president of the Australian Bird Banders Association, another male-dominated group. 'I remember Bill Lane was one who wanted me to do this,' she recalled, 'and I said to him, "Oh, Bill, they won't listen to a woman." And he said, "Yes they will."'[55] Reilly also had good support from Balmford, who was the first female judge of the Supreme Court of Victoria, the first female lecturer in the Law Faculty of the University of Melbourne, and a fanatical birdo. In the end, Reilly took on the task on condition that Serventy did the presidential address for the IOC. Serventy, who had a major speech impediment, reneged on this promise, but Reilly's presidential address, based on her own penguin work, was brilliant.[56]

In 1970 the RAOU had promised to match the government's grant of $10,000. When Reilly visited Frith in Canberra in 1972, just two years out from the congress, he said, 'You've got to get that money. The RAOU has promised it, but they've done nothing.' Time was running out. Reilly was no fundraiser, but she was a great inspirer of people and chose them wisely. She persuaded Norman Wettenhall to join the RAOU Council. He recalled:

Pauline came to me and said, 'Norman, you've just helped raise a lot of money for the university'—which I had, you know, half a million for the Dame Elisabeth Murdoch Chair of Landscape Architecture—'Do you think you could get $10,000, which is what Harry Frith says we need to show our credentials?' I said, 'That shouldn't be too hard,' so I tackled a few people … and we had that $10,000 in a month.[57]

Such philanthropic connections were extremely important in re-establishing the union's status as Australia's premier ornithological body. This was the sort of money that a publicly funded body like CSIRO could not raise, but that influential North American birders expected. The federal government and the RAOU had equal shares in the financing of the IOC, which was essential to showing both the government and the institutional establishment (CSIRO, museums and universities) that the RAOU was a serious partner in the ornithological venture.

It was the right moment for the RAOU to have a woman president. After all the ructions, there was an advantage in being so clearly different from the old guard. Reilly's talent lay in realising, as she had with the fundraising, that she did not have to do it all herself: 'You had to pick people's brains. You had a council of people who were reasonably concerned. I wanted to get some more dynamic people on to council.' Some councillors were already overcommitted and there were only nine of them, so 'I asked if they'd be prepared to stand down because I felt it needed new blood … They were most cooperative.'[58] Under Reilly's astute leadership, a new game plan was mapped out just in time for preparations for the IOC.

The RAOU survived. The professional ornithologists of the second reform committee, McEvey and Serventy, stepped back from day-to-day management and allowed the RAOU to define its new generational style without further interference.

An extraordinary moment to bring the rest of the world to Australia

Although the official sponsors of the 1974 congress were the AAS and the RAOU, the CSIRO Division of Wildlife Research was the key to its success. Harry Frith put an enormous amount of his own time into its organisation over the four years from 1970 to 1974. It is clear from his correspondence that by 1974 the congress represented a very significant part of his working week and that of his hardworking and intelligent secretary, Jan Finley, who serviced the executive committee.

Finley also wrote much of the routine correspondence for Frith about the congress, often working from just two or three cryptic handwritten words to create a full letter. Her work was indispensable in the period from December 1973 to January 1974, when Frith was hospitalised and then convalescing after a serious car accident that left him with a fractured pelvis. The congress business went along steadily despite his absence, and when he returned in February he was able to take the reins again seamlessly. Finley's efficiency meant that he had nothing to apologise for, and spared him the trouble of discussing the accident, which left him with ongoing pain.[59] The whole division swung in behind Frith on the IOC. During the congress itself, individuals were responsible for different aspects—for example, mammalogist John Calaby produced daily bulletins and led ornithological field expeditions. Younger staff were responsible for exhibits under the leadership of regional administrative officer Paul Magi (1927–2009), who had a talent for emergency management. Later the same year, he ended up managing the CSIRO Darwin labs and staff after Cyclone Tracy destroyed most of that city on Christmas Day.[60]

Neither the AAS (with very few paid staff) nor the RAOU (with none) could have shouldered such an administrative load. The IOC cost Wildlife staff (and their families) their weekends and evenings. As it turned out, the complications of transport strikes and other extraneous pressures meant that only an organisation the size of CSIRO, with officers in places like Alice Springs and Perth, could have rescued the congress. These were the 'young team which kept an everlasting smile all along the week'.[61] The men's wives ran a 'Ladies Programme' led by the able and hardworking Dorothy Frith, Daphne Fullagar and Jo Calaby. Dorothy was earmarked for this role not by her husband but by Serventy, who wrote in 1971 in his advice about organisation that 'ladies need a ladies committee (of which the Secretary-General's wife would be a prominent member)'.[62] The 'whole family' commitment that was part of the CSIRO culture in those years was a great boon in a crisis.[63] The Ladies' Programme was much appreciated by the international spouses and family members, and contributed significantly to Australia's good reputation as host nation.

Although the scientific crew took a high profile in leading the congress, they managed to do so in an informal and friendly way. Noel Gove (1920–2001), the RAOU treasurer and an amateur ornithologist, expressed appreciation that the 'precision of operations and timing of sessions' and 'the perpetual help and assistance to delegates ... allowed for so much discussion of equality between Professional and Amateur'.[64] The *Daily Bulletin*, edited by John Calaby, made last-minute changes to the program and tours possible, and all delegates felt that they knew what was happening. Gove wrote, 'I had many discussions with both the eminent and also-rans and without exception their sincere praise for the organisation and staging was wonderful to hear.'

Canberra itself was under scrutiny, and Canberra families were proud of their still-new city. In his bid, Frith described it cautiously as 'a planned and, hence, artificial city. Most people think it and its setting beautiful; some believe that it has everything but a soul.' Canberra's strongest claim for this particular congress was its wonderful birdlife:

> The city being at the bottom end of an altitudinal migration, it teems with birds in August. You can see a hundred or more cockatoos on the city lawns, king parrots in your garden and numerous passerines in the city streets. Lyrebirds and bowerbirds are twenty miles [30 kilometres] away. Honeyeaters abound close to the congress site.[65]

There is a defensive and slightly apologetic tone in Frith's claims for the university:

The Australian National University is new; some of the buildings the congress will use are not built yet. It has neither the charm of Oxford, the elegance of the Hague Congress Centre nor the opulence of Cornell. However it has everything that the average congress-goer needs, especially if he is familiar with young countries and with simple efficiency.[66]

As it transpired, the young volunteers from the ANU were essential to the success of the congress, and the congress itself inspired new directions in their future careers. Mike Fleming (1954–), who made his career as a parks and wildlife officer, was one of three or four undergraduate members of the ANU Biological Society who assisted the congress with local excursions: 'It opened my eyes for the first time to the fact that ornithology is an international thing, and that there were these people who were passionate about not only their own areas, but who could come to Australia and be equally passionate about seeing birds.' He made 'some interesting contacts' but it also made a connection for him between his childhood passion for birds and his new university science.[67] Penny Olsen, then a junior CSIRO Wildlife officer working on water rats (rakali), now a Serventy medallist, raptor specialist and natural history writer, declared: 'It made me an ornithologist.'[68]

Frith was impatient with condescension, particularly of the British variety. He was an Australian nationalist who was at times so anxious to avoid the colonial cringe that he came across with an Australian 'strut'. In a published reply to one British critic's early concerns in advance of the IOC, Frith wrote:

It is worth saying that Australians sometimes might be a bit rough externally, often do not like ill-informed criticism and, above all, do not suffer fools gladly but scratch one and you usually find a reasonably sensitive and extremely hospitable person underneath.[69]

He wanted passionately to put Australia's 'best foot' forward. This required small miracles at times to make a success of a congress dogged with more

than its fair share of administrative uncertainty. August 1974 came soon
after the global oil shocks, which affected many potential contributors
and caused a raft of late cancellations. Frith needed all the versatility and
strength of his full CSIRO team to cope with this and other vagaries.
Perhaps the secret of his own administrative success was that he organised
his work creatively to ensure that he never lost touch with his science (and
left the social activities to his very capable wife to organise). A journalist
who contacted him about the IOC just weeks before the congress got a full
report direct from the aviary Frith had installed next to his office. 'Right
now,' said Frith, 'I can see a bronze-wing, a wompoo, a top knot, a green-
winged pigeon, a red-crowned pigeon, a chestnut quilled rock pigeon ...'[70]
It certainly kept the congress's stresses in perspective.

Delegates on their way to the congress were stranded by a last-minute
transport workers' strike within Australia. Many who had travelled early
to see more of Australia while they were in the country were caught out.
Jean Dorst himself was stranded in Perth, along with others on an outback
excursion with Stephen Davies. Denis Saunders, who was acting officer-in-
charge of the CSIRO Perth Laboratory in the absence of Davies, managed
to charter two light planes, using his personal contacts in the aviation
industry. Dorst, Serventy and twelve other stranded delegates made it
from Perth to Canberra on the chartered flights, but eight hours late for
the planned opening on the Monday. The first day's proceedings had to be
rescheduled over the rest of the week, but the conference all went ahead.[71]
In the meantime, those who had arrived in time for the original start had
to be entertained. A busload of ornithologists went birding at Nanima near
Yass that afternoon at very short notice, and had a great time.[72]

Another group was stuck at Alice Springs, where the local CSIRO
Wildlife team (Colin Lendon, Bill Low and Laurie Corbett) rallied and
entertained them with an impromptu additional tour of that district while
they were awaiting their connections. The Alice Springs delegates finally
arrived in good spirits at 11 p.m. on the Monday night and were met by
Harry Frith himself, who had arranged a late dinner for them.[73]

Canberra scientist Henry Nix, returning for the congress after a
seven-week consultancy in Kenya, was stranded in Mauritius with many

of the Southern African participants. Qantas found a lateral solution to the strike, flying to Singapore to refuel and then to Perth and Sydney, but there was no transport from Sydney to Canberra. The travellers from Africa eventually arrived late on Sunday night in a VW Kombi van rented from an enterprising entrepreneur at Sydney Airport. Packed with jet-lagged Southern Africans, the elderly bus had encountered the aftermath of a major accident at a motor-racing circuit and the worst traffic jam ever seen between Sydney and Canberra. The normal four-hour trip took eight hours.[74] Such were the horrors that Jerry Price (1912–99), CSIRO chairman, commented that 'the transport difficulties may even have added to the spirit of the meeting'. His letter of thanks recognised the 'many hours overcoming problems which you no doubt hope will never have to be faced by those arranging such meetings in the future'.[75] Frith sent two desperate telegrams in the weeks before the congress: one to Bob Hawke, president of the Australian Council of Trade Unions, and the other to Clyde Cameron, the Minister for Labour.

EIGHT HUNDRED SCIENTISTS FROM ALL OVER THE WORLD WILL ATTEND 16th INTERNATIONAL ORNITHOLOGICAL CONGRESS IN CANBERRA 12–17 AUGUST. IF THEY HAVE TO LIVE IN UNHEATED ROOMS AND LECTURE THEATRES AND THERE IS NO PETROL FOR FIELD INSPECTIONS AUSTRALIA WILL LOOK POOR IN THE EYES OF THE WORLD. I WOULD APPRECIATE ANY HELP YOU CAN GIVE.

He also sent a special request for oil for the ANU to Gordon Bryant, Minister for the Capital Territory.[76] These last-minute machinations worked. No one complained of the cold in the congress facilities, despite the fact that it was a bitter week, with snow falling on the field excursions near Canberra.[77]

Even the publication of the proceedings faltered. Frith and Calaby sent the massive edited manuscript of the congress to EJ Brill of Leiden in the Netherlands, the publishers of the previous IOC proceedings, but international inflation and a rapidly devaluing Australian dollar meant that the cost of printing had risen steadily and the revised quotation for the publication was significantly more than the budgeted amount. Frith withdrew the manuscript. Fortunately, the AAS came to the rescue and published the proceedings locally. Because government supply had been blocked in the Senate, there was no prospect of a government subsidy, making the publication very expensive.[78] On 18 November 1975, a week after the governor-general had sacked the Australian prime minister, Frith reassured members of the Permanent Executive Committee of the IOC that the *Proceedings* were at the printers. The volume would be published in May 1976. 'I regret the delay,' he wrote, 'but May 1976 is not too bad after all.' Given the extraordinary circumstances, this was the understatement of the congress.

8

NOISY SCRUB-BIRD

The noisy scrub-bird (*Atrichornis clamosus*) was believed to be extinct for over half of the twentieth century. Archibald J Campbell, the future co-founder of the Australasian Ornithologists' Union, shot one on an expedition to Torbay in south-western Australia in October 1889 and there were a couple of doubtful nesting records in the 1890s, but no confirmed sightings of the bird were recorded for the first six decades of the twentieth century.[1] Occasional unconfirmed reports of mysterious loud calls in the Two Peoples Bay area near Albany kept alive the hope that the species would be rediscovered, but it was officially 'presumed extinct'.

Noisy scrub-birds were known as 'Jeemuluk/Tjimiluk' to Noongar Aboriginal people around the south-west coast of Australia. This name possibly related to the bird's complex triple-barrelled calls, sometimes referred to as 'zip da dee' or 'zit, squeak and chip'.[2] The first encounter between noisy scrub-birds and European ornithology, in 1842, was not in the Albany region but further north on the Darling escarpment. At Drakesbrook, near Waroona, a noisy scrub-bird met one of the great field ornithologists of the nineteenth century: John Gilbert, the most famous of John Gould's collectors. 'Its notes are so exceedingly loud and shrill,' Gilbert remarked, 'as to produce a ringing sensation in the ears, precisely the effect produced when a shrill whistle is blown in a small room.'[3] This one became the type specimen.

Despite its clamorous voice, the noisy scrub-bird was extraordinarily hard to collect because of its secretive habits and preference for head-high scrub. It was a mark of Gilbert's patience and skill that Gould was able to describe it so early, just over a decade after the founding of the Western Australian colony. It was not until 1866 that ornithologists described the related rufous scrub-bird (*Atrichornis rufescens*; also loud-voiced and secretive) that lives in the Gondwanan forests of northern New South Wales and southern Queensland.[4] Collectors had no success in finding nests, eggs or female birds. The females don't call; the loud, ventriloqual call is always the male protecting the nest. At the turn of the century, Campbell declared (of the rufous variety) that 'it is indeed remarkable that no collector has ever yet been able to procure a female'.[5]

Missing

Rediscovering *Atrichornis clamosus* became a dream of ornithologists east and west, including Campbell himself. Before the RAOU campout to Yallingup in 1920, he pleaded: 'Should any forest dweller believe the bird exists anywhere please advise Mr AJ Campbell.'[6] By the time of the 1948 RAOU Congress in Perth, the bird's status was mysterious, and known sites associated with it were 'significant'. As part of the congress, the Western Australians planned a celebratory 'pilgrimage' to Drakesbrook to dedicate a memorial tablet to Gilbert on the site of the discovery of the noisy scrub-bird.[7] Gilbert was regarded as the patron saint of Western Australian ornithology. 'With his coming,' wrote Dom Serventy and Hubert Whittell (1883–1954), 'Western Australian birds were to receive intensive study, and practically all the species inhabiting the southern portion of Western Australia were to be "discovered".'[8] Unfortunately, the Gilbert memorial dedication event was cancelled due to the stringencies of postwar petrol rationing.

Scrub-birds managed to find their way on to the congress agenda in any case. The problem was that there was no skin of a noisy scrub-bird in the Western Australian Museum. Gilbert's specimens had gone to Gould in England, while Campbell's 1889 skin was in Melbourne. Only twenty-one or twenty-two specimens survived in all the museums of the world.[9] Would the National Museum of Victoria give Western Australia one of its skins? Crosbie Morrison, speaking on behalf of the Victorian trustees, reported that 'as there were several skins ... the trustees decided to make one available to the local museum, but [only]... as a permanent loan'.[10]

Found!

In December 1961, Hargreaves (Harley) Webster (1909–?), an amateur ornithologist, teacher and bird artist, was on an excursion to Two Peoples Bay. Amid chest-high scrub thicket, he was astonished by a clear and unequivocal view of a noisy scrub-bird. Webster didn't know who to tell. His greatest worry was that the bird he had seen might be the very last of the species, the endling. This would prove too great a temptation for the collecting team from the Western Australian Museum, several of whom were passionately interested in what this bird could mean to international systematics.[11]

Webster's field notebook records his anguish: 'How can I record my discovery and retain re-discovery rights?' he wrote.[12] He thought of borrowing a portable tape-recorder to 'collect' the bird's distinctive territorial triple call. Six days later he returned to the site of the calls very early in the morning with his camera, in the hope of photographing the bird or its nest. Again he confronted the ethical dilemmas of his find. He wrote in his notebook: 'I almost held my breath when *Atrichornis* suddenly appeared in a (blue flowered) bush on the edge of the thick scrub ... I saw him for perhaps one minute. What am I to do about this discovery?'[13] His notebook lists the potential consequences of making the find public:

1. The bird will be collected by the museum;

2. Ornithologists will crowd the place;

3. Other people will crowd the place.

He agonised over his options. He could not collect the bird himself without a permit, and he could not get a permit without the museum team learning of the find. The state's senior professional ornithologists would 'almost certainly remove any credit and honour I may legitimately look for'.[14]

Webster finally broke his story to the *West Australian* newspaper. It was published on Christmas morning as a 'good news' story for the state, though the exact location was carefully withheld to protect the safety of the bird. Webster himself spent Christmas morning recording its calls. He immediately wrote up his rediscovery notes and offered them to the *Western Australian Naturalist*, where they were published in January 1962. With an eye to posterity, he lodged his field diary with the RAOU in Melbourne. Webster used the RAOU's national authority and its archive, which were at arm's length from tense Western Australian bird-politics, to protect his place in history.

Webster did not trust the professionals, but neither would he have his find dismissed as 'merely amateur'. The 1960s saw acute acrimony between old-school amateurs and the emerging class of new professionals. This friction nearly tore the RAOU itself apart (see Chapter 7). In fact, the team at the museum, especially Julian Ford (1932–87), who later undertook doctoral studies on the subject of speciation in the Australasian region, had been hoping for years to rediscover the bird.[15] Ford was the Western Australian secretary for the RAOU. In a short (competitive) piece in *Emu* in January 1963, he reported that Charles Allen and Peter Fuller had heard the bird on 5 November 1961, giving them bragging rights over Webster for 'the most exciting news of the century'.[16] The 5 November find was hotly disputed by Webster, who wrote to the *Albany Advertiser* on 19 July 1963 when it republished the Ford report from *Emu*:

You will remember when I first broke the momentous news of the rediscovery of the noisy scrub bird to you on the afternoon of Sunday

December 24 1961 and asked your advice whether or not to give the news to the press as I feared that an immediate attempt would be made to shoot this bird for the museum collection. You advised me to give it to the 'West Australian' and in fact, rang Perth and vouched for me.[17]

The editor published an apology: 'There has never been any doubt in our mind that Mr Webster was the first person to find and identify the noisy scrub-bird after its long disappearance.'

On 28 December 1961, Webster met Allen when Allen arrived with Ford and others to see the bird. There was, according to Webster, 'a heated argument between myself and the would-be bird collector [Ford] ... and I warned him for his own reputation to leave the bird alone'. For Allen 'I have nothing but respect', Webster commented, and observed that at this time Allen made 'no claim or mention of 5 November 1961'.[18] Allen did say that he had recognised the call as the same as one he had heard in 1942 in the same swamp. The swamp had been burnt in a major fire in the late 1940s, thus providing a retrospective 'record' of the bird. Dom Serventy also came to see the bird to confirm Webster's identification for the article in the *Western Australian Naturalist*. A total of seven men travelled to remote Two Peoples Bay from Perth on 28 December: Serventy, Ford and Allen were accompanied by JB Higham, Clee Jenkins, Gerlof Mees (1926–2013; the Dutch curator of birds then working at the Western Australian Museum), and the well-travelled American ambassador-ornithologist Don Lamm (1914–96). This bird was international news.

The ethics of 'collecting' were complex, especially in the case of an 'endling', the very last individual of a species. Dick Kimber's concern about the moral burden of taking the very last night parrot (see Chapter 2) was echoed in Webster's comment 'I hate the thought of killing this or any bird and will not do so unless driven to it—or asked to do it?'[19] It was not collected. But better still, it did not turn out to be the last noisy scrub-bird.

Webster's bird was one of a very small population with a tiny range, extremely vulnerable to fire, but there were both males and females in the area. The immediate problem was the plan for town development in the

Mount Gardner area, the centre of the birds' specialised habitat. The state fauna authorities were urged to proclaim Two Peoples Bay a faunal reserve and, after pressure from local, national and international conservationists, including the Duke of Edinburgh, the reserve was finally gazetted in 1967. The development was stopped. To rediscover the scrub-bird after so long and lose it before its biology was understood would have been a tragedy. The danger for the new reserve was fire. Recognising that unburnt post-mature scrub was the preferred habitat of the few birds left, the reserve's management concentrated its efforts on fire exclusion strategies.

Systematics

The noisy scrub-bird was not the first Australian species to confound the rules of systematics that were set up in northern lands, but it has been one of the most difficult to study. Alec Chisholm, reviewing the first 100 years of information about the bird, asked in 1951: 'Where does the group belong?'[20] He reminded *Emu* readers of the species' striking bone structure, which was first noted in the 1860s—in Australia by EP Ramsay of the Australian Museum and the collector John MacGillivray (1821–67), and in Europe by Cambridge ornithology professor Alfred Newton (1829–1907). The missing clavicle (wishbone) and the structure of the sternum were extremely unusual in passerine birds.

In 1965, the CSIRO Division of Wildlife Research seized the opportunity to work on the ecology and life history of the new-found species.[21] Norman Robinson undertook the early survey work, then in 1970 Graeme Smith (1938–99) transferred to CSIRO and began working with scrub-birds. He was keen to scrutinise the bird from a systematic point of view, but the tensions were so high that collection was impossible. With such a small population, its conservation needs were clearly the highest priority. Trapping and translocation offered a chance to give the birds more territory and would make them less vulnerable to fire. In the mid-1970s, four chicks were hand-reared in aviaries as the basis for a captive-breeding program, which in turn came to serve the systematic work.

On 15 August 1976, some ten years after the first CSIRO survey, a female bird was collected at a nest. Her chicks were transferred to the CSIRO captive-breeding program. This was the specimen the international community of museum taxonomists had been waiting for. It was not just a question of fitting *Atrichornis* into avian systematics: the question was also how *Atrichornis* and other Australian species (including lyrebirds) might influence and reshape international systematics. They threw out a challenge to the avian tree itself.

The systematists were very nearly overwhelmed by red tape as state and national governments enforced the rigid regulations designed to stop the ferocious international bird trade. Smith of CSIRO and Mary Heimerdinger Clench (1932–2011) from the Carnegie Museum of Natural History in Pittsburgh were frustrated that '*bona fide* scientific enquiry can be stifled by unyielding government regulations designed to regulate commercial trade'. Because the comparative birds were all in the United States, the systematics had to be undertaken there. Smith and Clench ended up taking out twelve Australian permits as well as import-export permits from the US Fish and Wildlife Service, which required shipments to particular ports in the United States. Having navigated the bureaucracy, they then set out to plan the scientific dissection work so that the greatest number of projects could benefit from the one rare specimen. Before the bird was preserved, blood samples were taken for examination by Charles Sibley. It was also photographed and measured. Once it had been preserved and exported, the sequence of study was crucial as each anatomist had to leave intact material for the following studies. Seven anatomists worked in sequence, including one who travelled from Belgium to work on the bird. The first three worked on the specimen at Pittsburgh, then it was sent to Washington, where it was divided: the head went to New York, the syrinx to the Peabody Museum, the bones of the inner ear to the Smithsonian. Its other bones were sent to the University of Kansas, where researchers had developed a special casting technique, usually used for 'small fragile fossils'.[22]

Another set of permits was required from Australia to allow 'replicas of parts of the skeleton' to be made. The permits required that the process did not damage the bones. The scientific team at the Kansas Museum of Natural History kept one delicate cast for themselves and then deposited casts with partners at the British Museum (Natural History), the Royal Ontario Museum in Canada, the American Museum of Natural History, four other US museums and the Australian Museum in Sydney.

In December 1978, just over two years after it had been collected, the original specimen, now partially disarticulated and 'down to bare bones' on one side but relatively intact on the other, was returned to its country of origin and laid to rest in the collection of the Western Australian Museum. The museum finally had its specimen. This one little bird had gone a long way.

Conservation

Graeme Smith's team made a thorough search of the gullies of Mount Gardner (now Two Peoples Bay Nature Reserve) and estimated that nearly 100 birds (approximately forty-four male territorial calls) were around at the time of Webster's rediscovery.[23] Scrub-birds are almost flightless, so they cannot move far from their original homes. Nothing was known of their breeding behaviour because they nest in impenetrable scrub. Since the population was so small, information about this aspect of their ecology was urgently needed. Smith and Robinson established over a series of seasons that the female noisy scrub-bird lays only one egg per season, and lays a second egg only if the first is lost, never after raising a chick. Population recovery would be a slow matter.

There was still the concern that the whole species could be wiped out by one bad fire. A very small population with a tiny range in a highly inflammable area of dense scrub is extremely vulnerable. By the end of the 1970s, the little population had grown enough for some birds to be moved to other likely habitats. Several translocations were made, the most successful being to Mount Manypeaks on the other side of the bay. Two decades later the Mount Manypeaks population had more birds than the parent population.[24] The successful translocation program, headed by

Alan Danks and sponsored by the Western Australian Department of Conservation and Land Management (CALM), was one of the great conservation stories of the last century.[25] Captive-breeding programs also saw the recovery-from-the-brink-of-extinction of the Lord Howe Island woodhen (in the 1970s, led by Peter Fullagar (1938–), John Disney (1919–2014) and others from the Australian Museum) and the Norfolk Island boobook (in the 1980s, led by Penny Olsen, with the support of local ranger Derek Greenwood).[26]

In 1997, the noisy scrub-birds were moved again as the Two Peoples Bay area was still vulnerable to wildfire. In a few decades their range had extended from just a gully on Mount Gardner to a stretch of nearly 50 kilometres of coast around Two Peoples Bay. Even this much larger area was still vulnerable to fire, and the growing population needed more habitat. The management team decided that the birds needed a new range further away. With a strong sense of history, they took some birds to a site near where John Gilbert had collected the type specimen, well north of Albany up in the Darling escarpment. In 1996, the total population was close to 1500.[27] However, because of changes in fire regime and the increase of wildfires, recent estimates place the population between 1000 and 1500 mature individuals, in decline again despite fifty years of research and management. Several translocations, some of which included the removal of introduced predators, have been attempted with some successes. Surveys are still being carried out to locate further suitable habitats for translocations.[28]

Bodies, blood and science

Individual noisy scrub-birds in this story have been crucial to what science knows about *Atrichornis clamosus*, but their cultural baggage is also fascinating in terms of understanding birdos. Gilbert's bird takes us back to the connections between ornithology and Empire. Campbell's bird reminds us of the changing practices of identification, moving from shooting to field glasses. Webster's bird is eloquent about the place of stories in bird observation, especially stories of hope, but his field notebook also reveals competitive tensions between birdos. Smith had to take the female bird to work out the place of Australian birds in international systematics; her nestlings were the beginning of the captive breeding recovery programs.

Systematics still relies on bodies, on blood, on the actual bird. Yet Smith's bird served many different scientific questions because the people involved planned together, and the half-and-half bird/skeleton now held at the Western Australian Museum is possibly the most revealing of all specimens, showing how one of the world's most arcane sciences can also provide practical data important for conservation of the species. The present status of *Atrichornis clamosus*, along with its cousin the rufous scrub-bird (*Atrichornis rufescens*), is in a small endemic family of passerine birds whose closest relation is the lyrebird (*Menura* spp.). DNA studies have suggested that scrub-birds differentiated from lyrebirds 30–35 million years ago. The Australian Foundation for National Parks & Wildlife considers the rufous scrub-bird a living fossil that evolved 97–65 million years ago. The scrub-birds have an ancient lineage, probably the 'corvid radiation' of the Australia–New Guinea region, according to the Evolutionarily Distinct and Globally Endangered (EDGE) of Existence program, which describes itself as the only 'global conservation initiative to focus specifically on threatened species that represent a significant amount of unique evolutionary history'.[29] The survival of noisy scrub-birds against the odds is a great tribute to translocation conservation.

The noisy scrub-bird is unique in having gone from 'extinct' to 'critically endangered' to 'vulnerable' in that order over just a few decades.[30] Alas, 21st-century climate-change-fuelled fires bring new threats to the southern populations near the south-west tip of the continent, and *Atrichornis clamosus* is now 'endangered' again. But it also has new Noongar carers and a new 'official' name: Tjimiluk.[31]

9

A CRISIS IN CONSERVATION

Thinking like a biosphere

The World Conservation Union, now the International Union for the Conservation of Nature (IUCN), was launched in Fontainebleau, France, in 1948. It was an initiative of UNESCO, with Pro Natura (the Swiss League for the Protection of Nature) and the French Government. Increasingly, UNESCO was looking at building conservation projects that transcended political borders. Non-governmental organisations stepped in to address the widespread threats to birds and other creatures as it became clear that national parks and nature reserves were not sufficient to prevent extinctions. Most NGOs were (and still are) limited by national structures dictated by tax and charity arrangements. However, the IUCN is a key international NGO for nature conservation and sustainable development. It maintains a strong ongoing relationship with UNESCO through its scientific programs.

The International Science Council (ISC) was one of the original links between UNESCO and NGOs and provided a platform for a range of international collaborations, including the International Biological Program (IBP; 1963–73). Two of ISC's component unions, the International

Union of Biological Sciences (IUBS) and the International Union of Microbiological Societies (IUMS), together with UNESCO's Natural Resources Research, hosted the IBP's Intergovernmental Conference of Experts on the Scientific Basis for Rational Use and Conservation of the Resources of the Biosphere in Paris in 1968. Soon after, the IBP launched its Man and the Biosphere program (MAB), which built on UNESCO's work in arid zone ecology, a project involving many Australians.[1]

UNESCO offered a major global convening power in education, natural and social sciences, culture and communication—a new 'integrated' way of understanding the natural world and the role of people in it. Ecologist G Evelyn Hutchinson (1903–91) popularised the term 'biosphere' in a special issue of the popular science journal *Scientific American* in 1970. The biosphere concept highlights how thin the space is for living matter on Earth, and the effects of human activities on chemical elements and all the global-scale cycles of energy. The 1972 United Nations Stockholm conference coined the term 'human environment', referring to the biosphere, the special part of the atmosphere where life is possible. It used the phrase 'only one earth' as the title of the book of the conference.[2]

MAB blended a new direction in natural and human sciences working together with an innovative site-based approach, the biosphere reserve.[3] There were other initiatives in the same period, including, in 1971, a new Convention on Wetlands with a strong bird focus, named for the city of Ramsar in Iran where it was designed. The Ramsar Convention recognised the 'interdependence' of humanity and the environment and focused on 'the fundamental ecological functions of wetlands as regulators of water regimes and as habitats supporting a characteristic flora and fauna, especially waterfowl'.[4]

These initiatives all fed into the mood of the International Council for Bird Preservation in Canberra 1974, held the week after the IOC. It was the first Southern Hemisphere congress of this group. The international and the local came together in such meetings in ways that sometimes had long-term ramifications for the host country. The ICBP was first established over a century ago (20 June 1922) as the International Council for Bird Protection by French–American aviarist Jean Théodore Delacour

(1890–1985) and ornithologist T Gilbert Pearson (1873–1943), who also founded the National Audubon Society in the United States. From 1928 until 1960, it was known as the International Committee for Bird Preservation, and in 1994 it was renamed BirdLife International, a name now familiar in Australia. The ICBP was based in Cambridge, England. Despite all the name changes, the continuities of the organisation were such that BirdLife International celebrated its centenary in June 2022.

The quest to find Australian birds

As we have seen in chapters 6 and 7, the RAOU was very keen to develop lively programs that would help birds and also engage new members. International initiatives were ideal for uniting local enthusiasts and professional scientists. Collecting 'data for conservation' became the backbone of national birding initiatives in the 1970s, 1980s and 1990s.

Pauline Reilly was concerned that the RAOU was not doing enough practical fieldwork to maintain a genuinely 'national' profile, especially among banding enthusiasts, who were the people she knew best. The IOC created a new capacity to work on different scales—local, national and international—and the coordination of these activities fell to the RAOU. Three presidents, Reilly (1972–75), Stephen Davies (1975–78) and Norman Wettenhall (1978–83), oversaw a transition that witnessed RAOU membership more than double from about 850 to over 2000 in a decade.[5]

The new big project, the *Atlas of Australian Birds*, assessing the location of birds, common and rare, in every last corner of the continent, became a driving force behind the massive membership growth.[6] It was seeded in Reilly's early years in office and laid out in her introduction to the special issue of *Emu* devoted to setting an agenda that both amateurs and professionals could 'own'.[7] She was well aware that the RAOU's new Field Investigation Committee had no resources and that research work cost money. Volunteer birdos were much less interested in theory than in the excitement of practical bird-handling through banding and meticulous observation. Such skills were also helpful to research questions.

Allan McEvey, who worked closely with all sorts of birdos in his professional life at the Museum of Victoria, acknowledged that people come to birds through very different routes. Not all ornithology was (or should be) science, he wrote.[8] CSIRO scientist Michael Ridpath wrote about international collaborative schemes, thereby laying the groundwork for an inclusive *Atlas* project.[9] The two 1974 international congresses (first ornithology and then conservation) brought a range of scientists, activists and bird enthusiasts to Canberra, including people with experience of coordinating amateurs in survey projects in Sweden, Britain and North America. Many of these came along to a discussion session orchestrated by Reilly and John Disney, curator of ornithology at the Australian Museum, developing ideas for what eventually became the *Atlas of Australian Birds*.[10]

Educating the amateur birdo was something field guides had targeted. However, other practical skills are needed for banding and atlassing. Rosemary Balmford, who had established the regular *RAOU Newsletter* in 1969, took up the challenge of writing a 'how-to' book, *The Beginner's Guide to Australian Birds*. It was first published in 1980, at the height of atlassing, and was reissued in 1990.[11]

One prequel project to the *Atlas* was a Nest Record Scheme, established in 1964 and led by the energetic English geologist Stephen Marchant (1912–2003). The NRS was based on a similar scheme in Britain, led by the British Trust for Ornithology. Schemes for recording detailed information on individual birds' nests had already been established in most European countries, North America, South Africa, Rhodesia (now Zimbabwe) and New Zealand. The NRS drew together independent and previously unpublished observations of breeding records from all over the country. Marchant saw it as a way to 'divert interest from the collection of eggs'.[12] By the end of the third year of the scheme, seventy-four individuals and three groups had contributed 5387 cards with information about the breeding of 396 species in Australia and Papua New Guinea (including eleven introduced species and five Papuan species). The nests most recorded were the minimal sand-scrapes of the masked lapwing (*Vanellus miles*), a particular interest of Hobart-based David Thomas (1927–), who took over the management of the NRS in 1967.[13] Participants came from every state and territory, with the Australian Capital Territory, where Marchant and Thomas were based, particularly well-represented.[14] The NRS became the longest continuous project sponsored by the RAOU in the twentieth century, apart from the publication of *Emu*. By 1999 the scheme could boast 90,000 records, with just fifty highly skilled and very committed annual observers. The NRS results were all incorporated into versions of the *Atlas*, but it was demanding work and didn't have the broad appeal to casual volunteers that the *Atlas* did. The *Atlas* was the project that brought badly needed new members into the national bird organisation.

In Reilly's words, the *Atlas* 'grabbed people. Everybody said, "Oh, there's no way you'll get enough people to do that. There are only about a thousand people who are birdwatchers or ornithologists in Australia." Well, we ended up with three thousand!'[15] Reilly and Wettenhall were both themselves 'amateur' ornithologists, and were actively concerned with attracting a wide range of people as well as generating good science for birds. Davies, a professional CSIRO scientist, was also deeply convinced of the importance of amateur enthusiasm for professional ornithology. Amateurs 'were a great deal more powerful' than professional research scientists, he argued, 'because they weren't limited by public-service rules. Time and again, we had to use political weapons to get things that we wanted done.'[16] Davies had built much of his own scientific work with the help of the local knowledge of practical people in remote communities, especially in the Western Australian inland and the Northern Territory. The commitment and skills of these three inspiring RAOU leaders over more than a decade (and beyond—all continued to support the club long after completing their terms as president) provided a new template for a merger between 'professional' and 'amateur', and for maintaining a local and human perspective in birding practices.

A national atlas pilot scheme was launched in March 1976 with an appeal to members to collate their own (historical) records in terms of standard one-degree squares on field cards.[17] These were coordinated by regional organisers on a state-by-state basis. Peter Curry became the RAOU's first paid staff member, with the task of compiling historical information from published sources, funded by a ten-month grant from the federally funded Australian Biological Resources Study.[18] His job was to comb the early *Emus*, translating vague geographical handwaving and such long-forgotten species as 'black and white campephaga, Mrs Morgan's parrot and Cloncurry honeyeater' into known species at known places. Nature writer and recently retired headmaster Tommy Garnett (1915–2006) was the RAOU's energetic honorary secretary, volunteering long hours. By 1976 Judy Gilmore (later McVicar) was appointed part-time to assist Garnett with the growing burden of correspondence associated with the *Atlas*.[19]

Prospects for national funding were still very uncertain when Davies bravely announced at the annual meeting in May 1976 that, 'rather than dismantle the organisational framework that had been set up, work on the Atlas should begin from January 1st 1977'.[20] Dom Serventy had prepared an atlas in the 1940s of all the known occurrences of birds throughout Australia, and Curry produced a map summarising Serventy's work in the August 1977 *RAOU Newsletter*.[21] This alerted people to the grid-squares where Serventy had found 'NO RECORDS OF ANY SPECIES'. Curry issued an appeal: 'Do *you* have any unpublished records of even the commonest species in the blank areas on the map?'

But in August 1976, Curry left the RAOU to take up an ongoing job in Western Australia. The RAOU was now committed to an atlas starting on 1 January 1977 but had lost its key staff member. It urgently needed 'someone who was mad enough to take it on', as Margaret Blakers (1951–) put it. With only months to go, Blakers was appointed Atlas Field Officer on a six-month contract to do what turned out to be a seven-year job. 'It was always insecure, but … once you've started, you have to finish it—so you've got to find the money from somewhere,' she reflected. Her steady hand and steady nerve saw the project through to the end, and her affectionate nickname, 'Big M', reflected the importance of her anchor role. 'I turned up at this office, and Judy was there, and that was about it. No stationery, nothing. Within [a matter of months] … we found a computer programmer, we designed the form, we got the forms printed and we designed the whole mechanism of the project with regional organisers.'[22]

The Field Investigation Committee met on 11–12 November 1976 and, under pressure from Serventy, took the major decision to computerise 'even though we had no money, no computer, nothing to make that real', Blakers recalled. The FIC appointed an *Atlas* committee, chaired by Reilly and comprising David Peters (the former RAOU secretary, and a CSIRO research scientist), Blakers and Simon Bennett, a qualified pilot and enthusiastic atlasser from the Australian Capital Territory, who was appointed to the RAOU staff soon after to continue Curry's historical background work for the *Atlas*.[23] By 1 January, with the help of a remarkable volunteer, Bob Rowlands (1930–2018) from CSIRO, the *Atlas* committee had access to a state-of-the-art computer. Rowlands' computer in 1976 filled a whole room. Everything had to be put on punch cards, and such specialist work was a continuing cost, but it proved a good decision. Rowlands, a keen birdo as well as a professional programmer, generously gave his time and supported the computing for the whole project right through to the end.[24] By the time the *Atlas* project was finished, the computer revolution had come and the data were in a form to be transferred to newer technologies, a task undertaken by Bennett.

As the *Atlas* grew, the RAOU found itself looking for bigger rooms to accommodate the staff, volunteers and interminable piles of punched cards and records. In July 1979, just over three years after it had bought its first headquarters for the century, the RAOU sold up and moved to a double-fronted Hawthorn-brick house at 21 Gladstone Street, Moonee Ponds. Here, there would be room for an 'Institute of Australian Field Ornithology'. At least the secretary would no longer have to work on a small table on the landing. Council resolved in October 1978 that 'since at the present time the Atlas is the union's major undertaking, ... Ms M Blakers ... would bear the title of Officer-in-charge'. The commitment to the institute was also a commitment that a director would eventually be appointed, something that took a further six years.[25]

Computers were not the only revolution to come just too late for the *Atlas* project. Most of the national field guides and maps were also published well after the start of the project. Blakers recalled: 'We had to design the way we'd refer to the grid blocks, and that they'd be ten-minute (one-sixth of a degree) and one-degree blocks. We'd refer to them by their centre point and so we had a cross-checking mechanism … The *Reader's Digest Australian Atlas* had only just come out—that was a one-to-a-million complete set of maps.'[26] 'There were no maps for the whole continent giving a higher level of coverage, and no Global Positioning System (GPS) to give precise locations. Every map was vetted by hand by Shane Parker (1943–92; South Australian Museum), John McKean (1941–96; CSIRO Wildlife) and Henry Nix (CSIRO Land System Survey), all professional field survey workers and ornithologists.[27]

Reilly, Davies and Blakers hit the road, calling meetings and inspiring local groups all over Australia to take up atlassing. The *Atlas Newsletter*, edited by Blakers and issued quarterly from headquarters in sixteen issues from March 1977 to December 1980, kept atlassers informed about the project wherever they were working. Eventually it merged with the *RAOU Newsletter*.[28]

The atlas success took over the whole organisation, even annual campouts. Sites at Ooldea on the Nullarbor Plain (26 August – 4 September 1979) and Top Springs, Northern Territory (26 August – 5 September 1981) were chosen for campouts because they were near blanks on the map. The Top Springs campout provided a base for thirteen one-degree blocks, five of which were visited for the first time. Distinguished RAAF veteran Cecil 'Boz' Parsons (1918–) provided a plane to make the trip possible, and Blakers organised the surveys.[29]

Wettenhall, who was president during this critical period, recalled that 'people went all over Australia in their own time and [with] their own funding to every corner of the 800 squares of the country'.[30] The rising popularity of four-wheel-drive vehicles in the 1970s and 1980s, especially among city-dwellers, made much of the remote work possible. The RAOU attracted support from all sorts of groups, including government conservation agencies, private mining companies, generous individuals and even the army. Sir Robert Law-Smith (1914–92), who had been an air-force pilot and was deputy chairman of Qantas and chairman of TAA, often flew Wettenhall to the Victorian Mallee to go birding with Western District conservationist-farmer Claude Austin (1908–?) and others.

Law-Smith and Wettenhall also joined forces for a major trip in Central Australia and the Great Sandy Desert. Law-Smith sent his Toyota on to Alice Springs, then he and Wettenhall flew in and set off in the vehicle up the Tanami Track to Halls Creek, where they joined a larger group. They came back through the Great Sandy Desert, mapping birds all the way. Fuel drops were provided by the army, thanks to Stephen Davies' considerable negotiating skill. Even two decades later, the excitement of the trip was evident in Wettenhall's recollections of the Toyota that 'charged the sand dunes'.[31] Four-wheel-drive vehicles were in demand for the project, as were experienced volunteers willing to lead bird trips in really remote areas. Some areas required more than just road transport. A group from Melbourne, including Margaret Cameron and *Atlas* staffer Julie Strudwick, were flown into a private airstrip by Argonaut International, a mining company drilling near Poeppel Corner (the south-eastern corner of the Northern Territory). The company lent them a vehicle for a day's birding to fill the crucial second-last empty square, and also fed them chicken Maryland and ice cream after a day of combing the Simpson Desert for birds. (They found thirty-eight species, many breeding.)[32]

In Alice Springs, the southern Northern Territory organiser, local doctor John Erlich, approached Mike Fleming, the newly appointed ornithologist at the Northern Territory Conservation Commission, to tackle the very last one-degree block on the *Atlas* map, an area to the north of Uluru that included the western half of Lake Amadeus, the eastern half of Lake Neale and the south of what is now Watarrka National Park. Fleming and Erlich were accompanied by Ken Johnson, Fleming's boss at the Conservation Commission, who was also an ornithological enthusiast. The traditional owners gave them permission to survey for birds in country crossed by nineteenth-century desert explorer Ernest Giles (1835–97) but where few whitefellas have trodden since. They were rewarded with a rare sighting of princess parrots (*Polytelis alexandrae*).[33]

The March 1982 *RAOU Newsletter* was the final *Atlas* issue. David Peters (1938–), the organiser for Victoria, captured in his column the emotion of finishing the surveys on 31 December 1981: 'It's strange but I'm sad! Just a few more checks and a few more URRFs [not French eggs, but Unusual Record Report Forms] to complete.'[34] The 'obsession of five years was over' for most of the atlassers. For the team back at head office, however, the 'Institute of Field Ornithology', a new sort of work had just begun.

Reilly, Davies, Blakers and their editorial advisers faced the task of pulling it all together. 'The pressure ... was incredible,' Blakers recalled:

> The last week or last few days, the postman turned up with sacks of mail—he had to drive a truck to the door because there was so much of it ... We knew it was coming, but ... the writing-up period was just horrendous because it was much harder to get money for that, because you are not actually [doing anything] visible.[35]

Wettenhall and Ian Sinclair persisted with fundraising and raised enough to complete the two-year 'backroom' task of consolidation. Reilly arranged all the illustrations and Davies wrote 'first drafts', but it fell to Blakers to cross-check all the records and edit and amend the text. Juggling the vision and the nitty-gritty, she worked grimly in a small, dark room with piles of records. It was with a huge sigh of relief that she handed the last of the *Atlas* to Melbourne University Press in October 1983. She resigned, exhausted, a few months later in March 1984.

On 12 July 1984, in the Audubon Room at the University of Melbourne, Robyn Williams of the ABC's *Science Show* launched the *Atlas of Australian Birds*, presenting Blakers with a leather-bound copy.[36] The book contained 3.5 million records, based on 190,500 bird-lists collected by more than 3000 ornithologists, including historical records in three classes: before 1900, 1901–50 and 1951–76. Records were accurate at least to a one-degree block, and many (all of Tasmania and Victoria for 1977–81, for example) to a ten-minute block (there being thirty-six ten-minute blocks in a one-degree block). By the end of 1986, the RAOU was offering *Atlas* information and maps from the larger database on a cost-recovery basis as a service to members.[37] A big initiative for a small organisation run almost entirely on voluntary labour, the *Atlas* brought together excellent observation and the latest in digital technologies and mapping (simple by today's standards, but pioneering in its time), and created a mountain of goodwill. It announced to the world that the RAOU was a lively national organisation, an NGO for birds in an era when Australian governments (state and federal) were downsizing public service conservation and moving away from supporting national science, even as international conservation initiatives were launched elsewhere.

There was still a thirst to 'do field ornithology' as the *Atlas* writing took place; and as the pace of the digital revolution gathered, a new RAOU project emerged: the Australian Bird Count (ABC). Like the *Atlas* it garnered widespread support, but the surveying system gathered information on *abundance*, not just presence or absence. This was the sort of data that needed computing systems to filter. The ABC ran from 1989 to 1995, collecting surveys from over 2000 sites across Australia. There were 1020 'surveyors'; some would just occasionally do a survey while others made regular contributions over the whole period. Three individual contributors (Kinglake, Victoria; and West Armadale and Norseman, Western Australia) submitted 2000+ surveys. The mountains of data were interpreted for the RAOU by Michael Clarke at La Trobe University, Richard Loyn at the Victorian Government's Arthur Rylah Institute and Peter Griffioen, then an independent consultant but now at Arthur Rylah Institute. A friendly summary of the results was published as a full-colour supplement to the popular outdoor magazine *Wild* in 1999.[38]

A science of crisis

Conservation biology is much more than a science, American ecologist Michael Soulé (1936–2020) argued in an important paper in 1985. Soulé called conservation biology the *science of crisis*, drawing an analogy with medical biology, particularly hospital emergency medicine. The natural world needed 'triage', a logical way to make choices about which species or ecosystems to save, given it was impossible to save everything. The triage principle focuses on the most serious cases and the ones that, if treated, will be most likely to recover.

The crisis that Soulé identified demanded concerted action on local, regional and planetary scales. The future of the biota depended on politics and people, ecologists realised: they were no longer documenting species in the wild but the survival of whole ecosystems. Making biological diversity urgent, rather than merely descriptive, directed attention to prediction and sharpened questions about extinctions. What happens to an ecosystem when a species becomes extinct? What are the knock-on effects for other biota? For individual species, extinction is the endpoint. But within the broader ecosystem, one extinction may lead to more as its functions become increasingly impaired.

Thus conservation biology applies biology to conservation but takes its 'questions, techniques and methods from a broad range of fields, not all biological'.[39] When the International Conference on Conservation Biology in 1978 defined the term, it was biology, specifically genetic diversity. By the time of Soulé's 1985 paper, 'biological diversity' was broader, with implications for the policy arena. His book *Conservation Biology* was published in 1986 with the subtitle *The Science of Scarcity and Diversity*. If 'diversity and rarity are synonyms for "everything" in ecology', Soulé observed in this book, practical conservation biology needs to start with what is 'nearly lost', with preserving futures for threatened species and using whatever tools will work.[40]

Biological diversity was shortened to 'biodiversity' in 1986 when the (international) Society for Conservation Biology was established. 'BioDiversity' was the title of a Smithsonian Institution teleconference in 1986 featuring Amazon ecologist Thomas Lovejoy (1941–2021), naturalist, ant specialist and Pulitzer Prize winner EO Wilson (1929–2021) and Nobel Prize–winning ecologist Paul Ehrlich (1932–), best known for his 1968 book *The Population Bomb*. Biodiversity quickly became a key concept for American conservation biologists and activists, and soon spread beyond America. It provided a framework for understanding both 'the phenomenon of life' and the impact of human activity on it. It is more than just 'nature': it is a *measure* that can be used to document change. While the term carried a veneer of scientific independence, it added a moral imperative to take action to avert environmental crisis.[41]

Soulé was not concerned so much about 'endangered' (cute, charismatic) species but rather 'keystone' species, the ones that make ecosystems work or crash. If the 'proper objective of conservation is the protection and continuity of entire communities and ecosystems', keystone species, 'complete' environments (for example, national parks and nature reserves) and 'top predators' have a special role. This is a philosophy that goes beyond the welfare of individual animals. Conservation biology is about 'the protection of the integrity and continuity of natural processes'.[42] Rather, its focus is species and genera, and the contexts that will allow them to thrive. Its outcomes must be defined in terms of whole populations and evolutionary futures.

Extinction has a long history. Fossils in the eighteenth century revealed extinctions that contradicted biblical ideas of creation, which challenged and deepened ideas about time and changed what was meant by the 'balance of nature'. Extinctions now are measured and counted as they have become a focus of conservation efforts. Increasingly, they are also a focus for museum and zoo education programs.[43] Extinctions are critical signs of a mismanaged world. Historian Dolly Jørgensen suggests that 'Extinction, in biological terms, is the end of an evolutionary line, a potential future cutoff'. If 'the generative capacity of the species is ended through extinction ... the possibilities for future biological generation are denied', disrupting whole ecological systems.[44]

Environmental managers everywhere grapple with the social and human dimensions of preserving the non-human biota. Biodiversity became part of broader management imperatives as the IUCN and other international environmental organisations with scientific roots worked to enlarge policy options for managers by ensuring that local and regional communities were part of the solutions, rather than just parachuting in global experts. What is different about what we now call the 'sixth mass extinction' is that human behaviours are changing the futures of other life forms, and that we *realise* that human developments affect the future survival of other species. Since it is people who manage conservation efforts and make the choices that fund conservation biology, political action becomes part of the moral imperative. As coastal resource manager

RA Kenchington put it, 'We do not manage the environment, only the human behaviours that affect its structure and processes.'[45] Ecology is a necessary, but no longer sufficient, expertise for biodiversity in a time of planetary crisis.

Biodiversity, as defined by the IUCN, now includes species diversity, genetic diversity and ecosystem diversity. 'Species richness (the number of species in a given area) represents a single ... metric that is valuable as the common currency of the diversity of life', but the IUCN also includes genetic diversity and ecosystem diversity in its brief.[46] While biological diversity had been used politically before this (for example, in the 1969 Victorian parliament in defence of wild country in the Little Desert[47]), by 1986 biodiversity was an urgent international cause. National governments, international lobby groups and NGOs joined forces, recognising that there was a global crisis of extinction. The IUCN published the Red List of Threatened Species in 1986. This was not its first list of endangered species, but it was now red, the colour of alarm. The Red List provided a new baseline for global assessments of the conservation status of species, and it continues to be regularly updated. It measures *changes* in status of biota (vulnerable, endangered, threatened, etc.), maintaining historical records and including data generated by 'public-private partnerships', such as bird organisations. It is interested in presence and absence, and also in fluctuations in abundance. These all require observers with a detailed sense of what *ought* to be in any place and when, and bird observers are both good at the history of seasonal changes and numerous enough to help provide solid data. It is much harder to get detailed reviews of other biota, especially nocturnal and microscopic elements of ecosystems.

In 1987, Conservation International (CI), a not-for-profit organisation, was established to enable the conservation of species such as migratory birds whose seasonal lifepaths demand international thinking. CI envisions 'conservation as a working model of the future' and urges the reconnection of people and nature.[48] Its tagline is 'Fighting to protect nature for people' and it is a union of over 1000 government and non-government organisation members, all of which have democratic voting rights. One of its early decisions was to prioritise work in the seventeen 'megadiverse countries'. These countries harbour more than two-thirds of the planet's biological wealth: typically, the richest biodiversity is in tropical rainforests and in the oceans. Among the crucial seventeen, only Australia and the United States have 'First World' economies, and as such they have led and financed much of the conservation effort in partnership with CI. CI works with governments, NGOs, corporations and local communities to fund scientific efforts in 'megadiverse' places that do not have other conservation resources. In the twenty-first century, it increasingly supports local biodiversity expertise: its website claims that 'By enlisting all parts of society—Indigenous peoples and local communities, youth and others—we seek to make the conservation movement more inclusive and harness the power of traditional knowledge, science and technology'.[49] The IUCN's benchmarks and its Biodiversity Convention, drafted for the United Nations 'Earth Summit' in Rio de Janeiro in 1992, drive government natural resource management policy in over 160 countries.

Changing national science

As NGOs took up more conservation work, Australian governments stepped back from supporting conservation biology both at state and federal level. An early sign of this was the CSIRO review committee that in 1980 ruled that bird-banding should no longer be a priority for the national science organisation. The Australian Bird Banding Scheme and the Australian Bat Banding Scheme (the latter established in 1957) were amalgamated and formally transferred from CSIRO to the Australian National Parks and Wildlife Service in 1984, the year that the *Atlas of Australian Birds* was published.[50] David Purchase (1934–2015), who had been officer-in-charge of both schemes since 1967, noted that in the time CSIRO had hosted the schemes, Australian banders had marked 1,770,000 birds of 850 species since 1953.[51] In all, 200,000 individuals of 520 bird species had been recovered on 310,000 occasions. The 1984 team comprised 456 banders (321 'A' class and 135 'B' class) undertaking a total of 388 projects, 240 of which were led by 'non-professional ornithologists', 66 by university staff and postgraduates, 52 by state and federal government agencies, and smaller numbers by CSIRO, museums, mining companies and 'other organisations'. While banding operations had grown exponentially, they were still essentially a 'non-professional' activity. Thus bird (and bat) banding was a place where government money could be saved as CSIRO's functions were downsized in the financial squeezes of the 1980s.[52]

Just as the CSIRO review committee was debating the future of the national banding scheme, an Australasian Wader Studies Group (AWSG) was established as a special interest group of the RAOU in 1981. Led by international businessman Clive Minton (1934–2019), an experienced cannon-netting specialist who had arrived in Australia in 1978, and spurred on by new techniques for aerial survey, the group grew quickly.[53] Cannon-netters use small 'cannons' to shoot projectiles carrying a net over a flock of shorebirds, catching large numbers when the tide is high and the birds are bunched on a narrow beach. The AWSG still uses this technique to coordinate its work banding birds so that international flight paths can be mapped right across the Asia-Pacific region.[54]

In 1980 the World Wildlife Fund sponsored a national survey of the range and status of rare birds.[55] RAOU pilot Simon Bennett and Tim Hunt explored north-western Australia and were astonished by the extent of the tidal flats around Broome and Roebuck Bay. Minton, launching the AWSG, and John Martindale, the RAOU's national wader organiser, followed up and organised a major aerial reconnaissance of the northern coastline from the Gulf of Carpentaria to Port Hedland between 21 August and 6 September 1981. They timed the survey to coincide with a Department of Health surveillance visit, and used aircraft chartered for the RAOU's congress in Katherine, Northern Territory, that year. They banded 1189 birds and assayed them for viruses, assisting the Department of Health, which was concerned about birds that might bring in psittacosis and other human/animal diseases from parts of Asia on the flight path between Australia and Siberia. Working together made for less stress on the birds: they needed only to be trapped once for both flyway studies and health information.

The reconnaissance group sent Minton's breathless radio reports from the air back to the RAOU: 'I just don't believe it ... it's incredible ... waders as far as the eye can see!'[56] Expeditions throughout the 1980s built the knowledge of shorebird arrivals and departures around Broome, Roebuck Bay and Port Hedland and relentlessly broke statistical records year after year. As seasons went on, banding recoveries revealed more and more about the life cycles of the birds and the threats to their breeding success.

The RAOU established a base for this work, the Broome Bird Observatory, with the help of many partners. The Western Australian Lands Department vested 2.5 hectares on the Roebuck Bay foreshore, while Mount Newman Mining donated a transportable ablution block and moved it to Port Hedland.[57] The participants in the North West Shelf natural gas project donated the main building, its transport from Karratha and its installation.[58] Lord Alistair McAlpine (1942–2014) also supported the observatory personally. The coordination of all these players was orchestrated by Minton, whose day job before he retired had involved large corporate mergers. The observatory was officially opened in 1990, with a plaque acknowledging the support of eight major corporate sponsors as well as the shire and people of Broome.[59]

The international imperatives were high: the site was listed under the 1971 Ramsar International Convention on Wetlands as a 'wetland of international significance, holding more than 1 per cent of the population of 20 species of migratory wader'. The sedimentology of the area generates many different microhabitats, and the tropical location fosters high biodiversity. The huge populations of migratory shorebirds supported by the tidal flats made it an ideal location for a bird observatory. The growing tourist industry in nearby Broome made it easier to bring observers into the area through commercial airlines, but also made the observatory's 'watchdog' role over the relatively pristine flats very important. In a 1997 preliminary assessment, the intertidal flats of Roebuck Bay were shown to be the most biodiverse in the world, because the enormous tidal range and the gently sloping seabed produce large areas of rich foraging habitat. BirdLife Australia still runs the observatory in Broome, which now has excellent longitudinal records of shorebird migration patterns over more than a quarter of a century. Rich foraging pickings make it possible for shorebirds to 'stock up' for their incredible migration to Siberia where they breed. The Arctic tundra is briefly so rich in insect life in the crucial northern summer months that the birds can fledge their young and fatten up to fly back to Roebuck Bay and beyond. Some Siberian breeding shorebirds spend the Australian summer as far south as the Western Treatment Plant, near Melbourne, which is the AWSG headquarters.

Although many banders had been RAOU members, the national and international focus of the new AWSG brought serious banding back to the union's jurisdiction. Some seven decades after its first tentative efforts, it embraced banding and thereby reconnected itself with many of the enthusiastic 'serious amateurs' of the Australian Bird Banding Scheme. Since the *Environment Protection and Biodiversity Conservation Act 1999*, the Australian Government (currently the Department of Climate Change, Energy, the Environment and Water) has formal responsibility for the national banding scheme, but operationally it falls under the National Environmental Science Program. The long-term continuity of the Australian Bird and Bat Banding Scheme (ABBBS) and other key field ornithology projects like the shorebird studies depends on the many volunteers from non-government groups.

The *Handbook* project

Not all birdos are keen on difficult fieldwork. Some are 'armchair travellers' who collect the literature of birds, while others focus on local studies close to home. As long ago as 1955, Dom Serventy was concerned that there was no Australian equivalent of the *Handbook of British Birds* and mused to Francis Ratcliffe that he might consider tackling such a project 'in my years of retirement'.[60] Harry Witherby's five-volume British *Handbook*, published between 1938 and 1941, was a benchmark publication in ornithology. Ratcliffe and Serventy both felt that Australia should have an equivalent, complete with 'coloured illustrations—preferably a plate for each species, showing adult and juvenile plumages (where necessary) and possibly also background figures of the birds perched or in flight to show the important diagnostic features for sight identifications'.[61] The problem in 1955 was not just the prohibitive cost of such illustrations but the lack of a sufficient knowledge base to make them useful. Serventy summarised his discussions with CSIRO Wildlife colleagues John Calaby and George Dunnet:

> We all think that the time is much too premature for such a work ... We haven't got the basic data for such a detailed book. In the UK a vast body of information has been accumulating, particularly during the last 30 years ... On this broad base the modern British *Handbook*, of 5 volumes, was built, and stands as a usable reference after many years. Should we in Australia, eyeing this sumptuous work with envy, attempt to short-circuit the British experience and bring one out forthwith, we would find it out of date before the printing ink dried.[62]

Serventy's insight proved prophetic. Another thirty years of knowledge was accumulated before an Australian handbook was considered again. Harry Frith, Ratcliffe's successor at CSIRO, suggested one in 1968, inspired by the forthcoming International Ornithological Congress, but nothing came of the suggestion.[63] A full and exhaustive reference book on Australian birds in the international tradition could only be attempted when Australian ornithology had come of age. The IOC had to make do with the excellent regional guide *Birds in the Australian High Country*, published in 1969, edited by Frith and with illustrations by Canberra-based scientific artist Betty Temple Watts (1901–92).[64]

The possibility of a *Handbook of Australian Birds* was first raised by the RAOU Field Investigation Committee in 1980 as the *Atlas* project was wrapping up.[65] The *Handbook* was a new and different project, with the aim 'to bring together the entire knowledge of all species occurring in the area and ... to foster and encourage ornithological research in Australia'.[66] Stephen Marchant was the driving force behind the proposals for an Australian handbook, and his model was Stanley Cramp's new nine-volume *Birds of the Western Palearctic* (published by Oxford University

Press between 1977 and 1994). The handbook would gather together state-of-the-art scientific knowledge on every bird species with excellent new illustrations, providing an accessible summary of all sorts of bird knowledge in one place. It would also be a highly 'collectable' book, something that serious bibliophiles, including international ones, would want. After twelve years of service as editor of *Emu*, Marchant turned to the gargantuan task of chief *Handbook* editor in 1982. It was he who defined the scope of the project and worked tirelessly to ensure that all contributors met his taxing standards.

Cramp's model was closely followed in the arrangement of sections: Field Identification; Habitat, Distribution and Population; Movements; Food; Social Organisation and Social Behaviour; Voice; Breeding; and Plumages and Related Matters.[67] With voluntary assistance from Peter Curry (field identification), Henry Nix (habitat), Stephen Davies (movements and food) and Peter Fullagar (voice), Marchant started recruiting contributors in January 1983. He himself undertook to write the section on breeding.[68] The cost was to be met by the 'generous voluntary co-operation' of many people. No pecuniary benefit was offered to contributors other than a discount on the eventual volumes. During the early years the geographical scope of the project changed, with Antarctica added in 1982 and New Zealand in 1985 at the suggestion of the Ornithological Society of New Zealand. In the end the geographical scope of the *Handbook of Australian, New Zealand and Antarctic Birds*, or *HANZAB*, was Australia, New Zealand, Antarctica, the subantarctic islands and Australia's island dependencies, but not New Guinea.[69] Until early 1987 Marchant managed the project with the team of volunteer subeditors, but as the task grew, a growing (paid) editorial team joined *HANZAB*, including Peter Higgins (who became managing editor from 1990, when the first volume appeared in print), the artist Jeff Davies, and Sid Cowling, who did all the maps. The number of artists grew with the project: Jeff Davies had been joined by Peter Marsack, Peter Slater, Mike Bamford, Nicholas Day, Brett Jarrett and Frank Knight by the time the final volume was published in 2006.[70]

An important spin-off of the handbook was the '1994 List' prepared by museum scientists Les Christidis (1959–) (then Melbourne Museum, now Southern Cross University) and Walter Boles (1952–) (Australian Museum), which updated the arrangement and nomenclature of Australian birds based on extensive published amendments in the literature.[71] CSIRO Wildlife scientist Richard Schodde had prepared a list in 1975 taking in some of the 1970s literature presented at the IOC, but many changes had occurred since, including Charles Sibley's taxonomic restructuring work that confirmed there had been a distinct Australian songbird radiation. By 1994 these bird groups had to be located at separate nodes on the avian tree.[72] Christidis is an expert in genetically based taxonomic studies and Boles is an expert in palaeo-ornithology, so the list drew together dispersed literature in a format suitable to guide the order in the handbook, which it did from Volume 3 onwards.[73]

The *HANZAB* project further blurred the distinction between the highly scientific ornithologist and the average birdwatcher. By contrast with the more technical systematic scientific work of Schodde and Ian Mason's *Directory of Australian Birds: Passerines* (1999), which appeared at about the same time as the fourth volume of *HANZAB* was published, the *HANZAB* format was designed to be accessible to amateur and professional alike as 'ordinary' bird observers sought more information than ever before. Marchant always regarded himself as an 'amateur' ornithologist, and his vision set the pattern for the whole set of volumes even after he retired.

The inclusion of New Zealand in *HANZAB* not only reunited the 'Australasian' of the original union but had an important effect on the RAOU itself. It was the handbook that attracted Philip Moors (1948–), then living in New Zealand, to apply successfully for the job of full-time RAOU director when it was advertised to start in 1989:

> I must say that it was probably the single most persuasive thing when I was considering applying for the position. I wanted to be part of it because for a decade in New Zealand I'd been reading about how successful *The Birds of the Western Palearctic* project had been in

Britain. I could see clearly how valuable such a publication would be for this part of the Southern Hemisphere.[74]

Moors, a zoology graduate of the Australian National University and Aberdeen University, had worked as a research scientist for fourteen years with the New Zealand Wildlife Service. He therefore had a good knowledge of both sides of the Tasman. It was fitting that the first volume of *HANZAB* was launched in New Zealand, at the International Ornithological Congress in Christchurch in 1990—the second time the IOC met in the Southern Hemisphere. Moors remained director of the RAOU until 1992. He then became the first zoologist to be director of the Royal Botanic Gardens Melbourne (now Royal Botanic Gardens Victoria), when bird knowledge was becoming integral to the understanding and management of public gardens (see Epilogue).

It is a mistake to limit any analysis of 'research' to 'funded research', particularly in the case of birdos—and also in conservation biology. The volunteer component and other in-kind contributions are often far more significant than the 'seeding grants' that start such projects, and the participation of the wider community is much more complex and enriching for society than the slotting of scientific factoids into narrow disciplinary knowledge systems. In 1996, when Stephen Ambrose compiled the *Australian Bird Research Directory*, he found ninety-three research groups or individuals working on a total of 223 funded projects for that year alone. But his list did not reflect all the research happening as there was no way to include the many unfunded and philanthropically funded projects that didn't fit his questionnaire.[75] The following year, his reach had grown to 127 respondents working on 301 funded projects. Half of these were conducted by university researchers, 18 per cent by state/territory government conservation agencies, 13 per cent by community groups, 9 per cent by independent researchers, 6 per cent by museums and 4 per cent by Commonwealth government agencies.[76] By comparison, the ABBBS report for 1996–97 recorded 458 projects for that year dealing with birds (and twenty with bats), giving some sense of the major contribution of unpaid work in ornithology.[77]

Penguins and other long-term projects

Official research projects usually have to finish within the life of a grant or two. It is always rare to maintain long-term research over decades. The international Long Term Ecological Research Network (LTERN) was established in Australia in 2012 in response to that difficulty.[78] Bird projects feature prominently on the LTERN list, not least because they are inexpensive (workers are generally not paid) and are seen as 'fun'. Research that starts with a geographically distinct project and willing volunteers is less limited by funding constraints over time.

In 1950, Roy Wheeler (1905–88) and Ina Watson (1909–92) decided to undertake a long-running study of the life history of the common silver gull (*Larus novaehollandiae*).[79] The Altona Salt-Works Survey involved a year-round survey of activity at the bird sanctuary near Melbourne, under the auspices of the BOC and RAOU (Melbourne). While silver gulls were the focus of banding activities, a hide built in May 1951 allowed for observation and censusing of all birds. 'Hours have been spent in this stout little hut by members working on displays and the nesting habits of the gulls,' Wheeler wrote affectionately.[80] The Altona Survey Group's work continued until 1962, when it broadened its efforts and became the core of the much larger Victorian Ornithological Research Group.[81] VORG continues well into the twenty-first century, is still a key participant in the ABBBS, and works closely with the Public Land section of the Victorian Department of Environment, Land, Water and Planning.

The studies of penguins at Phillip island, initiated by Pauline Reilly in the 1960s, are another example of long-term work. The threats to penguin survival posed by developments in the 1970s resulted in a new not-for-profit conservation organisation, Phillip Island Nature Parks, which is now responsible for penguin visitor services as well as science. This group maintains ongoing investigations of the island's significant populations of little penguins, short-tailed shearwaters, hooded plovers and Australian fur seals, and its threatened species as the pressure on breeding grounds has increased over the years. Peter Dann, who was the leader of the RAOU's Nest Record Scheme in the 1970s, was appointed

as a paid research director for this group in 1980, and retired finally from
Phillip Island Nature Parks forty-two years later in 2022.[82] While he took
on other consultancies and other unpaid tasks (including significant work
for *HANZAB*), he passed up many other scientific opportunities in order
to stay close to this very local long-term project, which has taken him in
many different directions for over four decades. In 1992 he published an
important paper consolidating the data from the 1960s to the 1990s, and
has since published hundreds of papers and book chapters and edited a
book on penguin ecology and management.[83] His main research interests
are population regulation, demography, climate change, foraging ecology,
mitigation of anthropogenic threats to seabirds, ecology of islands and the
conservation of threatened species. From his base at Phillip Island, he is
also a research fellow of the Department of Zoology at the University of
Melbourne and the Scott Polar Institute at Cambridge University, and
one of the editors of the journal *Marine Ornithology*. He is a past chairman
of the Australasian Seabird Group and is still a director of the Penguin
Foundation, which supports the work of Phillip Island Nature Parks.

In April 2022, on radio, Dann explained the importance of his new
work on climate change, which is already affecting the breeding behaviour
of penguins at Phillip Island. He measures heat stress at 'penguin height'
(33 centimetres above the ground)[84] and has created a heat map of the
Summerland Peninsula, near where he lives on the island, to identify the
coolest areas to build new burrows for the penguins, who are particularly
susceptible to heat stress during their moulting period. Dann's lifelong
commitment to science-based wildlife management and threatened-
species conservation has primarily been through one species in one place,
but it touches on many of the global problems of expanding populations of
humans and the limitations of locally breeding special birds.

10

WATCHING AND OBSERVING

Birdwatching

The term 'birdwatching' is internationally credited to a 1901 book of this title by British bird lover Edmund Selous (1857–1934).[1] Selous started as a conventional naturalist but developed a hatred of the killing of animals for scientific study, even for building museum collections. He wrote against the bloody traditions of his more famous older brother, Frederick, known as a fearless Zambesi hunter and author of several books, including *African Nature Notes and Reminiscences*, published in 1908 with a foreword by President Theodore Roosevelt.[2] Edmund actively opposed the collection of skins and eggs:

> For myself, I must confess that I once belonged to this great, poor army of killers, though happily, a bad shot, a most *fa*tigable collector, and a poor half-hearted bungler, generally. But now that I have watched birds closely, the killing of them seems to me as something monstrous and horrible … Let anyone who has an eye and a brain (but especially the latter), lay down the gun and take up the glasses for a week, a day, even for an hour, if he is lucky, and he will never wish to change back

again. He will soon come to regard the killing of birds as not only brutal, but dreadfully silly, and his gun and cartridges, once so dear, will be to him, hereafter, *as the toys of childhood are to the grown man.*[3]

By contrast with Frederick, Edmund was a solitary man. He did not keep company with people in birding circles—indeed, he was hostile to their activities. He even avoided reading ornithologists' reports. He strove to base his conclusions entirely on his own observations, treating birdwatching as a *scientific* method. Independently wealthy, he was able to travel to Southern Africa and India in his youth and later to Shetland, Sweden, the Netherlands and Iceland to observe and make notes on birds there. He had particular interests in behaviour, sexual selection and the problem of the coordinated flight manoeuvres of flocking birds. He continued birdwatching and writing his observations all his life, believing that every observed detail should be recorded.

Not all birdwatching pioneers were soloists like Selous and his more famous American counterpart, Henry Thoreau (1817–62). Some, like 'the Woodlanders', Charles Barrett (The Scribe), Claude Kinane (The Artist) and Brooke Nicholls (The Doctor), saw birdwatching and nature study as a social opportunity.[4] Their bush hut, 'Walden', named in honour of Thoreau's famous retreat, was in an old orchard in Olinda, a 'pleasant walk' from Lilydale, the most easterly station in Melbourne's metropolitan rail network. Like Waterfall station in Sydney, the train lines dictated which part of the bush became the favoured destination for birdwatching. At Walden, the Woodlanders were occasionally joined by Donald Macdonald, the nature writer we have already met (see Chapter 1), who was first president of the BOC and proudly 'amateur' in style. They, in turn, visited the bush acre at Black Rock (on a different train line) where Macdonald kept a 'book-lined study'. Unlike Thoreau, the Woodlanders and Macdonald 'carve homes for the heart out of "wilderness"', in the words of historian Tom Griffiths.[5] Birdwatching and nature study were, for these Australian contemporaries of Selous, reflective, practical and social all at once. Like him they shunned the gun, but, in Barrett's and Macdonald's cases, they replaced the hunt with lyrical prose, rather than Selous's functional scientific notes and educational essays.

Edmund Selous produced a number of ornithological books and papers as well as several books on popular natural history and a serious natural history series for children, part of the nature-study education that was popular in the first half of the twentieth century in Britain and Australia. The exhaustive ornithological library of Gregory Mathews that was later bequeathed to the National Library of Australia (see Chapter 3) ignored all of Selous's publications except one: his 1931 book, *Thought-transference (or What?) in Birds*, about telepathy and murmuration in birds.[6] *Bird Watching* was apparently not to Mathews' taste, but he did have Frederick Selous's hunting books in his collection.

Joining (and not joining) the club

Australia's first national birding club was established in the year of the publication of *Bird Watching*, but this was not its primary purpose. Australia in 1901 comprised just 3.7 million people—about the population of South East Queensland today. The new nation designed a 'minimalist' Constitution that ultimately swore allegiance to the British Crown. One chief justice of the High Court, Patrick Keane (1952–), called it 'a small brown bird', contrasting it with the ambitious 'bald eagle' Constitution of the United States.[7] Each of the six federated colonies operated out of its own 'London', a big central city with a port that created its connections with the world.[8] These colonial capital cities were often better connected to London than to each other. The new bird association, the Australasian Ornithologists' Union, looked to London, too. It sought international credibility more than national reach.

Alfred North, ornithologist and oologist at Australia's oldest museum, in Sydney, would certainly have had no interest in Edmund Selous. North was a competitive and active bird and egg collector. He avoided any enterprise that involved popular Melbourne-based journalist and oologist

Archibald J Campbell because they wrote competitively about the nests and eggs of Australian birds. North led trends in ornithology in Sydney in the late nineteenth and early twentieth centuries, but not through a formal organisation. He was a soloist, an expert for others, not 'clubbable'. His museum work was central to identifying and authenticating collectors' 'finds'. Campbell drew his authority from the museum itself and its excellent connections with other museums around the world. As a corresponding member of the American Ornithologists' Union from 1902 and the British Ornithologists' Union from 1903, he had no need of social birding to maintain his collections or those of the Australian Museum.

Sydney had an active local birding community interested in field observation, but none of these people joined the AOU in its early years, partly because the Royal Zoological Society of New South Wales (established 1879) already had an Ornithological Section. Sydney birdos were important lobbyists for the first legislated national park in the world (now called Royal National Park) in 1879.[9] Just 36 kilometres south of Sydney's Rocks community, the nature reserve was modelled on English reformer Octavia Hill's concerns about creating clean air for 'slum-dwellers'. Public-health-minded denizens of Sydney, most notably Sir John Robertson (1816–91), persuaded the government to support a bush reservation, and to support the important Waterfall railway station.

Sydney's early birding history foreshadowed the developments of the twenty-first century. There is now an increasing focus on preserving birding haunts in and near Australia's megacities as population pressures have increased. The national population doubled between Federation and 1945, then doubled again by 1970, diversifying through the massive postwar immigration program. In the 2020s both Sydney and Melbourne have over five million people, and future projections have Melbourne's population soon to become larger than Sydney again, as it was in 1901 when the first national bird association began and the Woodlanders were smoking pipes in their bush hut. Australia is one of the most urban nations in the world, with megacities built up from the capitals of the original colonies and densely populated regional areas close to them.

Educating observers

In 1979, a century after Royal National Park was reserved, the Cumberland Bird Observers' Club was formally established. It had an expanding vision for bird-education, including the Barren Grounds Bird Observatory further south, which it developed in the 1980s. Birdwatching was becoming an increasingly important and more professional activity, inclusive of adults and not merely 'improving' for children.

While the Gould League and John Leach's nature study in primary schools had been important in the early years of the twentieth century, in the 1960s bird-observing was becoming a formal skill for adults. In South Australia, the Workers' Educational Association (WEA) classes of Joan Paton (1916–2000) were a long-running favourite. Paton ran 'Beginners' Ornithology' classes every year from 1967 to 1999. She complemented these with adult education classes such as 'Birds of the Swamps and Sea' for the University of Adelaide, where she also taught biochemistry, nutrition and biology until 1983. Paton was a banding enthusiast and vice-president (1974–79) and president (1979–82) of the South Australian Ornithological Association.

Margaret Cameron (1937–), who was foundation librarian of Deakin University from 1977 until 1996, is a distinguished 'amateur' ornithologist, elected Fellow of the RAOU after serving as RAOU president from 1986 to 1990. She began birdwatching as a hobby in Queensland as a child with her enthusiastic grandfather and became a real birdo after she moved to South Australia in the late 1960s. There she attended Paton's classes at the WEA and the University of Adelaide. 'I did both of those one year,' Margaret recalled, 'and then you just got signed up to the SAOA.' She also joined the RAOU and became a regular bander.[10]

In 1998, Australia's first university-level graduate courses in the new ornithology were pioneered by David Goldney, head of the Environmental Studies Unit at Charles Sturt University (CSU); the courses combined bird-observational skills with environmental management. Goldney's team of enthusiastic ornithological academics included Rick Allen, who commented in 2000 on the importance of 'professional amateurs' and the high quality of the work they produced in the new course at CSU's Bathurst campus:[11]

> One of the things that has amazed me over the number of years that I've been involved with [what was then] Birds Australia is the complete spectrum between those two extremes [from amateur to professional], even to the point of publication in *Emu* and other journals ... there are very, very good publications coming from people who don't happen to be employed as scientists but are still doing very good scientific work.[12]

The CSU's first graduates were typically taking out a Graduate Diploma in Ornithology to formalise skills already honed through long voluntary service. They included Penny Drake-Brockman (secretary of the New South Wales Field Ornithologists Club, member of the Capertee Valley Regent Honeyeater Recovery Team, and BIGnet member), Judy Harrington (Sydney's Bicentennial Park and wetland species database, managed by the Sydney Olympic Park Authority), Roy Sonnenburg (Birding Services, Brisbane, and Queensland Ornithological Society Inc.), Nicci Thompson (Birds Australia councillor and *Atlas* regional organiser for Toowoomba), Peter Vaughan (a dentist who established a wildlife sanctuary in Newcastle) and Jo Wieneke (*Atlas* regional organiser for north Queensland and author of three local field guides). Such 'students' made the categories of amateur and professional seem arbitrary. Even the roles of teacher and student were sometimes reversed: Sonnenburg, an experienced A-class bander (ABBBS no. 1607), agreed to run the banding section of the course for his year.[13] The courses are still running successfully (now at CSU Albury–Wodonga as part of the vet school). They are now generally online with an intensive 'residential component', which makes them attractive to people from all over the country.[14]

Goldney found support for ornithology courses right across his colleagues at CSU, a collegiality that was important to the success of the whole interdisciplinary Environmental Studies course. Like Harry Frith, who had inspired support from CSIRO staff, administrators and senior management for the IOC in 1974, Goldney discovered closet birdos all over CSU and in the community. Birdos from all walks of life supported his course, and many of the most serious of them were known for other professional work. Goldney himself was always a practical environmental scientist, working for Cenwest Environmental Services and developing the Save the Bush Toolkit in the late 1990s. He also ran seminars for town planners on the implications of climate change in his 'spare time', alongside his academic career.[15] He retired from CSU in 2000 but remains an honorary adjunct professor and is now best known for his other popular conservation work: restoring platypus habitat at Duckmaloi Weir, a short drive from his home in Bathurst.[16]

Twitching and ticking

The term 'twitcher' started appearing in the *RAOU Newsletter* in June 1982. A 'twitcher' was defined as one who 'keeps lists of all the bird species they see. No effort is too great to extend the list.'[17] The twitching phenomenon was the fault of the British, where 'an elaborate grapevine exists ... to inform keen twitchers of unusual sightings'. North Americans, no less obsessive, called similarly afflicted individuals 'tickers'. Richard Jordan, a former schoolteacher who with his wife, Pat, was manager of Barren Grounds Observatory, claimed that the scientific name of both was *Ornifanaticus* spp. The term 'twitcher' took precisely two issues of the newsletter to become enshrined in the new 'Twitcher's Corner' column, a place for rare and unconfirmed sightings. The column became an outlet for what was known as the '600 Club' (people who had seen more than 600 Australian species of birds). Twitchers seldom wrote up their sightings at length, but at least such a column ensured that reports of rare birds and vagrants found their way into print.

Fundraising 'Twitchathons' followed soon after. The most fascinating aspect of this phenomenon for those unafflicted by it is the amount of trust involved. Why should one believe the twitchers' accounts of how many species they have ticked? The answer is that their fanaticism makes cheating inconceivable. Annie Rogers (1938–), a self-confessed bird addict, tells the charming story of the first Australian Twitchathon in 1984. A bemused journalist had been enticed along to cover the event by the presence of television personality and international super-twitcher Bill Oddie (1941–). She simply did not believe that ornithologists really trusted each other about their daily species count. Sniffing around for a story, she approached Kevin Bartram. 'It's not possible to get a really good total without cheating,' Bartram replied earnestly. The reporter turned to hear more. 'Well, can you believe that teams can drive 1500 kilometres in a day, count 200 species and not occasionally break the speed limit?'[18] The journalist switched off her tape in disgust. Speed limits might be optional for these crazy ornithologists, but 'cheating' on the ticks was inconceivable. Twitchathons and similar events attract all sorts of people interested in birds to raise money for worthy causes.

Melbourne-based comedy writer Sean Dooley (1968–) hails from close to Seaford Wetlands, where he has seen 180 species of birds. He was once told by a teacher that he could not be both a comedian and an ornithologist, but when he learned that Oddie, whom he knew from the BBC comedy *The Goodies*, did both, he decided that the combination was not just possible but worked really well.[19] Twitching is such a serious business that a sense of humour helps a lot. In 2002, Dooley took a year off writing to break the Australian birdwatching record. His year off was a success, with him seeing the most species of birds in one year, with a week to spare. He spent the next day, Christmas Day, recovering, watching birds alone for his own pleasure, and called it 'the best Christmas ever'. His book of that year, *The Big Twitch*, was a bestseller, popular with those who twitch and those who don't, because it is all about not just counting but also loving birds.[20] Dooley works as editor of the popular magazine *Australian Birdlife* and broadcasts regularly. On ABC Melbourne radio, he hosts 'Squawk-back'. Talkback radio became a lifeline for many isolated listeners during the pandemic, and birds close to home were news during lockdowns. The show is now a regular weekly segment on ABC Melbourne's afternoon show, and counts many people new to suburban birding among its listeners.

Living in the Anthropocene

The Anthropocene is the epoch in which human activities are considered a geological force, changing the earth's systems. The idea for it was proposed in 2000, but it has yet to be formally ratified by stratigraphers. Many scientists have observed the 'Great Acceleration' of anthropogenic change since the mid twentieth century, which has transformed land use, acidified the oceans and increased the pace of global warming. The Great Acceleration includes the extraordinary rise in the world's population from 2.5 billion to 8 billion in seventy-five years, just one human lifetime. The technological changes that feed such a population, bleaching of coral reefs, atmospheric pollution, melting of glaciers and polar ice caps, loss of clean water and air, and the plastic waste carried in the ocean all affect birds as well as humans. The greatest concern is the continuing loss of habitat, leading to the extinction of many birds and other animals, plants and fungi. At the time of writing, geologists and stratigraphers are still debating exactly what would formally mark the onset of the Anthropocene, but no one doubts that Earth is dealing with the multifaceted impacts of an unprecedented number of humans.

Many birds have adapted to live alongside humans and to live off the spoils of human excess. Such birds are often now seen as pests. The 'bin chicken' of Sydney's Hyde Park is an insulting new vernacular name that reflects changed human perceptions—the sacred ibis (*Threskiornis aethiopicus*) was a god in classical Egypt! But a bird with its head in a bin, strewing rubbish around, is not welcome in a tidy park manicured for human recreation. Birds who work out how to capitalise on human behaviours, whose numbers have increased rapidly alongside human numbers, are often denigrated. Sometimes they are actively hunted. In the twenty-first century, the urban 'wild' needs celebrating, too. Peter Slater, known for the 1970s 'Slater Field Guides' (see Chapter 3), recently joined forces with his son, Raoul, and artist Sally Elmer (1964–) to produce *Visions of Wildness*, a quirky artistic tribute to the birds and other animals, plants and fungi that 'exist and flourish despite the despoliation' of our times. More a celebration of persistence than a field guide, this is a new style of bird book for the armchair traveller in the urban wilds. Its images reveal remarkable behaviours: the bin chicken, despite 'regrettable habits' in city parks, can still look magical as it rolls onto its back while flying, rapidly loses altitude, then flips and quickly regains control.[21]

Stories of birds who get in the way of human expectations have emerged regularly for well over a century. People who care about birds have had to argue against farmers and orchardists for the birds' right to exist when livelihoods were threatened by sudden irruptions of birds and changing behaviours in response to human expansion. The protection of birds was the subject of many early presidential addresses to the RAOU, in 1906, 1907, 1908, 1909 and 1912. 'Economic ornithology' promoted the benefits of birds to the farmer and the orchardist. This was a nation-building reason to establish the RAOU, which campaigned tirelessly to add more birds to the 'protected' lists. Native birds, perhaps more than other native animals, were unprotected at this stage. Nineteenth-century colonial parliaments had passed game laws protecting *acclimatised* birds, but laws to protect indigenous species were slower to develop. As early as 1865, John Gould had commented on the Australian habit of giving preference to 'acclimatizing animals from other countries'. He sought 'protection for the emu, that it may not be extirpated from this continent as nearly as it has been from Tasmania'.[22]

Economic ornithology was sometimes inclined to exaggerate the 'ignorance' of the farmer as against the expertise of the ornithologist (apparently forgetting that many farmers are also good ornithologists), but the discipline's value to public policymaking could not be denied. Ornithologists began to analyse the crops and guts of birds to work out what they ate, and discovered that some supposed villains regularly shot by farmers or orchardists were actually eating insects and grubs harmful to crops.

Twenty-year-old Stanley Sharland (later better known as Michael) joined the Tasmanian Field Naturalists' Club in 1919. Initially, he did not know 'what particular branch of nature' to take up. His first natural history diary records his reasons for choosing to study the 'useful' discipline of ornithology:

The plover in Tasmania should be afforded total and complete protection under [the] Tasmanian Game and Protection Act from the so called 'Sportsman' and the 'Pot Hunter', on account of their usefulness in combating the dreaded enemy of the farmer, the grass grub ... Let us remember that the plover, more especially the black breasted variety, are practically outside the owl the only birds that work at night. And night-time is favoured by the grass grub, thousands of which wreak havoc on crops, grasses and the like. The birds do a service to the farmer [that] is far beyond his comprehension.[23]

Throughout the century governments of all sorts pitted themselves against 'pestilent birds', often without success, as ornithologists would occasionally gleefully record. Dominic Serventy's *Birds of Western Australia* tells the tale of the Commonwealth minister for defence who declared an 'emu war' in 1932, when the army took to emus with machine guns. The politician saw the eradication of emus as something to assist farmers and also to give the army target practice. The 7th Heavy Battery of the Royal Australian Artillery brought two Lewis guns and 10,000 rounds of ammunition to the 'war'. Fifty local settlers organised a 35-kilometre drive of emus to an ambush point on the No. 1 Rabbit Proof Fence. But alas for the honour of the army, the birds split into small parties, completely foiling the ambush.[24] The Western Australian Department of Agriculture, annoyed that it had not been consulted by the Commonwealth Defence Department, 'looked coldly on the whole campaign'. As the lack of success in the 'war' became more apparent, the Lewis-guns venture lost its political cachet and quietly withdrew. The state Agriculture Department took a different approach that proved rather worse for the emus: it offered a 'bounty', a bonus of a shilling a head for emus. In the economically depressed times of the 1930s, the slaughter of emus by local shooters provided extra income to many battlers, and the shooters were much more precise and accurate than the large and clumsy Lewis guns.

In the twenty-first century, emus are decreasing at an alarming rate. Many perish on their spring migration coastwards after winter breeding in the inland at the 'Emu Fence', built originally in 1907–08 as 'the rabbit-proof fence no. 2' or, more officially, the State Barrier Fence of Western Australia. The emu was known to be vulnerable, as its demise in Tasmania and Kangaroo Island in the nineteenth century testified, yet little was known of its ecology and seasonal migration. A century of research shows the problems fences pose for emus, yet the Emu Fence is still maintained because it keeps out not just emus but feral cats, dogs and other animals, thus protecting other significant biodiversity in the Wheatbelt, which has been the centre of major regeneration projects in the past three decades.[25]

The tension between conservation and progress

Nature study was an important part of peacemaking for many returned service personnel after World War II. Yet postwar reconstruction often threatened the places of retreat that would restore mental health. The postwar years coincided with the beginning of home movies, and talented natural history journalist Crosbie Morrison was one who used film and still photography, along with radio broadcasts and the magazine *Wild Life*, to enthuse new people about birds and their habitats. The war bred talk of 'enemies' but Morrison turned this around, adopting military language to defend nature against indiscriminate military activities, which he had secretly observed at Wilsons Promontory but for security reasons could not reveal until after the war was over:

> This remote area with its wide range and wild mountain country and extensive plains, and its short dividing fence, was the very place for certain military and air force purposes which at that time must at all costs be kept secret. The Commonwealth took it over for the period of the war. They made an aerodrome there ... They trained commando troops there—they had to learn to travel light, to make booby traps and to avoid enemy booby traps; they had to become accustomed to living off the land, and what better land could there be to live off than a region which had been preserved as a fauna sanctuary for nearly half a century?[26]

Morrison urged a 'stocktake' of wartime losses, reflecting a new concern for the preservation of habitat, not just individual birds. The first serious 'postwar reconstruction' work of natural history organisations was, for Morrison, the establishment of national parks and reserves. The RAOU enthusiastically joined his campaign. A special film night in partnership with the *Wild Life* magazine team in October 1945 attracted 'a very large attendance', something that would not have happened for an RAOU business meeting without the charismatic Morrison. The evening was 'devoted to colour films by Mr Norman Chaffer depicting the spotted and satin bower-birds in their natural surroundings'.[27] Before the films began, prominent Melbourne businessman and industrial chemist Russell Grimwade (1879–1955) opened proceedings with a speech on the preservation of native flora and fauna, including a particular plea for wedge-tailed eagles, which were being destroyed by graziers.[28]

There was a long history of bounties on wedge-tailed eagles (known as eagle hawks in many parts of Australia). Johann Knobel, a South African lawyer, described them as 'the most severely persecuted eagle species in the world' in the twenty-first century. Colonial and state governments had been paying bounties for their destruction since 1892, and postwar development and soldier settlement schemes created new dangers for eagles. In the period 1958–67, bounties were paid on 120,000 eagles in Queensland and Western Australia alone.[29] Throughout rural Australia, eagle carcasses were hung in rows on roadside fences, literally 'spreadeagled', boasting birds that had been shot, trapped or poisoned in accordance with various Vermin Acts and sometimes in spite of conservation legislation. Today, eagle populations are protected under law, with heavy penalties and even imprisonment for their persecution. Popular magazines such as *Australian Geographic* describe them as 'iconic'. Even so, the widespread use of industrial chemicals to kill the creatures that form their prey poses ongoing invisible threats through 'biomagnification', a process by which a chemical compound (such as a pollutant or pesticide) increases its concentration in the tissues of biological organisms as it travels up the food chain.

The effects of the accelerating use of industrial chemicals on humans and other 'top predators' went largely unnoticed until 1962, when Rachel

Carson published her bestselling book *Silent Spring*[30] and raised awareness and a new sort of activism. Global movements are powerful forces in changing local behaviours, but every place has its own local activism: birdwatching informs both. International networks are important, for example, to understanding threats to migratory shorebirds that travel halfway around the globe to breed in the Arctic summer and then back again to find food the rest of the year. But it is 'local extinctions'—for example, sedentary birds that no longer sing in places they used to frequent—that often stir up passions. Carson's parable about the spring without birdsong was a very local story in Middle America that alerted not just the local audience but also much of the rest of the world to the dangers of pesticides and the importance of insects in healthy ecosystems.

The 'unofficial' countryside

It has taken many years for ecologists to realise that megacities like London, New York, Los Angeles and Berlin have remarkable biodiversity. Historically, people chose places of high biodiversity to live because of the richness of the natural resources. Cities need ports and often navigable waterways, and they all need fresh water. River estuaries are resource-rich places. That is why the mangrove forests and shifting lands of the Ganges Delta can support an enormous population (in both India and Bangladesh) alongside the Bengal tiger in the Sundarbans: even places without reliable 'land' can provide important habitat.

Yet for most of the twentieth century, the focus of nature conservation was land, particularly land reserved for nature in national parks and similar reserves, mapped in fixed ways onto a landscape of other (mostly human) uses. This is changing as climate change moves ecosystems steadily towards the poles, and towards higher altitudes. Fixed boundaries are no guarantee against losing ecosystems. Conservation biologists work to help biota to survive threats from humans and from habitat loss; yet, paradoxically, they often choose to work in national parks and protected areas, not the threatened lands beyond. The demands of university jobs mean that they seldom venture into non-Western countries, despite the obvious fact that threats to biodiversity are so much greater in populous developing countries where there is less chance of reserving exclusive habitat for nature.[31] Historian Peter Alagona has noted this phenomenon within the context of the United States:

> Prior to European contact, Manhattan, an island of just twenty-three square miles [59 square kilometres], contained roughly the same number of species as now live in Yellowstone National Park, a vast region of mountains, valleys, forests and prairies covering some thirty-five hundred square miles [9000 square kilometres]. This means that the Manhattan of yesteryear housed around 150 times more plant and animal species than the Yellowstone of today. If European settlers had wanted to save North America's wildlife instead of getting rich from harvesting it, they would have built a great city in northwest Wyoming and set up a national park in the mouth of the Hudson River.[32]

The 'accidental' ecosystems of cities today are just a small part of the rich biodiversity of yesteryear, but even so, the estuarine and marine mix of the Hudson supports a surprising variety of biota, and even large animals.

What is conceived of as a biodiverse ecosystem is framed by human expectations, and sometimes limited by what humans notice. There may be surprises. Jens Lachmund tells the story of West Berlin ecologists who, finding themselves confined to the city limits in the Cold War years (when the Iron Curtain debarred them from the countryside near Berlin), began to survey the wastelands and neglected corners of the city. They documented hundreds of plant species, including some rare ones, in abandoned railway yards such as the Südgelände, where a 1980 survey revealed 334 species of ferns and flowering plants—about one-third of Berlin's total. This 'oasis of nature' was later preserved against redevelopment on the grounds that it was 'essential to the progress of ecological research'.[33] When the city reunified in 1989, a new railway station proposed for this area did not go ahead because of the unexpected cost of funding compensation 'for the loss of nature and landscape'. West Berlin ecologists would much rather have botanised in the countryside, but the political situation forced a reassessment of their city and created a new language of green planning.

Richard Mabey (1941–) evokes the persistent richness of the megacity of London despite its long history of industrial sprawl. His book celebrating the wastelands and forgotten corners of London, *The Unofficial Countryside*, was first published in 1973, when 'the idea of celebrating the impromptu wildlife of cities was regarded as mildly eccentric'.[34] By 1999, when the second edition was published, that idea was mainstream. 'The wildlife that thrives in cities—both green relics and opportunist newcomers—is now recognised as an important component in the country's natural diversity', he wrote. This is partly because human dwellings and businesses encroach everywhere, even the 'picture-postcard backcloths of wood and farm'. Indeed, natural history books in Britain celebrate 'unspoiled places'—a term less often used in Australia, where many wild places are 'spoiled' but remote and therefore remain out of sight.

In Australia, 'unspoiled' is sometimes replaced by 'unhurried'. Celeste Mitchell, Katie Gannon and Krista Eppelstun have assembled a coffee table book, *Life Unhurried*, that features 'slow and sustainable stays across Australia' for the stay-at-home traveller in the wake of COVID-19. It builds on the discovery of the joy of staying put and observing felt by owners and renters who have left (literally) 'high-flying' jobs to 'get their hands dirty', to 'live off grid'—to restore sanity to mad lives. 'Slow Stays' became 'sanctuaries for the mind and soul, as much as beautiful places to lay your head'.[35]

The sense of the world as 'mad' and a need to get off the treadmill of life is widely felt, but the contradictions between life as lived in Anthropocene times and life as it continues despite human-imposed incursions is still hard to unpack, to 'do something about'. London-based Mabey is a botanist, author of *Flora Britannica* and a popular nature writer. He has battled depression, and is watchful for things that trigger his own depression and that of others. He is an extraordinary writer because he doesn't so much write about 'nature' as people's emotional relationships with nature. These have become more intense and complex as climate anxiety accelerates in the Anthropocene.

Mabey argues persuasively that the people most in need of 'nature' are those deprived of it, confined to urban, indoor-office life. Long before COVID lockdowns, he wrote of his own 'normal working day' in an overheated and stuffy office that had no aspect. His day lacked rhythm but, rather, was patterned by 'bitching' and sadness: 'there was [not] much to see through [the office windows] but the damp and smoky air cowling the factory blocks'. At the end of a day of 'tense slouch[ing] at the desk one moment and tetchy to-ings and fro-ings the next', he jumped into his car to return home and found himself in gridlock: 'a creeping three-lane jam was about as much relief as if the office had been towed away on wheels. I was locked-up, boxed-in, and daydreaming morbidly. It was difficult to believe that there was any sort of world beyond all this.'[36]

He turned out of the traffic down a suburban lane. 'It was hardly the promised landscape', an 'area was pocked with working quarries and car dumps', but he had discovered it while developing his ideas of an unofficial countryside, where nature came back despite the best efforts of humans to make this impossible. Mabey realised that 'just to have seen some murky water lapped by non-air-conditioned wind would have set me right'. His black frame of mind made 'the unexpected late fruitfulness' of the canal and its towpath all the more remarkable: 'I had never noticed before that the canal here was as clear as a chalk stream', he wrote. Chalk streams – also called 'winterbournes' in Britain – only flow after rain, because they are based on limestone (or chalk) which absorbs the water quickly. The white base and the recent rain give them a transparent clarity.

> Yellow water lilies drooped like balls of molten wax on the surface. Near the edge of the water drifts of newly hatched fish hung in the shallows … My eyes began to relax a little, and, following the last swallows hawking for flies over the water, I caught sight of a brilliant spike of purple loosestrife [a wild British herbaceous perennial plant with towering purple flower spikes] in the distance. I had never before seen this plant so deep into suburbia … As dusk fell and the warning lights on [the roof of the local pumping station] began to flush the bellies of the roosting gulls, I went off home like a new man.[37]

Birding in the Anthropocene has taken on new, heavier psychological responsibilities. It is also full of happy surprises. Different sorts of people are calling themselves 'birdos', and for a wider range of reasons than ever before. Many are commenting on how their local birds saved their sanity in lockdown times. Reassessing the local, seeing the nature wherever you happen to be, is an old skill that has acquired new relevance in times where human encroachments can blind us to the ways nature pushes back.

Industrial science and post-industrial survival

Biomagnification is a crucial ecological process that was discovered largely through the ecological study of 'vermin' species in the interests of industrial agriculture. In 1932 Charles Elton (1900–91) established the Oxford Bureau of Animal Population and the *Journal of Animal Ecology*. Through his BBC radio broadcasts called *The Ecology of Invasions by Animals and Plants* (1957) and the book of the same title published the following year, Elton became famous around the world as the father of 'invasion ecology'.[38] The Bureau of Animal Population trained many of the specialist biologists that worked with the Empire Marketing Board, the enterprise that encouraged agricultural expansion within the British Commonwealth and in 1926 sponsored Australia's original Council for Scientific and Industrial Research (now CSIRO; see Chapter 6). Elton's best-known student in Australia was Francis Ratcliffe, whose CSIR ecological work on the grey-headed flying fox, a pest to fruit growers, became the basis for the popular book *Flying Fox and Drifting Sand: The Adventures of a Biologist in Australia*.[39] Ratcliffe ended up making his career in Australia, heading the CSIRO's Division of Wildlife in the 1950s and becoming the inaugural secretary of the Australian Conservation Foundation (established in 1963).

Under Ratcliffe's leadership, the approach to 'problem animals' became increasingly ecological. Paradoxically, the classification of some birds as pests allowed CSIRO Wildlife to undertake core projects on their life histories, biology and ecology. Ratcliffe argued to his industrially minded bosses that to control invasive species you had to understand their ecologies and life histories. Native ducks and geese, 'pests' for wet-land developments in the Murrumbidgee Irrigation Area and Northern Australia Development Program schemes, thereby became major official studies. Harry Frith's work on ducks around Griffith, New South Wales, and Stephen Davies' studies of magpie geese at Fogg Dam near Humpty Doo in the Northern Territory became leading international studies, much broader than simply methods to control numbers of pest animals.[40] Similarly, CSIRO supported detailed ecological studies of emus (Davies), ravens (Ian Rowley), and eagles (Michael Ridpath and Michael Brooker) because the birds were regarded as economic problems.

It is intriguing that many of the birds considered pests by people developing Western capitalist projects have long been considered impor-tant cultural figures by Indigenous bird observers. Some of the earliest papers in *Emu* were about Indigenous understandings of birds. In 1902, Katie Langloh Parker (1856–1940) contributed 'My Tame Wild Birds', which explored Noongahburrah Aboriginal names for birds around Walgett in Gamilaraay Country (New South Wales).[41] 'Walgett' is based on an Aboriginal word for 'the junction between two rivers' and is located where the Namoi and Barwon rivers meet. Parker (later Catherine Stow) was one of Australia's earliest ethnologists. Her contact with Aboriginal people went back to her early childhood: when she was six, a young Aboriginal woman saved her and two of her sisters from drowning in the Darling River. Later, as an isolated wife on Bangate station for over twenty years, she learned the local language (Noongahburrah) from the Aboriginal women who worked in her home, and based her paper on this knowledge. She was a rare female contributor to *Emu* in its early years. Parker was already a published author, contributing popular articles on Aboriginal myths and culture to other magazines as well as *Emu*. She also wrote two well-known children's books, *Australian Legendary Tales* and *More Australian Legendary Tales*.[42] After the very early years, *Emu* seldom reported on non-Western ways of observing birds. From the 1970s, it became more formally a 'science journal', without the reports of conser-vation efforts, bird-club activities and curious natural history observations that had enlivened its earlier pages.

Eagles and ravens are fundamental in Indigenous cosmologies. For Aboriginal peoples of Victoria, Eagle (Bunjil) is the far-sighted creator, while Crow (Waa) is clever and freewheeling, associated with the devastation and rebirth of fire, demanding respect but not always reliable. The same combination of raptor and corvid is important for Indigenous people as far away as the Bering Strait. There, Eagle is a creative force and Raven is a trickster who needs watching. These ancient and enduring parables of human/bird interactions are becoming ever more important as planet Earth groans under the weight of humanity.

As birdwatcher Edmund Selous advocated over a century ago, we all need more of the grown-up 'pleasure that belongs to observation and inference'.[43] Birds can teach humans ways to respond to the challenges of rapid change, if we learn to watch closely enough.

11

RAVEN

Who's watching who?

In a book about watching people watching birds, this is the chapter about birds who watch humans. 'There's always things in the air that watch us,' the traditional Koyukon people say. Alaskan anthropologist, linguist and broadcaster Richard K Nelson ('Nels', 1941–2019) wrote that:

> Koyukon people live in a world that watches, in a forest of eyes. A person moving through nature—however wild, remote, even desolate the place may be—is never truly alone. The surroundings are aware, sensate, personified. They feel. They can be offended. And they must, at every moment, be treated with proper respect.[1]

Nels' book about the Koyukon view of the northern forests of Alaska is called *Make Prayers to the Raven*. Everywhere he went, he paid attention to Raven, the local bird of a cosmopolitan family, a bird that watches, and watches over, humans closely.

Nels was an Alaskan but he was also an honorary Australian birdo. Every year for decades he followed the pathways forged by bar-tailed godwits and other migratory shorebirds, travelling from the Alaskan end of the East Asian flyway to Australia.[2] Australia was, for Nels, a way to spend February outdoors in nature, camping, listening and watching—things that were impossible deep in a dark Alaskan winter. He was always watching, even at night, with his motion-sensor camera, catching ringtail possums and other nocturnal animals in action, surprises even in my own garden. When you travelled with him, you saw things you'd have never seen otherwise. Sometimes he gave talks about nature writing, sometimes he made broadcasts about nature for Raven Radio, the community radio station in the town of Sitka, where he lived for many years. The Australian Broadcasting Commission also picked up his *Encounters* broadcasts.

As a true 'observer', more than just a watcher, Nels was guided by sound. He listened carefully to people and spoke several of the Athapaskan languages of what is now Alaska. He recorded the joy of a dawn bird chorus wherever he could, particularly loving the opening notes of the morning from Australian magpies, with their glorious carolling. The raucous cockatoos, especially the yellow-tailed black cockatoos that warned of coming storms, were another favourite, because he loved storms, too. One of his best broadcasts was made up a tree in a howling gale, where he shared the full force of the wind with his listeners. He listened to birds, to the rustling of the wind, to the cracking of glaciers. He learned as a young man sent to Wainwright on the Alaskan north coast that survival depended on listening.

Nels' commitment to listening grew stronger in his later years. He was a wonderful writer, but in his final decade he stopped writing and devoted himself to being in nature and recording its sounds. He and his parabolic microphone were inseparable. He collected sounds for himself, for the Cornell Lab of Ornithology's Macaulay Library, for films and for his radio broadcasts.[3] He was a brilliant interviewer, recording in situ an interview about zebra finches (*Taeniopygia guttata*) at Oceans Bore in the Channel Country with Australian ecologist and author Steve Morton (1951–). The interview was nearly drowned out by the 'nyii nyii' sounds of the zebbies, the sound that gave them their Ngaanyatjarra name.[4] But whether Nels was in Alaska or Australia, everywhere he went he listened up to Raven.

Ravens are creation beings in Koyukon forests, clever and witty like the humans they created. They love to play, but they need watching as they are tricksters, too. The big corvid family is widespread in the world, originating in the Southern Hemisphere, but the birds themselves are very local. They know their people well. It is striking that the traditional stories told by Woi Wurrung people of the Australian raven (*Corvus coronoides*) and those of the Koyukon people about the Alaskan raven (*Corvus corax*), so far away, share an understanding of a bird who watches and 'watches over' humans. Nels' seasonal travels took him over 12,000 kilometres ('as the crow flies') each way, yet he was watched at both ends of his long trip by ravens.

Wominjeka

The Melbourne Museum (now part of Museums Victoria) has been at the heart of the bird clubs in this book—it hosted the early RAOU and purchased some of its collections at a time when the club needed money. The museum has a new building now: it left its old building in 1997 due to an expansion of the State Library of Victoria and moved to the Carlton Gardens, a short walk away. The new building opened in 2000. It is modern and light-filled with a striking architectural blade, an iMax theatre and solar panels on its roof, quite unlike the original neoclassical building modelled on the British Museum. Ravens perch on the very urban blade, and their cawing echoes around the grand public space below where locals bring their skateboards to do tricks, and impromptu tai chi classes pop up.

The new museum has a very different emphasis from the old 'natural history museum'. As you enter, you encounter a massive artwork across the entrance: *Wominjeka*, it declares. That is 'Welcome' in the language of the Woi Wurrung and Boon Wurrung nations, on whose land the museum stands. Museums are cultural places. Of course, they always have been, but now they are taking pride in this and taking Indigenous curatorial leadership seriously. Entangled with the letters of *Wominjeka* are Bunjil the ancestral eagle and Waa the crow, the protector.[5] These are the birds that created the Country now known as south-eastern Australia. The creator and the protector work slightly differently in different places, but birds with distant vision and a protective voice are a guiding force widely shared across peoples who care for Country in traditional ways. Brendan Kennedy, a Tati Tati artist and Aboriginal linguist, designed the entrance art. Kennedy is Dindi Thangi Wuthungi (River Country Man). He comes from a place where Bunjil is called *Wiripil* and *Wangi* is Crow, but he worked collaboratively with the people from exactly the place where the museum stands, and used their words. 'Stories of Bunjil and Waa together provide meaning to south-eastern Aboriginal people. A person's affinity with either Bunjil or Waa defines their kinship relationships, marriage partners and social responsibilities,' he explains in the caption.[6]

Inside the museum, in the Bunjilaka Aboriginal Cultural Centre, we learn more of Waa's creative spirit and meet fire and free will. According to the *jimbayer* (learning) of Jaara woman Justice Nelson, Waa was once a beautiful many-coloured bird who could sing and sing and sing, but he was jealous of Bunjil. He went away and brought back fire and set fire to all the Country, and himself. Waa inhaled the smoke and lost his voice, and burnt all his feathers black. He is the trickster who outsmarted himself, the creator of free will, which leads to danger, to mistakes, to consequences.[7]

Crow

While the scientific community has long argued about the distinction between ravens and crows, the difference is not so significant to the general public, who often use 'crow' for both. The international collective term, 'a murder of crows', reflects a negative perception, and perhaps also the bird's predisposition for eating carrion. The British poet laureate Ted Hughes (1930–98) explored the depths of grief and despair in *Crow: From the Life and Songs of the Crow* (1970). According to the literary blog *The Examined Life*, Crow is 'a metaphor for our torn complex selves and an often absurd universe', but playful, too: 'A user of tools and technologies that can be both creative and destructive, as human technologies are.'[8] 'Eating crow' is bad news in the United States, where the phrase means that one has been shown to be wrong. However, in Australia 'crow' is more complicated. South Australians proudly use 'crow-eaters' as a demonym, reminding them of the tough pioneering pastoralists who resorted to crows when there was nothing better to eat. Today both the Adelaide AFL football club and a South Australian poetry magazine take the moniker as a badge of honour.[9]

Crows and ravens are sometimes taken for granted because they are common, noisy and too interested in human activities. They are certainly not rare challenges for wild expeditioners with binoculars. The Sydney-based Foundation for National Parks and Wildlife has a 'Backyard Buddies' program that attunes people to the value of ordinary, common birds as environmental indicators. It distinguishes carefully between crows and ravens, and between native and non-native crows:

> The five native species of Corvids (crows and ravens) in Australia are the Australian Raven, Little Raven, Little Crow, Forest Raven, and the Torresian Crow. They are all quite similar—ravens being perhaps slightly larger—and some can be difficult to tell apart in the field without close scrutiny. Another, introduced species, the House Crow, makes an occasional appearance. It is the only Corvid in Australia which has white in the plumage and is a declared pest in some states.[10]

Backyard Buddies declares crows sometimes 'infuriating' but resourceful and ingenious, too. Their nest-building can include 'pulling the rubber strips out of car windscreen wipers to line their nests and stealing letters from letterboxes to shred'. They are not favourites with golfers when they steal golf balls, mistaking the balls for eggs. The birds 'drop them from a roof, hoping to smash them open to eat'. Crows and ravens are 'good buddies' to gardeners when they eat lots of snails. For birdscapers, there is advice to plant spiky shrubs to protect small native birds from marauding ravens. However, crows and ravens are a problem on farms, where they 'have a particular liking for grapes, soft fruits, potatoes, nuts and grains. They remove fruit directly from trees, land on trellises which collapse under their weight, and despite their size, can perch directly on stalks of grain, snapping off plants such as wheat and sorghum'. Their reputation for attacking lambs is disputed: 'many believe they only go for sick animals or those abandoned by their mother'.[11] They are not always considered pests: carrion-eating birds help clean the environment of rotting carcasses. Common birds can be important to ecological understanding, too.

Presence and absence

The Western Australian Wheatbelt runs from Kalbarri to Esperance. Its inner boundary, the 600-millimetre isohyet, roughly runs from New Norcia/Moora to Tenterden/Stirling Range, while the outer boundary, the 300-millimetre isohyet, runs through Merredin and Hyden. The industrial-scale land clearance can be seen from space. In the words of literary historian Tony Hughes-d'Aeth, the Wheatbelt is 'like nothing on this earth'.[12] In 1984, the CSIRO Division of Wildlife and Ecology began to study the dynamics of remnant vegetation and associated fauna in this post-apocalyptic landscape, a project that started with the work of Richard Hobbs, a pioneering 'ecological restoration' specialist who is now a world leader in this field.[13] After being intensively cleared and farmed for nearly two centuries, it is truly an Anthropocene landscape, terraformed by human activities. The aim of the CSIRO research was to establish the conservation potential of remnants of native vegetation, and the incentive to involve the community came at least in part from the problems of salinity and land degradation in the area.

Birds were one of the groups chosen for study, and CSIRO sponsored 'a community-based observer scheme to map the distribution of birds in ... the wheatbelt, to gauge their abundance in the period 1987–90, and to examine changes in their distribution and abundance this century'.[14] The 'community' included observers over the whole century. Denis Saunders and John Ingram made use of historical records to construct a baseline against which to measure changes in the monitored period. Although the early collectors and natural historians rarely recorded 'abundance', these 1980s scientists combed their records for clues. Saunders commented in an interview that *Emu*'s annotated bird-lists were 'terribly important … if you want to look at change from then to now … You can almost *see* the way that people are saying this bird was common for the following regions and this bird wasn't.'

Alex Milligan (1858–1921), an excellent observer and an important collector for the Western Australian Museum, was one of a number of writers in *Emu* whose annotated lists gave 'benchmark data' for an analysis of change between the first wave of farming (before 1937) and the major expansions in the Anthropocene epoch. Saunders gave the example of Milligan's early work in 1903:

> He went by train from Perth down to Tenterden. Then for three weeks, he spent most of the time camping in the Stirling Range, which is now the Stirling Range National Park. Shot his way through the south west corner for the WA Museum and then went back to Perth.[15]

Milligan wrote: 'It is worthy of note that not one crow (or raven) was observed during the journey.'[16] This was a crucial observation: Saunders, eight decades later, knew them only as very common birds for that region.[17] An absent raven can speak volumes to humans about how the environment works.

Family stories

The caption in the Bunjilaka Centre about clever Waa, who pushed his limits and lost his song, weaves the personality of the bird deep into cultural knowledge. Raven is a complex figure, drawing out the rich ways humans and birds know their place in the world. Caring about ravens is caring for place, for the world, for life itself. The visionary bird (Eagle) and the clever bird (Crow), each with very specific stories, complement the cosmologies of our own species. As Indigenous knowledge keepers share their stories, they help us all to better understand the natural world and the deep and important culture that birds and humans share.

Evolutionary biologists in the 1970s were surprised to learn that the corvid family, a familiar northern bird, started in the south. It radiated north, something that contradicted expectations of the time. It is a Gondwanan superfamily. Some of the 'core corvine' family members are key exponents of cooperative breeding.[18]

After Robert Carrick, who had started the CSIRO banding work in Canberra on magpies (see Chapter 6), left to work for the Antarctic Division in Adelaide in 1960, Ian Rowley took over and expanded Carrick's program. Rowley colour-banded ravens (*Corvus coronoides* and *C. mellori*) and white-winged choughs (*Corcorax melanorhamphus*) near Canberra, studying their territorial and cooperative breeding behaviours for the next ten years.[19] Cooperative breeding is a distinctive evolutionary strategy that maximises resources at the nest. Rowley identified it as an overwhelmingly 'southern' breeding strategy, occurring in over 20 per cent of birds who evolved in ancient Gondwana, compared with just 3 per cent of birds worldwide. It is a strategy that works well for birds who breed in places with precarious food and shelter, who live with boom-and-bust ecologies. Choughs remain to this day highly localised, with closely defended territories.[20] Looking rather like crows until they take off in flight and expose the white on the underside of their wings, choughs are world leaders in cooperative breeding. One seldom sees a lone chough.[21]

Corvids that went north found plenty of resources, so they evolved different breeding strategies. But Australia's white-winged choughs are only distantly related to European choughs—a case of convergent evolution. The Australian birds are members of the special mud-nest builder family Corcoracidae, another southern group that is now placed in the narrower 'core corvine' group, which contains the crows and ravens, shrikes, birds of paradise, fantails, monarch flycatchers, and drongos—most of which would never be confused with a raven.

Listen carefully

Arcane evolutionary systematics, with its new genetic technologies, can reveal surprising stories about the voice of the raven. The latest science places the lyrebird family, the birds with such remarkable voices, close to the corvids on the evolutionary tree.[22] There are signs of 'convergent evolution' in cultural stories, too. The idea that Australian ravens might be birds who once sang, birds who 'lost their song', has echoes in the latest science.

While the voice of a raven is not melodious, it is complex and it is loud. Raven is definitely communicating with other ravens. Raven is watchful. For those who listen, Raven speaks to humans, too, as Nels celebrated. Perhaps, as *jimbayer* suggests, Raven has a special relationship with fire. We all must be watchful as fires become more dangerous, wilder and more unpredictable, as climate changes.

12

BIRDING ABROAD AND AT HOME

Joining forces

In 2011, Australia's two biggest bird organisations, Birds Australia (BA) and Bird Observation & Conservation Australia (BOCA), joined forces and became BirdLife Australia. Both had existed in various forms for over a century, and many birdos belonged to both. Their unification marked the merging of the interests of scientific ornithologists, field ornithologists (both professional and amateur) and general bird-enthusiasts.

Reflecting its rich diversity, BirdLife Australia manages a range of publications, including the original *Emu*, now with the subtitle *Austral Ornithology* and published through a big international scientific publishing house.[1] BirdLife Australia marked its new status with the launch of *Australian Birdlife* in 2012, a popular quarterly magazine that features 'interesting articles and all the latest news and views on birds, birdwatching, conservation and the people behind it all'.[2] This replaced a host of different club magazines over the years, including *Wingspan* (BA) and *The Harrier* (BOCA).

Between the international science journal and the popular club magazine sits *Australian Field Ornithology* (*AFO*), a peer-reviewed publication inclusive of non-professionals, with a focus on Australasian birds and their ecology, behaviour and species histories. Natural history observations, data and field observations are also published, notably those that support *HANZAB*. *AFO* also reviews other ornithological publications. It traces its origins to the *Australian Bird Watcher*, first published by the BOC in 1959. (*AFO* took its present title in 2003, before the merger.) There is also a lively and 'instant' publication, *Birds E-news*, a free monthly newsletter for subscribers. The Publications Section of BirdLife Australia is rounded out with the important *State of Australia's Birds* report series for long-term trends, published as needed since 2002.

Birdos see themselves differently in the twenty-first century. Under the new banner of BirdLife Australia, they have a peak Australian group that simplifies working with other international NGOs. It is a diverse body, as its publications and other activities suggest, and it is branded to reach beyond Australia through BirdLife International.

BirdLife International, first established in 1922 as the International Council for Bird Preservation and renamed in 1994, is an international network working to conserve birds and their habitats. It has a membership of more than 2.5 million people across 116 country partner organisations, some of which carry the 'BirdLife' name (for example, BirdLife South Africa), but many of which don't. The Royal Society for the Protection of Birds (in the UK), the Wild Bird Society of Japan and the National Audubon Society (in the USA) are among its biggest and oldest national partners.

In a time of rising threats and extinctions, conservation of habitat has become a leading priority for bird lovers all over the world. BirdLife International's mission includes preventing the extinction of bird species, identifying and safeguarding important sites for birds, maintaining and restoring key bird habitats, and empowering local conservationists wherever they work. It has identified 13,000 Important Bird and Biodiversity Areas (IBAs) and is the authority for the IUCN's Red Lists for birds. The 2015 Red List, which was the most recent at the time of writing, identified 1375 bird species (13 per cent of the total) as threatened with extinction (critically endangered, endangered or vulnerable). The BirdLife partnership operates on the principle that many more species can be saved by working together than by any one organisation alone. No other international conservation NGO has such a broad membership. Birds have a special power to unite diverse interests.[3]

Birds and social justice

As the new millennium has unfolded, social justice has become an increasing concern as rich, multinational corporations expand rapidly. In 2005, journalist Mark Dowie's paper 'Conservation Refugees', published in *Orion* magazine, took many conservationists by surprise when it reported tensions building between Indigenous peoples and biodiversity activists. At one United Nations meeting in 2004, an Indigenous activist commented that 'while extractive industries were still a serious threat to their welfare and cultural integrity, their new and biggest enemy was *conservation*'. CI, The Nature Conservancy (TNC), World Wide Fund for Nature (WWF), the Wildlife Conservation Society (WCS) and even the IUCN found themselves on a blacklist of 'culture-wrecking institutions' with oil companies Shell and Texaco, mining company Freeport and engineering and construction company Bechtel.

Dowie documented the rise and rise of what have become known as BINGOs (big international non-government organisations) with what often seemed to many First Nations leaders a one-size-fits-all approach to the conservation of biodiversity. In some cases, this process left too little space for Indigenous and local engagement in conservation practices. In extreme cases, it gave rise to 'soft eviction' or 'voluntary resettlement': conservation refugees forced to move by the aspirations of BINGOs.

Not all the protests about one-size-fits-all conservation methods have come from Indigenous peoples. At a conference of the Oceania Section of the Society for Conservation Biology in Sydney in July 2007, Dick Watling (1951–), a consultant ecologist from Fiji, gave an impassioned keynote address on the changing priorities of conservation in his country. Funding from cetacean-minded BINGOs had resulted in almost all of it (government and non-government alike) being redirected to marine species, yet his research showed that the most endangered endemic species in Fiji were forest animals. Only one marine species was 'vulnerable', and it was not endemic to Fiji. Meanwhile dozens of uniquely Fijian species were on the brink of extinction as their habitat was cleared by big forestry operations that had no obligation to respect environmental concerns. The government's regulation of conservation was limited to sea-dwelling animals because of international conservation priorities.

BINGOs and the hyper-success of private international conservation initiatives are changing conservation practices. They create new stresses, often in places where people can least cope with them.

A case in point: Crater Mountain

The anthropologist Paige West (1969–) has documented the environmental and social history of the creation of Crater Mountain Wildlife Management Area in New Guinea, an example of an 'integrated conservation and development project'. It had its origins in the 1970s, long before BINGOs such as CI were formed. West's fieldwork, undertaken in intensive periods between 1997 and 2004, traced a shift in the balance between conservation and self-determination.[4] She treated both the Indigenous Gimi-speaking people and the local biodiversity scientists as 'subjects' in her anthropological study. The scientists were surprised by this, asking 'Why would you question the worth of conservation?' West's work unpacked the tensions of a society where the conservation budget was greater than the national economy, yet where traditional ways of looking after nature were excluded from conservation plans. These were unwelcome but important research findings for her multinational sponsors, the Biodiversity Conservation Network (BCN) and the WCS, which were major supporters of international conservation projects linking biological conservation and economic development, in line with the Sustainable Development Goals of the United Nations conference in Rio de Janeiro in 1992.

Crater Mountain Wildlife Management Area, like many international conservation initiatives, has a complex colonial backstory. The Gimi people were the subjects of a study by American medical anthropologists Leonard B Glick and Nansi S Glick in 1960–62. The Glicks were based about 40 kilometres from the Australian colonial station at Lufa (now part of the Eastern Highlands Province of Papua New Guinea). A decade later, between 1973 and 1975, Gillian Gillison, a student-anthropologist from the City University of New York, returned to work with the people the Glicks had studied. Her then husband, David Gillison, was a photographer and conservation activist who documented the decline of birds of paradise in the area. Returning alone in 1979, he negotiated with local landowners in Ubaigubi to identify conservation sites, and then launched the Crater Mountain Project in 1986 with the Research and Conservation Foundation of Papua New Guinea, the WCS and the PNG Government.

West arrived in 1997, after the project had been up and running for more than a decade, and observed that 'biological capital' was not the only value in Crater Mountain. The local Gimi people, particularly the women, had found their own understandings and management of the nature of their place sidelined by the sheer level of funding afforded such a large Western conservation initiative. The democratically elected PNG Government was only a junior partner. The Gimi people declared, 'Conservation is our government now', which statement West took for the title of her powerful book. If conservation becomes a big colonial business initiative, greenwashing multinational brands, it misses the opportunity for shared moral obligation. The conservation of birds of paradise was the focus of the scientific work, but for senior Gimi man, Kabi, there was no focus: *it is all context*. Kabi told West that he knew the place through 'my eyes, my ears, my nose, my mouth, my teeth, my skin, my father, my bones'.[5]

An anthropologist can throw new light on how best to maintain a local sense of place in a grand international project where local people and distant supporters share concerns about the future of nature but express their understanding of that place in very different ways. In the past decade it has quickly become apparent that more listening to local people will only help and improve outcomes for global conservation, especially where Indigenous people and biologists can join forces on an equal footing, with humour and compassion on both sides. Kabi's philosophy endorses an approach that takes more care with habitat restoration, rather than putting too much focus on iconic species. The fact that birds of paradise are charismatic species (and therefore important to Western fundraising models) might mean that their habitat needs are overlooked in favour of more exciting conservation practices, including controlled-breeding programs.

Indigenous knowledge and biodiversity management

Getting the best protection for birds does not always mean buying or reserving land. Global ideas of what wilderness means, and nationalist rhetoric, sometimes get in the way of caring for ecosystems and whole landscapes. As Australia's interior has depopulated, there is a growing recognition that 'people are good for biodiversity', something Aboriginal activists have known all along.[6] Indigenous understandings of Country in Australia are often very different from those of Western thinking. Country owns the people, not the other way around. Country includes the sea, the land and the sky. Some Indigenous people regard wilderness as a 'whitefella word' (and have used these words on a bumper sticker). Wilderness is, for them, a term for Country that is sad: it has no one caring for it. One Indigenous elder described cities in this way to anthropologist Deborah Bird Rose (1946–2018). She recalled that when the elder arrived in Canberra from the Northern Territory in the 1990s, he called the city a 'wilderness area'. It lacked cultural care, in his view.

Biodiversity management in Australia is gradually shifting to be more inclusive of Aboriginal world views. The *Natural Heritage Trust of Australia Act 1997*, No. 76, identifies Indigenous Protected Areas (IPAs): areas of land and sea managed by Indigenous groups for biodiversity conservation, with the work undertaken through voluntary agreements with the Australian Government. Australia's National Reserve System at the time of writing includes eighty-one dedicated IPAs. That's over 85 million hectares of Country—or about half the current National Reserve System. The environmental benefits (as expressed in the government's language) are 'pest plant and animal management, fire management, marine and coastal clean-ups, threatened species research and protection, and development of management plans'.[7] IPAs provide some Aboriginal livelihoods in remote places. Where biodiversity management can include Indigenous knowledge and engage people on Country, it benefits birds and people together and is done in different ways.

Indigenous communities can continue to protect the cultural values of Country for future generations when they can make a living at home. Employing IPA rangers on their own Country provides financial stability in the community. The rangers become positive role models and teachers. Traditional bush-tucker and medicine knowledge is regularly taught on Country to younger generations and also to paying visitors. Thus the additional funding for biodiversity conservation has significant health, education, economic and social benefits. While 'wilderness' distances people from Country, 'rewilding' involves them in conservation practices that support healthy communities.

The Pakana project, an Aboriginal-led collaboration with the WWF to 'rewild' lungtalanana (formerly known as Clarke Island), is a new plan to return 'nature, culture and sovereignty' to a depopulated island near Cape Barren Island in the wilds of Bass Strait.[8] The Tasmanian Aboriginal Centre (TAC), WWF-Australia's Rewilding Australia team, and researchers from the University of Tasmania are working together to identify the locally extinct species lost on lungtalanana, 'to restore culture and heal an island ecosystem'. This is not just about birds: the first work is likely to involve a wombat subspecies unique to Bass Strait islands, once present but now extinct on both lungtalanana and Cape Barren Island. Predator-proofing the island and revegetating it after years of sheep farming and neglect is a conservation plan, but it is more importantly cultural, as Andry Sculthorpe, Land and Heritage Coordinator at the TAC, explains. Repatriating 'culturally significant species back into lands that have suffered the ravages of invasion' is part of holistic care: 'It's about animals, plants, fire, community on Country and creating cultural knowledge development pathways to understanding healthy Country'. These Bass Strait islands are, historically, places of pain. Sculthorpe comments: 'There wouldn't be any Aboriginal people in Tasmania who haven't had family members with experiences in these islands, whether good or bad.'[9]

This is a project that would have delighted Dom Serventy, who worked with Indigenous people on Fisher Island shearwater sites for so much of last century. The traditional owners there call the nocturnally active shearwaters 'moon birds'. Fisher Island is another tiny granite island in Bass Strait, part of the Great Dog Group between Flinders and Cape Barren islands. Those Fisher Island birds are still the subject of longitudinal monitoring, and the formal engagement of Indigenous leadership in rewilding is an important ongoing conservation practice.

Biodiversity management is increasingly blurring the distinction between natural and cultural management practices. This is true for non-Indigenous practices, too. Conservation now includes all sorts of privately owned reserves. Diversity of management strategies is also essential to urgent action on climate. Working agricultural properties often include important woodlands. Agricultural and pastoral enterprises are being managed to help birds, and sometimes local Indigenous people are joining the 'ecological restoration' and 'rewilding' projects and making them cultural as well.[10] Thus birds help bring other biota and people together, by inspiring the restoration of 'lost' places. Changing business practices, keeping birds in mind, can also keep carbon emissions down. Climate change is putting increasing pressure on whole ecosystems. Nature restoration can improve the situation, but reserves alone cannot scale up quickly enough to avoid disaster. New research shows how real action on climate is still limited by *existing* uses of land. So wherever ecosystem restoration can modify agriculture and pastoral businesses, such opportunities must be seized and added to the mix.[11]

BirdLife Australia and its partners

In its *Bird Conservation Strategy 2023–2033*, BirdLife Australia works to develop a network that builds evidence through science, research, information management and inclusive partnerships of all sorts. Beginning with existing conservation, research and citizen science programs and partnerships with governments, universities and research bodies, BirdLife Australia has ambitious aims to 'expand, consolidate and maintain a robust evidence base that will guide and support our conservation work. This will include, for example: identifying knowledge and capacity gaps, identifying priority species/sites and their threats, optimising current monitoring programs and implementing new research initiatives.'[12] In these ambitions, the organisation is partnering with a range of other conservation NGOs, both Australian and international, including the WWF, Bush Heritage and the Tasmanian Land Conservancy.

While science underpins BirdLife Australia's conservation work, it now also recognises traditional knowledge—the innovations and practices of First Nations peoples. The BirdLife Australia website acknowledges that 'Indigenous knowledge of native Australian birds, their life cycle and habitat needs is profound and has made a substantial contribution to the scientific study of birds in this country'. It offers a grant to support Indigenous rangers, community groups, schools and organisations and those who work directly with Aboriginal and Torres Strait Islander people to undertake research and conservation work in Key Biodiversity Areas (KBAs).[13] In 2022, for example, its tenth Indigenous Grant for Bird Research and Conservation was awarded to the Mithaka Aboriginal Corporation in south-western Queensland. On 27 October 2015, the Mithaka people were awarded native title over a huge area of Queensland land and water. The Federal Court, sitting in Windorah in the south-west of the state, made the native title ruling over 55,425 square kilometres, slightly less than the area of Tasmania and slightly more than the area of Croatia. The non-exclusive native title area includes 33,752 square kilometres (roughly the area of the Netherlands) of pristine rivers, rolling gibber plains and sandhill country.

Caring for this Country is a complex job on a grand scale. The Mithaka people have already welcomed partnerships with conservation NGOs, including Bush Heritage Australia and the Australian Wildlife Conservancy (AWC). The Mithaka traditional lands border Ethabuka— the Bush Heritage reserve of Wangkamadla Country, which bridges the ecotones between the Simpson Desert and the vibrant ephemeral waters of the Diamantina and Cooper floodplains and Kalamurina reserve in South Australia, acquired in 2007 by the AWC. Mithaka people are also working with archaeologists from the University of Queensland and presented their work in museum forums in 2022.[14] The area around Sandringham station (including the former Ethabuka and Craven's Peak pastoral stations) has been a long-term ecological research site of the University of Sydney and has the benefit of decades of excellent scientific research.[15]

Mithaka rangers are already working on Country, and the BirdLife Australia grant will support the ranger group to undertake further research that traverses and benefits both Western and traditional knowledge. BirdLife Australia publicly acknowledges the privilege of being invited by the Mithaka rangers to work with them as they negotiate how to best look after their vast Country. Mithaka Country is of exceptionally high value for both KBAs and threatened species, important to BirdLife Australia's strategic conservation. The Diamantina and Cooper floodplain KBAs are part of Mithaka Country. These are very significant for waterbirds as well as inland specialties, including the letter-winged kite and grey falcon. There is also excellent night parrot habitat in this Country, with the Pullen Pullen Reserve co-managed by Bush Heritage, Mithaka people, and the neighbouring Maiawali traditional owners. Bush Heritage also works in Martu Country in Western Australia on the Birriliburu IPA, another important site for night parrots, where night parrot Dreaming stories are part of cultural life (see Chapter 2).[16]

Partnering with Indigenous rangers makes great sense for bird conservation. The areas of Australia under Indigenous management (including IPAs) in 2022 cover about 60 per cent of the land area (equivalent to the area of the whole European Union).[17] Native title (as formally recognised under the *Native Title Act, 1993*, No. 110) accounts for almost half of this. At the time of writing there are 81 dedicated IPAs covering 85 million hectares, according to the official website. In addition there are IPAs over crown land, and Country in joint management arrangements.

Greening our cities

In terms of area, there are vast regions where conservation plans are needed. In terms of population, however, cities and peri-urban areas account for the overwhelming majority of *people* in Australia. Australia is one of the world's most urbanised nations. Bird conservation begins at home, as Robert Hall recognised as long ago as 1900.

Hall, a scientific ornithologist and museum worker (later director of the Tasmanian Museum and Art Gallery in Hobart), produced *The Insectivorous Birds of Victoria* in 1900. Its frontispiece was a map of the Australian continent and its biogeographical regions were as recently described by University of Melbourne professor of zoology Baldwin Spencer. But the span of the map is misleading. The birds Hall described were all local to Victoria, which was still a separate colony. He called his practical little book a 'handbook' rather than a field guide. Although his descriptions are enlivened by 'observations in the field', they are designed for observations at home—not 'fieldwork' in the sense of a trip to the bush to see birds, which might warrant a 'field guide'. The birds were situated in suburbs such as Box Hill (where Hall lived) and Hawthorn (nearby) or in Victorian country areas such as the Wimmera, the Mallee and the basalt plains in the west, where correspondents wrote to him about their birds. They were personal notes by Hall and friends, not a statistically balanced survey. In a sense, his method was an early recognition of the importance of 'citizen scientists'. His book is important now because it reflects the abundance and variety of the birds of the city and its surrounds when the Greater Melbourne population was only about 400,000—the crash of the 1890s had sent many people back to the regions. Yet Melbourne/Narrm itself, like so many great cities, was built on a river estuary, *birrarung*, a place of high biodiversity. It had already lost many species as it expanded.

Most passerine (perching or singing) birds are insectivorous, but Hall's handbook also included fruit-eaters, such as cockatoos, that 'have proved themselves troublesome in summer'. His aim was to protect birds by showing how useful they are 'to the fruit-grower, the agriculturist, and the naturalist'. His correspondents constituted his imagined audience for the book—birdos at home, not afield—and he advocated bird study that would aid their businesses and their gardens. The book was a work of economic ornithology. Hall quotes one correspondent who declared: 'the study of small birds is profitable as well as healthy, for we would be starved off the land if it were not for our bird friends, both large and small. As much as possible I leave cover to protect and preserve them.'[18]

In this millennium, cities have become sites of other, very different rewilding initiatives as leaving cover has been increasingly rare in the vast monocultural agricultural estates of our times. It is also an important principle of birdscaping, or landscaping gardens to protect small birds from predators in urban areas. And engaging birdos-at-home is a big part of the newest trends in Australian birding practices. It is easy to capture on phones video, sound and images that can be posted to social media and become helpful to major research initiatives. BirdLife Australia balances its work supporting remote communities to care for birds in traditional ways with other activities that appeal to its metropolitan members.

The millennium began with the 'Birds in Backyards' research, educa-tion and conservation program that focuses on the birds who live where people live. It started in and around Sydney, sponsored by BA's Southern New South Wales and ACT Group (SNAG), working in partnership with the University of Wollongong, with data management undertaken by university students funded by scholarships. Observers were volunteers. With changing digital options, the project is now more geographically inclusive; it has accumulated more than two decades of data generated through online surveys.

Birds in Backyards has picked up on the enthusiasm of gardeners offering tips on how to 'create bird-friendly spaces in your garden and local community', and information about Australian birds and their habitats that is accessible to suburban observers and children, including through apps and other digital tools. The idea of school gardens emerged a century earlier, at about the same time as the Gould League. Bird Day and Arbor Day were being celebrated in schools (see Chapter 3). The state schools gardening movement was led by Cyril Isaac (1884– 1965), a Victorian primary school teacher who, in 1900, dug up the asphalt in the grounds of the Lee Street primary school in North Carlton and planted dahlias and other bright flowers. He inspired a generation of teacher-gardeners to collect and share seeds and help each other, following the serious drought of 1908 when his own school garden (by then at Barnedown, near Bendigo) lost every plant. School gardens beautified public spaces, attracted birds and at the same time educated and 'improved' the schoolchildren who worked in them. The director of education, Frank Tate, supported Isaac's work, and the Victorian State Schools' Horticultural Society was established in 1910. Isaac went on to a career in horticulture, politics and conservation activism, establishing the nursery of the Natural Resources Conservation League (NRCL), an NGO that still grows much of the tree and shrub stock for local council roadside revegetation projects throughout Victoria.[19]

Starting with the birds at home and with children is, of course, a recurrent story. Joan Paton (see Chapter 10) and her son, David, set up banding studies in their Adelaide backyard in the 1960s, when David was just ten. For children too young to drive or travel alone to distant parts, backyards and schoolyards became launching pads for bigger birding careers. David Paton (1953–) grew up to become an evolutionary biologist and ecologist at the University of Adelaide, devoting his paid and unpaid time to birds and to conservation. Now David and his wife, Penny Paton (née Reid), the daughter of another enthusiastic Adelaide bird family, run Bio-R, a grassroots charity that reconstructs habitats to support native wildlife in the Mount Lofty region. The nursery that grows stock for Bio-R's revegetation projects is in the backyard where David's birding adventures with his mother began over fifty years ago. The sequence of field ornithology (banding), professional science and horticulture for habitat regeneration in David's personal history reflects the shifting efforts of birdos, as birds become increasingly crowded by cities, suburbs and industrial agricultural practices.

In 1970, enthusiastic suburban birdos Tess Kloot (1923–2016) and Ellen McCulloch (1930–2005) developed a guide for birdwatching at home. *Some Garden Birds of South East Australia* offered bird identifications and advice to city-dwellers on how to make their gardens work as 'a link with the countryside'.[20] Densey Clyne (1922–2019), a prominent Sydney nature writer, featured 'Nature in the City' in her newspaper columns and other writings, which from 1982 were collected in the *Wildlife in the Suburbs* book series.[21] These women were important in creating an inclusive culture of birding. By offering hints about what ordinary people at home could do to help the natural world, they made birdos of us all. This was a big change from the 'bird nerds' who dominated ornithology in the early twentieth century.

Birdscaping gardens

Birds offer a lively connection with the natural world and, as nature study slipped out of school curricula in the postwar years, gardeners stepped into the educational space, creating enthusiasm and new bird-observers among adults rather than children. For example, the enthusiastic birdo and forester Bill Middleton (1926–2018) created a very different sort of 'gardening' program for his country radio listeners on 3WV and 3WL (northern and western Victoria and the Riverina). Between 1970 and 1983 he made 350 radio broadcasts educating his listeners about plants and plantings, particularly in the drier inland country where he ran the Forests Commission's arid zone nursery at Wail, near Dimboola in Victoria. His arid zone saplings were growing up on country that was 'in-between' the temperate cooler south and the hotter, drier interior, and he realised that his local bird fauna had elements of both. His garden, his nursery and the nearby Little Desert attracted international visitors. There were so many different species to see in his special ecotone.

One of Victoria's great plant specialists, Jim Willis (1910–95), the government botanist at the Melbourne Herbarium, brought Ernst Mayr (see Chapter 7) to visit Middleton when Mayr came to Australia in 1959. Mayr was then a world leader in evolutionary theory and director of the Agassiz Museum of Comparative Zoology at Harvard University. Willis knew Mayr was interested in 'barrier species'—birds that crossed over between different biogeographical regions—and that Middleton was a terrific birdo. Middleton and Mayr became firm friends.

Middleton's professional expertise was in plants, but his passion was birds. Most of his broadcasts encouraged planting and restoring of native habitat as he used his own garden primarily to watch birds. He talked about plants that encouraged birds to come into the backyard, but also campaigned for shelter for birds in the wider landscape.[22] His radio shows extolled the virtue of natural cover in public parks and of remnant roadside vegetation, defending natural bushlands from 'tidy-minded' council workers.

From the 1970s onwards, Middleton developed a passion for ecological restoration right across the vast basalt plains between his home in the Little Desert and the Bass Strait coast, where he retired to in the 1980s. The Western District of Victoria was mostly native grasslands that in the nineteenth and early twentieth centuries had been replanted with imported pasture grasses for sheep. Paddock and roadside trees and shrubs had also been cleared, destroying ecological corridors for birds. Middleton was a founding member of the charity Trust for Nature Victoria (now Trust for Nature Australia), which from the 1970s bought up private land for conservation and placed a 'covenant' on sections of the land parcels to ensure that valuable conservation areas could never be cleared, then on-sold the properties to fund the purchase of the next conservation property. Middleton's excellent knowledge of good birding haunts in western Victoria, where he grew up and lived for most of his working life, enabled Trust for Nature to build up the Hindmarsh Biolink, offering private-land reserves that connected public reserves and roadside plantings. Hindmarsh Landcare Network still manages this system today, with strong support from the Melbourne-based Victorian National Parks Association.[23]

Despite water shortages and very hot summers, European sensibilities about what gardens are 'for' shaped the tastes of Australian suburbanites. Polymath historian and planner George Seddon (1927–2007) once commented wryly that the most irrigated crop in Australia was the suburban lawn. But lawns have limited interest for birds, and their maintenance is a particular problem in long, dry summers. The Australian Native Plants Society has, since 1957, encouraged planting 'native' Australian plants and, later, locally indigenous ones in city and suburban gardens, and many birdos appreciate the value of native plants to birds.[24]

Gardening for birds has developed in style and variety since George Adams coined the term 'birdscaping' in 1980, meaning to design landscapes specifically to attract birds.[25] BOCA started a 'Birds & Gardens Survey' in 1988, mapping the relationships between birds and plants and trying to discover which plants attract native birds to gardens.[26] BirdLife Australia still runs an annual survey in spring, the 'Aussie Backyard Bird Count', where observers choose their favourite outdoor space and simply note all the birds they see in twenty minutes, submitting the results via an app or online form. The 'favourite outdoor space' for those without a private garden might be a city park or a birding haunt. As gardens have shrunk in the twenty-first century, books, podcasts and apps have become available to enable birdscaping of even small gardens, balconies, courtyards and rooftop gardens. Adams writes of how even the smallest spaces can 'contribute to the greening of our environment, and the creation of habitat'. He encourages the use of native species for 'creative birdscaping', beginning with a windowbox or involving neighbours to 'convert an apartment block rooftop into a beautiful native garden space for you and the birds to enjoy'.[27]

It turns out that indigenous plants survive better in unpredictable climates. The 2000s have brought more extreme events, including the long Millennium Drought in south-eastern Australia, which resulted in water rationing in megacities. Plants are an excellent defence against heat stress in urban 'heat islands', which are expanding in times of global warming. Birds come in for shelter and become 'family' for isolated urban dwellers. Chloe Hooper writes of the importance of the honeyeaters that chose to nest on her suburban back veranda at a time when her partner was grappling with treatment for cancer, and she was anxiously watching him with their young sons, aged four and seven. The whole family defended the nestlings from their natural predators as the survival of the baby birds became personal for the humans riding the emotional roller-coaster of chemotherapy.[28]

In 1992, zoologist and former director of the RAOU Philip Moors was appointed director and chief executive of the Royal Botanic Gardens Melbourne (now Royal Botanic Gardens Victoria), a venerable institution first established in 1846. By the time he retired twenty years later as the second-longest-serving of all directors in the RBG's 175-year history (and the only professional zoologist), he had cemented both birds and backyards into the mission of the RBG. Under his leadership, the Australian Garden at the RBG Cranbourne site (acquired in 1970) was developed. Reflecting on his two decades in the job, Moors particularly highlighted the 'revitalisation and major capital projects', singling out 'the creation of the Australian Garden at Cranbourne and the Ian Potter Foundation Children's Garden' (the latter in Melbourne) and the work of the Australian Research Centre for Urban Ecology (ARCUE) that complemented the RBG's traditional curatorial work in the National Herbarium of Victoria. His initiatives included water conservation projects, one of which was harvesting stormwater for the Working Wetlands project.[29]

The Australian Garden opened formally in two stages, Stage 1 in 2006 and, just in time for Moors' retirement, Stage 2 in 2012.[30] It was billed as a 'journey into the Australian landscape'. The site extends across 363 hectares, ten times the size of its senior partner, the RBG Melbourne, established in 1846, with 'picturesque' landscapes designed by William Guilfoyle (1840–1912) in the 1870s. The Australian Garden's Stage 1 covers 11 hectares, contains 100,000 plants of over 1000 species, and features 1000 mature trees—the oldest of which, the slow-growing grass-trees (*Xanthorrhoea*), were transplanted there after growing elsewhere for nearly half a millennium. Stage 2 added a further 10 hectares.[31] The visitor's journey begins in the Australian Garden's large Red Heart—a massive red-sand sculpture featuring grey-blue saltbush and crescent-shaped lunettes, designed by landscape architects Taylor Cullity Lethlean in association with plant designer Paul Thompson. The desert sands threw up some surprises: soon after the sculpture had been installed, tracks appeared—not part of the original design, but very welcome. The nationally endangered southern brown bandicoot (*Isoodon obesulus nauticus*) was unexpectedly prospering in the fenced, cat-free security of the Cranbourne gardens.

The Australian Garden project emerged during the decade-long Millennium Drought, which made the task of establishing plants in the sandy terrain a particular challenge. The stresses of the drought were also apparent beyond the garden fence: all remaining vegetation in the 'desert' of new houses in the fastest-growing suburban corridor in Melbourne (the local government area of Casey, which has a population of over 340,000 people, including a high number of families with young children) became a haven for birds and other animals.

The Cranbourne gardens always took their role as a 'good neighbour' very seriously. Planning for the local community was a priority, including through a range of programs, from bush-kindergarten playgroups, to Indigenous-led activities, to water-conservation planting and hardy garden designs offering suggestions for surrounding suburban areas. The 'nature strips' in some streets nearby have been replaced by stony soils and shrubs more effective than mown (or dead) lawn in times of water restrictions, something that would have delighted George Seddon.

Within the grounds of the Cranbourne gardens there is a vast 'Woodland Picnic Area' of local bushland, some of it never cleared but much restored from the area's previous use as a sand mine. Managed with paths and tracks and reserved areas, this is an important resource for local and visiting humans, birds and other creatures. It is right in the middle of Casey, where few other parcels of land are available to bushland birds. The housing in the area is mostly single-storey and densely packed. In the sea of concrete, small gardens, balconies and even roundabouts and other 'road furniture' are important spots for biota, but plants in these places have to be hardy to survive the conditions.

The Cranbourne gardens have sought to improve water efficiency despite the heat effects of the suburban sprawl, both within their fences and, through education, beyond them. The exhibition gardens provide examples of how people can save water and improve heat stress through what they plant in their private gardens. There are, for example, examples of 'cottage gardens' and 'kitchen gardens' created with native plants to suit different generations of Australian homes, including 'heritage' homes. By replacing traditional European plants with pretty and hardy indigenous shrubs such as westringia and native poas, gardeners can save water and bring a variety of birds into the neighbourhood. Indeed, the horticultural efforts of Cranbourne have become part of the story of the important eastern bristlebird (*Dasyornis brachypterus*) translocation program, a great example of gardens working for birds. After the 2019–20 bushfires destroyed much of their habitat near Mallacoota in East Gippsland, seventeen endangered bristlebirds were brought from Jervis Bay in New South Wales to Wilsons Promontory, the southernmost point of Victoria. The long overnight drive was rendered less stressful for the birds by purpose-built transportation boxes that contained tasty insect snacks and hummocks of specially grown native grass, *Poa labillardierei* (tussock poa), which they like to hide in. This grass was grown and nurtured by the horticulture team at RBG Cranbourne, who ensured it was healthy and pest-free.[32]

Sometimes the birds at the Cranbourne gardens remind us that the landscape doesn't quite belong there. The 'Desert Discovery Camp' on the far side of the desert garden from the visitor centre features sandy soil dotted with the silver-grey foliage of *Eremophila*; it is a good vantage point from which to enjoy the stately grass-trees in the mid-distance. However, when I was there in 2021 the extended pebble gardens of various shapes and sizes around the camp carried the constant ringing of bell miners (*Manorina melanophrys*) and the twitter of superb fairy-wrens (*Malurus cyaneus*). These 'wrong birds' were obvious reminders that the splendid desert landscape, however visually persuasive, is in fact an artwork, a 'landscape sculpture', not an ecosystem. Local birds, however, are important for the garden's public programs: volunteer birdos regularly lead the popular 'Breakfast with the Birds', which explores how birds use the Cranbourne gardens.[33] The message that ordinary backyard gardens are important to the future of birds and other creatures, especially in densely populated cities, is well told in this special public garden.

EPILOGUE
THE CANARY
IN THE COALMINE

Australian birds face unprecedented threats in the twenty-first century with the encroachment of human activities into all aspects of their lives. Their land, sea and sky habitats have been altered beyond anything that might have been envisaged by the early followers of John Gould. The birds that have survived and adapted are more precious than ever in our globalising world. They lift up our eyes to the freedom of the sky, take us into strange places, wet and dry, and offer a glorious reminder that the natural world is still there as we face the very challenging next three-quarters of the twenty-first century, with accelerating global warming already locked in from unsustainable lifestyles.

In the bad old days of underground coalmining, a canary in a cage alerted the miners to treacherous gas leaks, thereby saving lives. Today's birds are caged by the biosphere, the thin layer of habitable sea, land and atmosphere that supports all life on the planet. The mining impacts in the biosphere are huge, indeed 'terraforming': they affect the stability of Earth's crust, the deepest trenches of the oceans, the polar ice caps and gla-ciers. Humans are mining the soils, too, turning forests into hamburgers, depleting soil nutrients and despoiling clean water in an ongoing mission to feed the world. Birds continue to alert the observant to the shifting baselines of our human environmental support systems.

The people who watch the birds—the ones with the binoculars around their necks, as my Aboriginal radio host called them at the beginning of this book—are more diverse than in the past. Gregory Mathews' 'portraits of ornithologists' project, donated to the National Library of Australia in 1949, comprised 200 images of ornithologists important to birding east of Wallace's line, a set of white male faces with British names that would be inconceivable as a collection today. There were no Aboriginal faces, although First Nations people's work as collectors was crucial to Mathews' *Birds of Australia*. Only three women are named: Elizabeth Gould, Ada Fletcher (1870–1956) and Margaret Wigan. JA Ross is one of a few pictured with his unnamed wife. Few portraits included children. The long-suffering Ethel White, who endured and documented long camel trips exploring northern South Australia with her husband, Captain SA White, is missing from his portrait. International ornithologists included John and Elizabeth Gould and some European museum systematists. Dominic Serventy is the sole representative of non-British Australians. Born in Boulder, near Kalgoorlie in the goldfields of Western Australia, his parents came from Croatia. His portrait was taken with visiting Polish ornithologist Kazimierz Wodzicki (1900–87), head of the New Zealand Department of Scientific and Industrial Research's Ecology Division—perhaps even Mathews noticed new international connections beyond London by 1941, when that photo was taken?[1]

Until the 1940s, 'international connections' in Australia meant London. Despite his Croatian heritage, most of Serventy's connections began with his 1933 Cambridge doctoral studies, at a time when Australian universities did not offer doctorates. But his Eastern European forebears alerted him to other dimensions of international networks a generation before the massive postwar immigration schemes that changed the face of Australia. 'Birdos' are not quite the same as the serious ornithologists in the Mathews gallery, who were chosen to fit with Mathews' obsession with systematic lists. Birdos rather than systematists lead conservation campaigns these days, though in recent years the documentation of formal extinctions and the arrangements of Red Lists of rare and threatened species depend on all sorts of science as well as observation. Birdos place the highest value on fieldwork, watching birds' behaviour and how they live, and often care more about vernacular names than technical ones.

Harry Frith, the chief of CSIRO Wildlife Ecology and host of the 1974 International Ornithological Congress, was an expert on the pigeons and doves of Australia. He also worked in the 1950s and 1960s on the waterbirds of the Murrumbidgee Irrigation Area. He might have been surprised to find his serious ornithological and applied ecological science framing a new sort of environmental history of Australia in the twenty-first century. Emily O'Gorman has returned to Frith's very practical and well-preserved documents to craft *Wetlands in a Dry Land: More-than-human Histories of the Murray Darling Basin.*[2] Good observation makes good science. It also makes new histories possible—histories that imagine a place co-created by birds and humans, and that give us a 'bird's-eye view' of the changes in the land. The treasure trove of field journals and documents, bird-lists and photographic records that Frith and other birdos created at the beginning of the Great Acceleration of change are precious in times when baselines are shifting rapidly, when places meet constant 'unprecedented' fires, floods and other crisis events.

Distinguished fisheries biologist Daniel Pauly (1946–) coined the term 'shifting baseline syndrome' in 1995 to describe the fact that each new generation of scientists begins its study of a population with a baseline stock that is poorer than the last generation. This results in cumulative research that masks the creeping disappearance of species, underestimates economic losses and creates unambitious targets for rehabilitation measures.[3] Shifting baseline syndrome is a framework that applies equally to amateur birdos. 'The olden days' are always personal, and the point of reference for the future is the moment of the first observation of a significant bird, or the listing of it. Thus older people hold in their heads a baseline for the presence or abundance of birds in a particular haunt that is different from the reference point for younger people, even when they are talking about the same place. The idea of a 'place in time', not just a place, makes oral testimony and private lists important. Shifting baselines are formed from precise observation, from what you *notice*. They differ across scales and cultures. Indigenous observers are looking out for birds for different reasons from twitchers or life-listers.

Melbourne urban ecologist Erin Lennox no longer calls herself a 'birdo': that means that others depend on her for information, she says. She doesn't want to compete to get the best list or photograph or be the first to make a rare field record. Rather, she celebrates her passion to 'just notice' birds in her own suburban surrounds:

> I let birds into my life accidentally when I stopped one day to read an interpretive sign along the Yarra in Ivanhoe. Apparently, on my daily walk, I could hope to see white-faced herons, eastern yellow robins and red-browed firetails. I thought I may as well look out for these creatures seeing as I was there already and, lo and behold … I beheld them.[4]

The act of noticing is a release from the daily humdrum. Lennox is an ecologist, but she also researches the ways people alert each other to birds, to the social world of birding. Knowing there is *something to see* changes the way we walk and think about other creatures we meet.

In the increasingly urban environment, bird people are not so much recording rare species as the presence or absence of familiar species, or changes in the timing of seasonal migrants. It is chilling that sparrows are becoming locally extinct in London. Birds that have long been taken for granted are becoming the new canaries in the cage. The project of creating environments in private gardens and streetscapes that are meaningful to birds has become a new and urgent task even for people who can recognise or name only a handful of species. Good gardeners 'notice' bird behaviour, and plant to support it. This sort of birding community is a long way from the obsession with nests and breeding that created the passions of the early years. It is much more diverse in membership and motivation.

Citizen science—that is, partnerships between communities, government authorities and technical scientists—adds an essential volunteer labour force to scientific quests and often forces scientists to ask new sorts of questions. The term originally gained popularity because it was adopted by the Environment Protection Agency in the United States (established in 1970), which now has a major program in participatory science.[5] The Queensland Museum, recognising the significance of volunteer observers, hosted a citizen science workshop in 2014 where the Australian Citizen Science Association (ACSA) was launched. Volunteers came together and formed working groups to build awareness of Australian citizen science locally, nationally and internationally.

Academic science has long depended on volunteers for time-intensive fieldwork. Birdos have featured prominently because they reliably identify what they see and hear. Zoologist David Lindenmayer, for example, studies the fragmented landscapes near Tumut, New South Wales, where patches of native vegetation are embedded in plantation forests of radiata pine. He has worked across 165 sites documenting the behaviour of ninety species of birds in multispecies bushland and monocultural non-native forests. Such a comparative study of how animals use anthropogenic landscapes was only possible because knowledgeable people from the Canberra Ornithologists Group volunteered to walk his transects regularly and systematically, recording observations. Lindenmayer found a complex reassemblage of bird species in relation to landscape context, rather than any fixed community of birds. Some birds replaced others, so formal biodiversity change per se was difficult to assess.[6]

The Lindenmayer study supported the importance of remnant vegetation to birds, but also noted that change was complex. Different species use habitats differently and 'edge effects' are important.[7] As other forests have increasingly been disturbed, most notably Victorian remnant forests scarred by the massive 2009 'Black Saturday' bushfires, Lindenmayer has been increasingly called upon as an expert 'fire ecologist' assisting with salvage operations, and as a 'conservation biologist' testifying in court about managing remnant forests, especially last remnants that support near-extinct species. Long-term ecological data are critical for informing trends in biodiversity and environmental change. Bird data are important because of the quality of long-term records in *Emu* and elsewhere, and the private life lists of good, local birdos.

The Terrestrial Ecosystem Research Network (TERN) hosts infrastructure and open-access data for ecological researchers in Australia and, since 2012, internationally (through LTERN, see Chapter 9). Effectively, TERN is an Australian land observatory 'structured around three aspects of observation: landscape observation, ecosystem observation, and ecosystem processes'.[8] Ecosystem observation in Australia dates back to the Koonamore research station in South Australia, established in 1926. Birdos, plant specialists and photographers have worked together to document detailed changes in these special places. Long before 'citizen science' was a concept, volunteer observers were a key to maintaining multi-generational understandings of changes in local places. Koonamore's quadrats (marked field sites) have now been observed and photographed for almost a century.

Lindenmayer has also been part of another emerging conservation partnership. In 2006, at a black-tie dinner in Melbourne raising money for environmental research, he was to receive the Australian Environmental Research Award for leadership. On the way to the podium, he surprised himself by making a quick decision. In his acceptance speech, he said he was 'honoured to be recognised as a leader in outstanding environmental research' but there was other important leadership that needed honouring, too, and announced that the $30,000 cheque would support Indigenous leadership in his fire ecology project at Booderee National Park (Jervis Bay) on the coast south of Sydney. He had been working closely in partnership with the Wreck Bay Aboriginal Community, but the government funding for Darren Brown, a senior Wandandian man who was radio-tracking bandicoots and diamond pythons as part of Lindenmayer's research group, had just been slashed. Through Brown's research, members of the group had in turn been learning about Wandanian knowledge of Country. 'We're not doing enough ... to use the incredible environmental knowledge and skills of Indigenous people in this country,' Lindenmayer argued in his award speech.[9] He felt that by transferring the $30,000 associated with such a prominent and prestigious award, he could show governments the value of Aboriginal traineeships to conservation biology. 'People like Darren are the future,' he said. 'The environment is their passion and if they get the right opportunities, conservation in this country will really take off in some exciting new directions.'

Working with Aboriginal people 'cuts two ways', Lindenmayer told the environmental managers, supporters and private donors sitting at the $100-per-head dinner. An Aboriginal training program offered employment and scientific skills to local people, as well as Indigenous knowledge for practical science. At just thirty-four years old, Brown was younger than Lindenmayer but already an elder in an Aboriginal community where people, particularly men, died young. Understanding the Australian environment is a complex and unfolding task: science and Aboriginal knowledge can learn much from each other. Brown was excited about the possibilities that conservation biology held for cultural perspectives— what he called 'bringing the science to broaden out the picture'.[10] Alas, Lindenmayer's passionate speech failed to sway the government of the day, which flatly refused to reconsider the Booderee program. His gift bought time, but not much. While the orthodoxy of 'small government' dictates outcomes, all projects become short-term.

Yet Aboriginal health issues are a major problem in Australia's otherwise 'First World' society. Caring for Country and having a passion for the bush are good for both health and the environment. This connection is acknowledged explicitly by Indigenous people, but non-Aboriginal environmental managers have been much slower to make the link, to listen to the wisdom of Country and not just manage its 'resources'. Conservation work and Aboriginal health tend to sit in different ministerial portfolios, and whitefellas still don't really understand the connection between health and Country. Country is essential for Indigenous futures, and conservation partnerships can be transformative both for people and for Country.

Biodiversity isn't confined to national parks. It is deeply cultural in diverse ways. Biodiversity depends on reserves, but also remnants, 'wastelands', suburban gardens and other unlikely resources.[11] It needs research into 'nature' that has survived under farming, forestry and urban regimes. Lindenmayer is one pioneer in the study of animals in fragmented landscapes.[12] Thinking beyond and outside park boundaries reveals that a national park such as Booderee is itself a 'production landscape' for Indigenous peoples. Reserves are cultural and not just biophysical places.

Australia's long tradition of 'public good' science has evaporated in the twenty-first century. As Commonwealth and state governments have steadily divested themselves of the tasks of managing reserves for conservation since the 1970s, private players have been plugging the gaps. Biodiversity research is now a 'charity' that depends on philanthropic funding and free volunteer labour. Indigenous collaboration in bird conservation science has been identified as important, but it has taken years to develop and shape the many private scientific conservation and ecological restoration initiatives that offer a hopeful future for our birds in the face of accelerating pressures of human activities. Bush Heritage Australia, Gondwanalink, the Tasmanian Land Conservancy and many others are developing new ways to partner with Indigenous corporations as they care for Country, including Sea Country. But the archives created by public service initiatives in conservation and natural resource management over decades are often lost in the transition. Research continuities and baseline records are hard to recreate. As new initiatives work on a project-by-project basis, beginning with a land purchase, they depend on published records of birdos and other ecological observers not just to establish baselines, but also to select suitable properties for their investments. Often Indigenous oral histories, from people on the ground who have an intergenerational connection to Country, are crucial to understanding ecological challenges.

The changing wilds of the twenty-first century

The complexities of the Anthropocene, its global thinking, its grief for places lost and the sheer number of people pressing into all environments have changed the idea of 'wild' in every generation. Birdos have changed, too, often choosing more international terms like 'birder' or 'birdwatcher' to accommodate the influx of international bird-tourists. Even at a time when international tourism was well down because of pandemic restrictions, bird tourism was a big business. BirdLife Australia reported research in 2022 that shows that bird-tourists often stay longer and spend more than others in regional Australia.[13] Exploring remote and forgotten places, near and far, has always been a hallmark of birdo behaviour, and that continues today with Twitchathons, specialist bird tours and solo wanderers carrying binoculars in the bush or setting up field telescopes at sewage works.

This little field guide has featured birdos of all sorts. It has also included chapters on the birds themselves. What did they make of the people that watched them? Poor Jack the lyrebird was perhaps too trusting of humans. Did he recognise that the chainsaw he could imitate so perfectly was a death warrant for his beloved forest, his habitat, his way of life? But lyrebirds did learn to nest up high to avoid foxes, and perhaps humans, too. They learned the remarkable practice of burying their marvellous feathers so they could not be found, probably long before chainsaws attacked their habitat and the foxes arrived. Raven was, and still is, most observant of human behaviour, capitalising on opportunities to share in human bounty, to clean up roadkill left by humans, to engage with human social moments so as not to miss the picnic pickings—even to live and nest in the very heart of megacities.

Birds are metaphors, art forms, ways for humans to fly and to dream. Filmmaker Rob Nugent decided to make the night parrot the central character in his 2016 film of the Anthropocene, *Night Parrot Stories*.[14] It was to be a requiem, an elegy to the lost creatures of our strange times. Nugent visited many dingy back rooms in old-style European museums, sites where the few sacred specimens of night parrots have been preserved for over a century. Following in the footsteps of John McDouall Stuart and Frederick Andrews, he took his camera on long pilgrimages to the sites of night parrot finds, driving thousands of kilometres in remote parts of Australia where roads are dusty and unsealed and go on interminably. He cast himself in the film as one of the crazed people who chase the nocturnal bird, the holy grail, reading his own night parrot field notes by the light of a head-torch in the desert nights, tormenting himself with 'if onlys'. But Nugent is a Centralian, and his instinctive love of the desert with its samphire claypans, desert oaks and spinifex makes this a very beautiful film. Its lightest moments are also its most serious, when the birds' traditional stories are retold in language and in English by

Martu and Pitjantjatjara elders, when the bird itself seems to fly. Here *Night Parrot Stories* is dignified, hopeful, surviving. At the point where the film was all over the cutting table in 2013, Nugent learned of the secret rediscovery of the bird. Life, in this case, caught up with art, and the obsessive and competitive politics of rediscovery was out of keeping with the elegiac tone of the film and its careful crafting. Such a rediscovery brought no closure. The night parrot still symbolises loss, and perhaps new grief as the Anthropocene epoch rolls on, crushing cultural interventions that are designed to heal.

The definition of an Australian bird is changing: in Gould's era, only the birds that breed here technically counted as Australian. Now migratory flight paths and pelagic vagrants are revealing how birds' lives are changing all over the world in response to natural and unnatural disasters and other human pressures. Australia's birds are world birds, too. A bird's rarity is an international phenomenon, but it is also an intensely local one. Local extinctions are a clue to bigger problems further afield. Birds allow environmental change to be scaled right up and right down, to include official and unofficial environmental management strategies, global and local contexts, and all sorts of participants in managing the environment.

The idea that a bird is good news and needs all our support is probably the only thing amateur birdos, professional zoologists and birdscapers have in common.[15] But these diverse people together form a community—a conservation community—who care about the future of birds and their habitats, who are working to heal the damage wrought by those who don't notice birds. Noticing is important. The story of birdos is not just about the 'ones with the binoculars around the neck'. The bigger, more inclusive birdo community supports all sorts of nature. By nurturing habitats that attract birds and make them sing, birdos conserve lively habitats for humans as well.

ACKNOWLEDGEMENTS

I was watching birds before I could read. Dad would take me to his favourite bird haunts before breakfast to give Mum a sleep-in, as I was always the first awake in the family. The chilly mornings rang with birdsong and strange names. The names he used then are the ones I still tend to use when I identify birds, although many bird names have changed since the 1960s. Dad carried field glasses: they were the signal that we were off on a birding adventure, not just a walk in the bush. Occasionally he shared them with me. I never did work out how binoculars focused, but I didn't have the heart to tell him that I could see the bird better without them. The passing of the field glasses was like a tea ceremony, a formal moment when I was admitted to his secret bird world, and I respected that. At four years old, I tuned in to watching humans watching birds.

This book had its origins many years later in the 1990s, when Norman Wettenhall invited me to write a centenary history for the RAOU. This became *The Flight of the Emu*. The project introduced me to birding nationally and internationally. Many people who had a role in shaping the course of the national bird club gave their time generously in formal and informal reflections for their 'birthday book'. They were proud of their organisation, but increasingly I realised that much of birding is private, personal and passionate. It is not always 'clubbable' or 'professional', even for those who join clubs or make their living as ornithologists. This book, a quarter of a century after the first, explores the private passions of birdos rather than their institutions and clubs.

Organisations like BirdLife Australia (and its staff and volunteers) foster big team projects and engage in very diverse ways to support birds. They build on many of the concerns of those who pioneered the early bird clubs, but also must grapple with the new circumstances of our times, which constantly challenge birds. Bird-people come from all walks of life and many different backgrounds. The private ways they care about birds motivate some to work in teams, and some alone. Together they have power, perhaps even to change the world. Human behaviours now affect all Earth's systems and life is stressful, yet birdwatching is, for many, a way to relax. Irish nature writer Dara McAnulty says in his *Diary of a Young Naturalist* that he needs to spend time watching birds in the wild just to recover from the 'noise' of humans. He started watching birds at a very early age and began writing *Diary* when he was just fourteen.

Wild places are very different from what they were in the last century, but there are deep historical roots in the ways we care about birds, and these can motivate all sorts of people to work towards imagining the world in ways that help birds survive, even thrive with change. I am grateful to the many birdos who shared stories that have enabled me to trace both the changes and constancies in birding over time.

Gwynnyth Taylor (neé Crouch) (1915–98) created gardens planted richly for birds. She first studied the work of landscape designer Edna Walling (1895–1973) at Burnley Horticultural College, when Neville Cayley's *What Bird Is That?* first appeared, and later worked with her for seven years. The 'bush garden' sensibility shaped the way she led the Save Our Bushlands Action Committee in the 1960s, as the activist group opposed state-sanctioned habitat-clearing for agricultural development. When she and I sat together in her garden in the 1990s to talk about environmental activism, her eyes lit up as a honeyeater attended the grevillea right next to her well-placed wheelchair. Birds, gardens and activism were all part of the same story. The artist Ern Hoskin was keen to talk to me about Keith Hindwood, his great friend and the doyen of Sydney's birding community for many decades. But Ern also reminded me what birding was really all about when he went to his suburban back door and whistled up a wild eastern spinebill. Travelling with professional land-system scientist Henry Nix when he was president of Birds Australia, I could see the great loss of bird habitat across swathes of landscape caused by dieback (*Phytophthera cinnamomi*), but without his well-tuned ear, I would have completely missed the distinctive call of the collared sparrowhawk far in the sky, crying out before we had even left suburban Canberra. It was barely a dot in a vast cloudless blue sky, yet its notes immediately drew his excited attention. Sounds, smells and the moods of the bush itself are all tied closely to birding. This book could never have been written without all the people who have shared their diverse bird knowledge with me, consciously and unconsciously, as we have talked together, exchanged letters, emails and visual material.

Talking is important, and so are documents, especially for under-standing birdwatching before living memory. Thank you to the curators of the wonderful bird libraries at BirdLife Australia (the HL White Library), State Library Victoria, which holds much of the historical material for the early RAOU, the National Library of Australia in Canberra, which holds the very significant Gregory Mathews collection, and the Mitchell Library in Sydney, where the Hindwood and Chisholm collections are preserved. The National Archives of Australia (Perth and Darwin) were also impor-tant, especially for Dom Serventy's extensive material. A wide range of materials are curated by museums: I have been grateful particularly to the Melbourne Museum, the South Australian Museum and the Australian Museum in Sydney, which not only made early archives available but also facilitated interviews and over the years have presented stimulating exhi-bitions about bird-people, historical and current.

Special thanks to the environmental humanities scholars and museum curators of Australia, Germany, Norway, Sweden and beyond, who have explored with words and objects how humans and birds and other life forms can co-exist in ways that are good for us all. Local and international conversations about emotional and material ways of knowing have sustained this project and opened up unexpected avenues of research. Local stories, it seems, sometimes have far flung echoes in distant places. I especially treasure conversations about birding during unlikely excursions to Orkney, Texel and south-western Australia with my South African friend, historian and birdo, Jane Carruthers.

Thank you to the kind and generous team at MUP, especially Nathan Hollier, Cathy Smith and Katie Purvis, who have made the publishing journey a joy.

My family has tolerated, even aided and abetted, my efforts to watch people watching birds over the past quarter of a century. This field guide is dedicated to the youngest members of the family, whose lively interest in birds is already apparent. I am especially indebted to Tom, who counted among the best childhood Christmas presents his binoculars and his Cayley. He suggested the title that provoked this book.

NOTES

Prologue: This Eccentric Field Guide

1   The RAOU is now known as BirdLife Australia, and *Emu*, the journal of Australian ornithology, continues to be published with CSIRO Publishing.
2   William George Dyer (Bill) Middleton, OAM (1926–2018), transcript of interview with the author, 8 March 1998, p. 2.

1   Birding for the Nation

1   DL Serventy, 'A Historical Background of Ornithology with Special Reference to Australia', *Emu*, 72(2), 1972, p. 45.
2   Gould League, 'Mission', Gould League website, 2018.
3   JH Calaby, 'The European Discovery and Scientific Description of Australian Birds', *Historical Records of Australian Science*, 12(3), 1999, pp. 321–4.
4   Clemency T Fisher, *The Importance of Early Victorian Natural Historians in the Discovery and Interpretation of the Australian Fauna, with Special Reference to John Gilbert* [unpublished PhD thesis], Liverpool Polytechnic, 1992.
5   EM Webster, *Whirlwinds in the Plain: Ludwig Leichhardt: Friends, Foes and History* (Melbourne University Press, Carlton South, Vic., 1980), pp. 40–2.
6   A bird-skin is the external part of a bird prepared for study or museum display by removing most of the innards and replacing them with cotton or tow. Usually rolled cotton is placed in the eye socket for a study skin, but for display, a glass eye is added.
7   Calaby, pp. 315, 324.
8   *Emu*, 1(2), 1902, p. 33, and 1(1), 1901, p. 5.
9   Kerryn Herman & Katherine L Buchanan, 'Emu evolves', *Emu: Austral Ornithology*, 117(1), 2017, pp. 1–3.
10   *Emu*, 1(1), 1901, pp. 1–3.
11   'Cotton, John (1802–1849)', *Australian Dictionary of Biography*, National Centre of Biography, Australian National University, 1966.
12   The organising committee comprised Ryan, Le Souef, Hall and Campbell, plus Joseph Gabriel (1847–1922) and George Arthur Keartland (1848–1926).

13 D Le Souef, 'Proposed Australian Ornithologists' Union', printed notice, RAOU Archives, State Library Victoria (hereafter SLV), MS 11437, Box 6(a).

14 *Emu*, 10(3 Special), 1910, p. 154.

15 5 November 1894, RAOU Archives, SLV MS 11437, Box 12(a).

16 Six of the union's first members were women, including the first life member, Miss Amelia Pike.

17 *Emu*, 3(2), 1903, p. 117 reported *The Times* without comment.

18 *Emu*, 3(4), 1904, pp. 247–8.

19 Carl Lumholtz, *Among Cannibals* (John Murray, London, 1889), pp. 325–7. The period referred to would have been 1881–82.

20 The state museum of Victoria has gone through several name changes since it was established. It was the National Museum of Victoria from 1862 to 1983, Museum of Victoria 1983–98 and Museum Victoria 1998–2016. In 2016 it took its current name of Museums Victoria.

21 Rod Fisher, 'Silvester Diggles: Brisbane's Pioneer Musician, Scientist, Artist and New Churchman', *Journal of the Royal Historical Society of Queensland*, 17(6), 2000, pp. 271–86.

22 Penny Olsen, *Feather and Brush*, 2nd edn (CSIRO Publishing, Clayton, Vic., 2022).

23 Calaby, p. 324.

24 Patricia Vickers-Rich, 'The Mesozoic and Tertiary History of Birds on the Australian Plate', in P Vickers-Rich et al. (eds), *Vertebrate Palaeontology of Australasia* (Pioneer Design, Melbourne, 1991), p. 722.

25 WRB Oliver, *New Zealand Birds* (Fine Arts, Wellington, 1930), p. 5.

26 *Emu*, 6(2), 1906, pp. 79–81.

27 John Truran, 'The Foundation Period 1899–1933', in R Collier et al. (eds), *Birds, Birders and Birdwatching 1899–1999* (SAOA, Adelaide, 2000), pp. 18–56.

28 Richard Fitter & Peter Scott, *The Penitent Butchers: The Fauna Preservation Society, 1903–1978* (FPS, London, 1978); Harriet Ritvo, 'Visualising Extinction', in Valérie Bienvenue & Nicholas Chare (eds), *Animals, Plants and Afterimages: The Art and Science of Representing Extinction* (Berghahn Books, New York, 2022), pp. 77–90.

29 *Emu*, 1(1), 1901, p. 5.

30 Ibid., p. 3. There is a veiled suggestion here that not all members and potential members were happy with the so-called 'science of egg collecting'.

31 Ibid., p. 2.
32 Mark V Barrow Jr, *A Passion for Birds: American Ornithology after Audubon* (Princeton University Press, Princeton, NJ, 1998).
33 AJ North, *Descriptive Catalogue of the Nests and Eggs of Birds Found Breeding in Australia and Tasmania* (FW White, Sydney, 1889); AJ Campbell, *Nests and Eggs of Australian Birds including the Geographical Distribution of the Species and Popular Observations Thereon* (Pawson & Brailsford for AJ Campbell, Sheffield, 1900 and 1901) and *Nests and Eggs of Australian Birds: Embracing Papers on 'Oology of Australian Birds'* (AJ Campbell, Melbourne, 1883). On nomenclature, see also Chapter 3.
34 Colonel WV Legge, 'Presidential Address', *Emu*, 1(2), 1902, pp. 36–8.
35 Alfred Wallace, 'The Geographical Distribution of Birds', *Ibis*, 1(4), 1859, p. 450. *Tropidorhynchus* later became *Philemon* (friarbirds, a genus of honeyeaters).
36 Legge, 'Presidential Address', *Emu*, 1(2), 1902, p. 38.
37 Legge, 'Presidential Address', *Emu*, 3(3), 1904, p. 145.
38 AG Campbell to FC Morse, 8 July 1922, National Museum of Victoria (hereafter NMV), unlisted green box of 'Early Correspondence'.
39 AJ Campbell to Morse, 22 July 1922.
40 EJ Court to Morse, 15 April 1921. There were letters from seven others concerning egg purchases and swaps.
41 JA Ross to Morse, 2 March 1922. Ross's diaries of egg-collecting trips between 1905 and 1929 were purchased by NJ Favaloro for the NMV in 1964. His companions included F Howe, A Mattingley, F Godfrey, T Tregellas and C Ladwig. He also mentions Russell and Neuendorf but does not include their first names or initials.
42 HL White to Morse, 9 November 1921.
43 The *RAOU Bulletin* (published in five parts from 1910 to 1915), probably funded privately by HL White, reported on acquisitions to the HL White collection.
44 Charles Ryan, 'The President's Address: The Protection of Native Birds', *Emu*, 6(2), 1907, p. 96.
45 International Ornithological Congresses were held in Europe until 1962, when Ithaca, New York, was the venue (see Chapter 7).
46 *Emu*, 7(2), 1907, p. 102.
47 *Emu*, 5(1), 1905, p. 41.
48 D Le Souef, 'The White Oological Collection', *Emu*, 9(2), 1909, p. 91.

49   HL White to Frank Smith, 11 May 1911, quoted in Judy White, *The White Family of Belltrees* (The Seven Press, Scone, 1981), p. 76.

50   Le Souef, pp. 90–1 (with plates).

51   L H[arrison], 'Catalogue of the Jacksonian Oological Collection', *Australian Naturalist*, 1(10), 1908, pp. 118–19.

52   White, *The White Family of Belltrees*, p. 78. On Jackson's photography, see also Judy White (ed.), *Sidney William Jackson: Bush Photographer 1873–1946* (The Seven Press, Scone, 1991).

53   Le Souef, pp. 90–1.

54   White, *The White Family of Belltrees*, pp. 182–6.

55   HL White to AJ Campbell, 27 July 1917, quoted by J White in *The White Family of Belltrees*, p. 83.

56   NMV Green Box 'Correspondence' contains many such letters. AR McEvey, 'Notes on the HL White Collections', Appendix 3 to Chapter 6, in White, *The White Family of Belltrees*, p. 189.

57   *Emu*, 15(3), 1916, p. 206.

58   *Emu*, 16(4), 1917, p. 246.

59   *Emu*, 18(3), 1919, p. 233. and 16(4), 1917, p. 245.

60   'Report on the RAOU Oological Collection', *Emu*, 18(3), 1919, p. 231.

61   His full name was Edward Dunham Brooke Nicholls. Seventeenth Annual Report 1916–17, *Emu*, 17(3), 1918, p. 161.

62   Captain SA White, 'Narrative of the Expedition Promoted by the Australasian Ornithologists' Union to the Islands of Bass Strait', *Emu*, 8(4), 1909, pp. 195–207.

63   Ibid., p. 204.

64   *Emu*, 8(2), 1908, p. 112.

65   SA White, p. 205.

66   Ibid., p. 195.

67   Australasian Ornithologists' Union, *Expedition to the Islands of Bass Strait* (AOU, Melbourne, 1908). This is a very rare volume: Norman Wettenhall kindly showed me his copy on 10 March 1998.

68   The Flinders Island wombat is smaller than the mainland *Vombatus* ursinus and is today recognised as one of three subspecies of common wombat.

69   SA White, pp. 200–1.

70   AJ Campbell, 'After Mutton Bird Eggs', *The Australasian*, 2 January 1897.

71   AJ Campbell, 'Camp-Out on Phillip Island', *Emu*, 8(4), 1909, p. 207. Cost of the Bass Strait expedition from note in *Emu*, 8(2), 1908, p. 112.

72 Council meeting, 27 August 1910 [Minute Book], RAOU Archives, SLV MS 11437, Box 12. The detailed minutes of the Brisbane meeting (held on 5 October) were not included in the Minute Book.

73 Bird Observers' Club, *Monthly Notes*, 10 May 1932. GM Mathews' collection of 200 portraits of ornithologists (1900–49), National Library of Australia (hereafter NLA) picture collection. On Gilbert White in Australia, see Tom Griffiths, 'The Natural History of Melbourne: The Culture of Nature Writing in Victoria 1880–1945', *Australian Historical Studies*, 23(93), 1989, pp. 339–65.

74 Thomas Carter, 'Birds Occurring in the Region of the North-West Cape', *Emu*, 3(1), 1903, pp. 30–8; 3(2), 1903, pp. 89–96; 3(3), 1904, pp. 171–7; 3(4), 1904, pp. 207–13.

75 Robert Hall, 'Notes on a Collection of Bird-Skins from the Fitzroy River, North-Western Australia', *Emu*, 1(3), 1902, pp. 87–112; see also *Emu*, 2(2), 1902, pp. 49–68 and 3(1), 1903, pp. 40–3.

76 Sunday 12 July, Siberian Diary of RE Trebilcock, RAOU Archives, SLV MS 9247, p. 71. Libby Robin & Anna Sirina, 'Siberian Ornithology, Australian Style 1903'—website project in association with Manuscripts Collection, SLV, June 2003 (in English and Russian).

77 Robert Hall, 'The Eastern Palæarctica and Australia', *Emu*, 19(2), 1919, pp. 82–98.

78 PR Sweet, JW Duckworth, TJ Trombone & L Robin, 'The Hall Collections of Birds from Wonsan, Central Korea, in Spring 1903', *Forktail*, 23, 2007, pp. 129–34.

79 Letter to Miss H Tymms (later Mrs H Trebilcock), Adelaide, 6 November 1903. Correspondence from Siberia, RAOU Archives, SLV MS 9247.

80 Letter to 'Jack' from Jarkutsk, 25 June 1903, p. 4.

2 Night Parrot

1 Bush Heritage Australia, 'Ghost of the Outback', *Bushtracks*, 21 September 2015.

2 DL Serventy, 'A Historical Background of Ornithology with Special Reference to Australia', *Emu*, 72(2), 1972, pp. 41–50.

3 Joseph M Forshaw, Peter J Fullagar & J Ian Harris, 'Specimens of the Night Parrot in Museums Throughout the World', *Emu*, 76, 1975, pp. 120–6.

4 Penny Olsen, 'Night Parrots: Fugitives of the Inland', in Libby Robin, Robert Heinsohn & Leo Joseph (eds), *Boom and Bust: Bird*

Stories for a Dry Country (CSIRO Publishing, Melbourne, 2009), pp. 121–46.

5   Andrew Black, 'Collection Localities of the Night Parrot *Pezoporus (geopsittacus) occidentalis* (Gould, 1861)', *Bulletin of the British Ornithologists' Club*, 132(4), 2012, pp. 277–82.

6   Olsen, 'Night Parrots: Fugitives of the Inland', p. 129.

7   Frederick William Andrews, 'Notes on the Night Parrot (*Geopsittacus occidentalis*)', *Transactions of the Royal Society of South Australia*, 6, 1883, pp. 29–30.

8   Herbert Massey Whittell, *The Literature of Australian Birds* (Paterson Brokensha, Perth, 1954), p. 14.

9   Penny Olsen, *Feather and Brush*, 2nd edn (CSIRO Publishing, Clayton, Vic., 2022), p. 132.

10   In Australia, the arid zone is generally defined as the area where rainfall is less than 250 millimetres per annum in the south and 500 millimetres in the north; this corresponds closely to the edges of Spencer's Eyrean region.

11   Rob Linn, *Nature's Pilgrim: The Life and Adventures of Captain SA White, Naturalist, Author and Conservationist* (South Australian Government, Adelaide, 1989), p. 56.

12   Archibald James Campbell, 'Missing Birds', *Emu*, 14, 1915, p. 167.

13   Hugh Wilson, 'Notes on the Night Parrot, with Reference to Recent Occurrences', *Emu* 37, 1937, pp. 79–87 (quote pp. 83–4).

14   F Lawson Whitlock, 'Journey to Central Australia in Search of the Night Parrot', *Emu*, 23(4), 1924, p. 248.

15   Ibid., p. 249.

16   Olsen, 'Night Parrots: Fugitives of the Inland', p. 141.

17   Whitlock, p. 263.

18   Ibid., p. 264.

19   Forshaw, Fullagar & Harris.

20   Dal Stivens, *A Horse of Air* (Penguin, Ringwood, Vic., 1986; originally published in 1970), p. 156.

21   Ibid., p. 163.

22   Rex Ellis, *Bush Safari* (Rigby, Adelaide, 1982), pp. 217–19. I am grateful to Richard Jordan for this reference. Jordan's Emu Tours also offered a trip, 'Atlassing and Night Parrots', which promised visits to 'an area known for recent night parrot sightings' from 22 May to 4 June 2000 (*Bird Observer*, 802, November 1999).

23 Graham Pizzey & Frank Knight, *Field Guide to the Birds of Australia* (Angus & Robertson, Sydney, 1997), p. 274.

24 All quotes from Dick Kimber, 'Seeing What You Want to See: The Night Parrot that Wasn't', unpublished typescript, 4 March 2000, kindly provided by the author.

25 'The Night Parrot Exists', *Australian Geographic*, 23, 1991, p. 17.

26 *RAOU Newsletter* (hereafter RN), 75, 1988, pp. 1–2.

27 Walter Boles, interview with the author, 7 February 2000.

28 'The Night Parrot Exists', p. 21.

29 Stephen Garnett et al., 'Notes on Live Night Parrot Sightings in North-western Queensland', *Emu*, 93(4), 1993, pp. 292–6.

30 Adjectives from 'Pezoporus occidentalis', in *Handbook of Australian, New Zealand and Antarctic Birds, Volume 4: Parrots to Dollarbird* (Oxford University Press, Melbourne, 1999), pp. 606–12.

31 Bush Heritage Australia was founded in 1991 by environmental campaigner Bob Brown to buy land for conservation purposes. See 'Our History', Bush Heritage Australia website, 2020.

32 Ann Jones, 'The Night Parrot and the Scientists, Indigenous Rangers and Naturalists who Search for Australia's Most Elusive Bird', ABC Science, 10 February 2019.

33 Olsen, 'Night Parrots: Fugitives of the Inland', pp. 122–3.

34 Kim Mahood, *Wandering with Intent: Essays* (Scribe, Melbourne, 2022), pp. 195–215.

3 Nature Study and Names

1 *Emu*, 10(2), 1910, p. 160.

2 Russell McGregor, *Idling in Green Places: A Life of Alec Chisholm* (Australian Scholarly Publishing, Sydney, 2019).

3 WW Froggatt, 'The Aims and Usefulness of Field Naturalists' Societies', *Australian Naturalist*, 1(1), 1906, p. 6.

4 'The Gould League of Bird Lovers', *Emu*, 38(2), 1938, p. 240.

5 JA Leach, *An Australian Bird Book: A Pocket Book for Field Use* (Whitcombe & Tombs, Melbourne, 1911). This was initially published as a descriptive list of Victorian birds by the Education Department in 1908.

6 Russell McGregor, 'JA Leach's Australian Bird Book: At the Interface of Science and Recreation', *Historical Records of Australian Science*, 33(2), 2022, pp. 97–109 (quote p. 98).

7   *The Gould League of Victoria*, 1976 (Education Department brochure, typescript). The Gould League has been variously 'of Bird Observers', 'of Bird Lovers' and 'of Nature Lovers'. It is now simply the Gould League, and focuses on environment and sustainability education.

8   Bryant letter in *Education Gazette*, 20 October 1909; AHE Mattingley, 'Origins and Aim of the Gould League', *Monthly Notes*, 14 May 1935.

9   'The Gould League in Australia', in CFH Jenkins, *John Gould and the Birds of Australia* (Gould League of Western Australia, Perth, 1983), pp. 45–7.

10   Bruce Mitchell, 'Webster, Edward (1866–1928)', *Australian Dictionary of Biography*, National Centre of Biography, Australian National University, 2005.

11   Jenkins records its initial membership as 2000; by 1955 it had risen to 18,000. The Western Australian Natural History and Science Society was also a critical supporter.

12   Jenkins, p. 42.

13   Frank Tate, 'Foreword', in Victorian Education Department, *The Education Department's Record of War Service 1914–1919* (Education Department, Melbourne, 1921).

14   AG Hamilton's 'How to Study the Birds', first published in the *Gazette* of 30 September 1911, was reprinted in *Australian Naturalist*, 2(9), 1912, pp. 121–3.

15   Frank Tate, 'Introduction', in Leach, p. 3.

16   Ibid., p. 4. See also Jenkins, p. 39.

17   Hamilton, p. 122.

18   The first meeting of the inaugural committee was held on 25 June 1914, but the first Bird Day was not until 1916.

19   3 November 1922. AH Chisholm Papers, Mitchell Library, Sydney (hereafter Mitchell) MS 6245/1 'Correspondence'. Soon after Chisholm left, the Gould League amalgamated with the Queensland Naturalists' Club to form a 'Nature Lovers' League', later superseded by the Wild Life Preservation Society of Queensland.

20   'Very Strange Voices', in AH Chisholm, *Bird Wonders of Australia* (Angus & Robertson, Sydney, 1948), p. 199.

21   Jenkins, p. 43.

22   'With Children in Birdland', in AH Chisholm, *Mateship with Birds* (Whitcombe & Tombs, Melbourne, 1922), pp. 70–1.

23   Quoted by Chisholm in ibid., p. 74.

24 Oliver Fuller, 'The SAOA 1940–1960', in R Collier et al. (eds), *Birds, Birders and Birdwatching 1899–1999* (SAOA, Adelaide, 2000), p. 58.

25 Edwin Ashby, 'The Educational Value of the Study of Ornithology', *Emu*, 27(3), 1928, pp. 169–72 (quotes pp. 169–71).

26 Editor, *Emu*, 27(3), 1928, pp. 172–3.

27 Dr A Chenery, 'The Study of Birds by the Nature Lover Apart from the Scientist', *Emu*, 31(3), 1932, p. 227.

28 Neither name is now in use; the preferred name is Bassian thrush (*Zoothera lunulata*).

29 V Legge, 'Memorandum Relative to a Vernacular List of Names for Australian Birds', in John Shirley (ed.), *Proceedings of the Australasian Association for the Advancement of Science (Brisbane, Queensland)*, vol. 6 (AAAS, Sydney, 1895), pp. 445–9.

30 Ibid., p. 446.

31 Committee no. 5, *Proceedings AAAS*, vol. I (AAAS, Sydney, 1888), p. xxxiii.

32 Motion passed 5 May 1899.

33 SAOA Minutes 7 July 1899.

34 SAOA Minutes 11 September 1899. Emphasis in original.

35 *Emu*, 3(2), 1903, p. 159.

36 DL Serventy, 'A Historical Background of Ornithology with Special Reference to Australia', *Emu*, 72(2), 1972, p. 47.

37 Tom Iredale, 'Introduction: The Work of Gregory Mathews', in GM Mathews, *Birds and Books: The Story of the Mathews Ornithological Library* (Verity Hewitt Bookshop, Canberra, 1942), p. 7.

38 Compare, for example, the checklists of 1926 and revisions; Leslie Christidis & Walter E Boles, *The Taxonomy and Species of Birds of Australia and Its Territories* (RAOU, Melbourne, 1994). The notable exception is *HANZAB*, which includes New Zealand and Antarctic birds in its brief (see Chapter 12).

39 Mathews, 'Preface', in GM Mathews, *Handlist of the Birds of Australasia* (Walker, May & Co. Printers, Melbourne, 1908).

40 John Truran, 'The Foundation Period 1899–1933', in Collier et al. (eds), p. 47.

41 JH Calaby, 'The European Discovery and Scientific Description of Australian Birds', *Historical Records of Australian Science*, 12(3), 1999, p. 325.

42 Ibid.

43   Serventy, p. 47.

44   R Schodde, 'The Mathews Collection and the Birds of Australia', *National Library of Australia News*, February 2000, pp. 3–6.

45   Allan McEvey, 'Literary Notes no. 6', *Emu* 67(2), 1967, pp. 150–1.

46   Iredale, p. 8. See also Tess Kloot, 'Gregory Macalister Mathews (1876–1949)', *Australian Dictionary of Biography*, National Centre of Biography, Australian National University, 1986.

47   Barbara & Richard Mearns, *The Bird Collectors* (Academic Press, San Diego, 1998), p. 301.

48   'Mystery Birds of the Jungle', in AH Chisholm, *Birds and Green Places: A Book of Australian Nature Gossip* (JM Dent & Sons, London, 1921), p. 1.

49   *Emu*, 10(3), special, 1 December 1910, p. 160.

50   Ern Hoskin, interview with the author, 19 May 1998.

51   The rare first edition is available online at the NLA's Trove website.

52   Peter Slater, *A Field Guide to Australian Birds: Non-passerines* (Rigby, Adelaide, 1970) and *Passerines* (Rigby, Adelaide, 1974). The 'Slaters' of the 1980s were written by Peter Slater, Pat Slater and Raoul Slater (Rigby, Dee Why West, NSW, 1986, 1988; Weldon, Sydney, 1989).

4   Campouts and Cameras

1   B463–488 inclusive.

2   CE Bryant, 'The Excursion to Marlo', *Emu*, 35(3), 1936, p. 219. Despite an extended description of the camp, the birds seen and the challenges of photographing oystercatchers and their eggs, Bryant made no mention of collecting activities or of the departure of ten people.

3   'SCARLET ROBIN Shot by Collector: Trouble at Bird Lovers' Camp' was the headline in the *Sydney Morning Herald* of 28 October 1935.

4   J Keith Dempster, 'Index' card for Royal Australasian Ornithologists' Union, SLV MS 12401, Boxes 3202–3. See also 'Ornithologists Celebrate', *Wild Life*, April 1951, p. 348.

5   Thomas A Darragh, 'Mahony, Daniel James (1878–1944)', *Australian Dictionary of Biography*, National Centre of Biography, Australian National University, 1986.

6   'Proceedings of Congress', *Emu*, 35(3), 1936, pp. 283–5.

7   Ibid., p. 284.

8   AH Chisholm, *Mateship with Birds* (Whitcombe & Tombs, Melbourne, 1922), p. 77.

9   *Emu*, 36(1), 1936, pp. 65, 68.

10   Experienced eggers would have been aware that the 'legality' factor
      could potentially raise the price asked for eggs (especially those sent to
      enthusiastic oologists in the United States). The union had to be careful
      not to set in place a policy that made egging financially more attractive.
      The only state that allows egg collecting today is Western Australia, and it
      has a strict policy of requiring collections to be endowed to the Western
      Australian Museum.

11   Serventy completed his PhD at Cambridge in 1933.

12   The first six universities (established between 1852 and 1913) were Sydney,
      Melbourne, Adelaide, Tasmania, Queensland and Western Australia.
      No new universities were established between the wars; the Australian
      National University was established as a research university in 1946.

13   Jane Marshall, *Jock Marshall: One Armed Warrior* (Australian Science
      Archives Project / Bright Sparcs, Melbourne, 1998).

14   See Judith M Heimann, *The Most Offending Soul Alive: Tom Harrisson and
      His Remarkable Life* (University of Hawai'i Press, Honolulu, 1999).

15   Marshall, Chapter 13, pp. 1–2/6. Jan Mayen is now part of the
      Norwegian Arctic.

16   Quoted in Marshall, Chapter 4, pp. 6/12.

17   James W Warren, 'Alan John (Jock) Marshall 1911–1967', in *Australian
      Dictionary of Biography*, National Centre of Biography, Australian National
      University, 2000.

18   *West Australian*, 30 October 1920. Cuttings file collated by Mr PE
      Petherick, Cottesloe, and deposited in RAOU Archives, SLV MS 11437
      Box 11(a), 'WA Visit and Conference Press Cuttings'.

19   Description of site in administrative brochure for the conference, National
      Archives of Australia (hereafter NAA) (Perth) K1344/5, Item 11, Box 1.
      Serventy: RAOU Conference Perth 1927.

20   Arrangements for getting into the site were complex, but Frank Skinner-
      Thompson, an enterprising settler at Tinglewood, Nornalup, arranged for
      transport by buggy from the railway 80 kilometres away.

21   DL Serventy, 'A Historical Background of Ornithology with Special
      Reference to Australia', *Emu*, 72(2), 1972, pp. 41–50 (quotes p. 48).

22   BOC, *Monthly Notes*, 8, 1932.

23   Carolyn Pettigrew & Mark Lyons, 'Royal National Park: A History',
      Parks and Wildlife, 2(3–4), Centenary Issue, 1979, p. 18.

24   Colin R Harris, *The National Parks and Reserves of South Australia* [MA thesis], University of Adelaide, 1974, p. 19.

25   Libby Robin, *Defending the Little Desert* (Melbourne University Press, Carlton, Vic., 1998), pp. 29–32, 76.

26   Raine Island, Hinchinbrook Island, Gould Island, Garden Island, Agnes Islet, Eva Islet, Channel Rock and the Barnard Group were all 'reserves for the protection of birds': *Emu*, 15(3), 1915, p. 171.

27   'About O'Reilly's Rainforest Retreat: Our History', O'Reilly's Rainforest Retreat website, 2022.

28   Betty Crouchley, 'Lahey, Romeo Watkins (1887–1968)', *Australian Dictionary of Biography*, National Centre of Biography, Australian National University, 1983.

29   'The Gould League of Bird Lovers', *Emu*, 38(2), 1938, pp. 240, 241.

30   BOC Annual Report, March 1928 [handwritten, signed NAR Arnold, Hon. Sec. BOC, 5.3.28].

31   Norman Wettenhall, transcript of interview with the author, 10 March 1998, p. 7.

32   Bird conservation is still prominent in the aims of the Trust, which also include support for citizen science, long-term flora and fauna conservation, and threatened-mammal conservation.

33   Tom Griffiths, *Hunters and Collectors* (Cambridge University Press, Melbourne, 1996), pp. 118–49; Hugh Anderson, 'Macdonald, Donald Alaster (1859–1932)', *Australian Dictionary of Biography*, National Centre of Biography, Australian National University, 1986.

34   Alec Chisholm, 'Why do Birds "Ant" Themselves?', in Chisholm, *Bird Wonders of Australia* (Angus & Robertson, Sydney, 1948), pp. 163–75.

35   AH Chisholm, 'The History of Anting', *Emu*, 59(2), 1959, pp. 101–30.

36   The campout was cancelled in 1937, then two were held (in Adventure Bay, Tasmania and Leeton, New South Wales), and then there were neither campouts nor congresses from 1940 to 1946 inclusive.

37   Chisholm to Hindwood, 12 August 1941, Mitchell MS 2364, Box 1.

38   Chalk, Hanks, Chisholm and Morrison debated this point at the 1943 AGM. *Emu*, 43(3), 1944, p. 157.

39   CE Bryant to Charles Barrett, 15 February 1951. Charles Barrett Papers, Australian Manuscripts Collection SLV.

40   Graham Pizzey, *Crosbie Morrison: Voice of Nature* (The Law Printer, Melbourne, 1992), pp. 114–17.

41 From Macdonald's 1903 book *A Flake of Wild Honey*, quoted in Nick Drayson, *Early Developments in the Literature of Australian Natural History* [PhD thesis], University of New South Wales, 1997, p. 179.

42 Traditional (1744) see 'Cock Robin', *Wikipedia*, 2022.

43 The death of Keith Murdoch was the death knell for *Wild Life*, something Morrison had predicted.

44 Libby Robin, 'Visions of Nature: *Wild Life*, 1938–1954', *Victorian Naturalist*, 102(5), 1985, pp. 153–61; Stuart Brash, Anne-Marie Condé & Libby Robin, with Gavan McCarthy & Tim Sherratt, *Guide to the Records of Philip Crosbie Morrison (1900–1958)* (Australian Science Archives Project, Melbourne, 1993).

45 'Wild Life' broadcast, Script No. 149, 'Stocktaking', 4 April 1946, SLV, Philip Crosbie Morrison Archive, Series 3/010.

46 Editorial, *Wild Life*, January 1941, p. 4.

47 The AGM report included a plea for more observers in western New South Wales, western Queensland and north-western Australia. *Emu*, 49(4), 1950, p. 238.

48 This date is as early as the photography 'pioneers' in Britain (RB Lodge) and the United States (Frank C Chapman).

49 AHE Mattingley, *The Story of the Egret* (Royal Society for the Protection of Birds, London, 1909). British Museum of Natural History (Tring), 'Plumage Collection', Box 1, legislation files.

50 RAOU Archives, SLV MS 9247, Box 110, 'Nature Photographers Club of Australia', and MS 11437, Box 27, 'Jubilee Photographic Exhibition 5–13 October 1951'.

51 Norman Chaffer, 'The Development and Progress of Bird Photography in Australia', *Emu*, 56(1), 1956, p. 62.

52 *Emu*, 61(2), 1961, p. 113.

53 E Sedgwick, 'Annual Congress', *Emu*, 48(3), 1949, p. 179.

54 RAOU Council, 21 April 1949; Chisholm to Hindwood, 10 March 1947, Mitchell MS 2364 Box 1.

5   Lyrebird

1 'A Confiding Lyre-Bird', *Emu*, 7(2), 1907, p. 104 (reprinted from *The Argus*).

2 LC Cook, 'Notes on the Lyre-Bird at Poowong, South Gippsland', *Emu*, 16(2), 1916, p. 101. Cook also reports a 'controlled' experiment in which he trained the birds on his property not to build on the ground by himself removing their eggs as soon as they were laid there.

3   HV Edwards, 'The Nesting of Lyre-Birds', *Emu*, 18(4), 1919, pp. 298–9.

4   'Knapping' is reported by Edwin Ashby from Cowra Creek, New South Wales, in *Emu*, 7(2), 1907, pp. 94–5. Chainsaw and crosscut saw stories abound. The six-blast story appears in *Australian Geographic*, 5, 1987, p. 3.

5   FP Godfrey, 'Domestic Lyrebirds', *Emu*, 5(1), 1905.

6   Pauline Reilly, *The Lyrebird: A Natural History* (UNSW Press, Kensington, 1988), p. 5.

7   RT Littlejohns, *Lyrebirds Calling from Australia* (Robertson & Mullens, Melbourne, 1943), p. 10.

8   Spencer Roberts, 'Prince Edward's Lyre-bird at Home', *Emu*, 21(4), 1921, p. 242.

9   JA Leach, *An Australian Bird Book* (Whitcombe & Tombs, Melbourne, 1911), p. 114.

10   *Sydney Morning Herald*, 3 June 1909, reported in *Emu*, 9(1), 1909, p. 45.

11   LC Cook, 'Lyre-birds' Habits', *Emu*, 15(1), 1915, p. 52.

12   The lyrebird featured on a New South Wales postage stamp as early as 1888.

13   Elizabeth Willis, 'The Beauty and Strength of the Deep Mountain Valleys', boxed text in Tom Griffiths, *Forests of Ash: An Environmental History* (Cambridge University Press, Cambridge, 2001), pp. 126–7.

14   RT Littlejohns, 'Filming Lyre-birds', *Emu*, 25(4), 1926, pp. 271–4.

15   AH Chisholm, 'Lyrebird Revels', in Chisholm, *Bird Wonders of Australia* (Angus & Robertson, Sydney, 1948), p. 22. Jeremy Boswall, 'A Catalogue of Tape and Gramophone Records of Australasian Region Bird Sound', *Emu*, 65(1), 1965, pp. 65–74.

16   *The Romance of the Lyrebird* first appeared as a reprint from the *Journal and Proceedings of the Royal Australian Historical Society*, 43(4), 1957, then as a separate book published in Sydney in 1960 by Angus & Robertson.

17   LH Smith, *The Life of the Lyrebird* (William Heinemann, Richmond, Vic., 1988); LH Smith, *The Lyrebird* (Lansdowne, Melbourne, 1968).

18   The film was edited by David Cooke and reviewed by Stephen Davies in *RN*, 71, 1987, p. 12.

19   Birdlife Photography Awards 2022 (website).

20   Tom Tregellas, 'Further Notes on the Lyre-bird (*Menura superba*)', *Emu*, 21(2), 1921, p. 95.

21   A Chas. Stone, 'Porosity of the Lyre-bird's Egg', *Emu*, 16(2), 1916, p. 109.

22   Leach, p. 113.

23   Order XX in Bowdler Sharpe's list, as reported by Leach in 1911.

24   In Australia, the pittas are the chief representative of the less complex
      syrinx or 'suboscine' group, though some have suggested that lyrebirds and
      scrub-birds belong there, too. See Reilly, p. 74.

25   Michael Sharland, 'Memories of Tom Tregellas', *Australian Bird Watcher*,
      9(4), 1981, pp. 103–8.

26   Jeffrey Boswell, 'A Catalogue of Tape and Gramophone Records', *Emu*,
      65(1), 1965, pp. 65–74 (quote p. 72).

27   Michelle L Hall & Robert D Magrath, 'Duetting in Magpie-larks:
      Territorial Defence or Mate-guarding?' in Lee B Astheimer & Michael
      F Clarke (eds), *Second Southern Hemisphere Ornithological Congress*, Birds
      Australia Report 9 (BA, Hawthorn East, Vic., 2000), p. 69.

28   F Norman Robinson & H Sydney Curtis, 'The Vocal Displays of the
      Lyrebirds (*Menuridae*)', *Emu*, 96(4), 1996, pp. 258–75.

29   *Emu*, 8(2), 1908, pp. 111–12; MSR Sharland, 'The Lyrebird in Tasmania',
      Emu, 44(1), 1944, pp. 64–71.

30   John Schauble, 'Safeguarding the Living Heritage of Sherbrooke Forest:
      Lyrebird Watcher Seeks a Successor', *The Age*, 29 March 1999. GG
      Carmichael, 'Superb Lyrebird *Menura novaehollandiae* Nesting in Sherbrooke
      Forest, 1974 to 1996', *Australian Bird Watcher*, 17, 1998, pp. 290–6.

31   Alex Maisey et al., 'A Lyrebird Tale', *Australian Birdlife*, 19 June 2018.

32   Roberts, p. 243.

33   Sandy Gilmore, pers. comm., 25 November 2000.

34   The relevant concession is approximately 3000 hectares. Alex (Sandy)
      Gilmore, 'Distributional Ecology of the Albert's Lyrebird *M. alberti*
      in North-east New South Wales', presented at Southern Hemisphere
      Ornithological Congress, 29 June 2000.

35   Willis, in Griffiths, p. 126.

36   Reilly, p. 80.

6   Scientists and Citizens

1   Libby Robin, 'From the Environment to the Anthropocene: A History of
      Changing Expertise 1948–2018', in Manuel Rivera, Anna Barbara Sum &
      Frank Trentmann (eds), *Work in Progress: Economy and Environment at the
      Hands of Experts* (IASS, Potsdam, 2018), pp. 184–203.

2   Libby Robin, 'Radical Ecology and Conservation Science: An Australian
      Perspective', *Environment and History*, 4(2), 1998, pp 191–208.

3   *Bulletin of the British Ornithologists Club*, 27, 1906, and reported in the *Australian Naturalist*.

4   Paul Warde, Libby Robin & Sverker Sorlin, *The Environment: A History of The Idea* (Johns Hopkins University Press, Baltimore, MD, 2018).

5   Dr Spencer Roberts, 'The RAOU and the CSIR', *Emu*, 36(4), 1937, pp. 294–5.

6   David M Richardson & Petr Pyšek, 'Fifty Years of Invasion Ecology: The Legacy of Charles Elton', *Diversity and Distributions*, 14, 2008, pp. 161–8.

7   Quoted in George Main, *Of Beauty Rich and Rare: Fifty Years of CSIRO Wildlife and Ecology* (CSIRO Wildlife & Ecology, Canberra, 1999), p. 2.

8   Head Office Circular 55/42, 'Publication of Research Results', as cited in Ratcliffe to FG Nicholls, 16 August 1955, Ratcliffe–Serventy correspondence, Ratcliffe Collection, NLA (reference copy sent to Serventy).

9   Ratcliffe to FG Nicholls, 16 August 1955, Ratcliffe–Serventy correspondence, Ratcliffe Collection, NLA, p. 1.

10 Ratcliffe to Serventy, 22 July 1960, p. 2.

11 Margaret H Friedel and Stephen R Morton, 'A history of CSIRO'S Central Australian Laboratory, 1: 1953–80: pastoral land research', *Historical Records of Australian Science*, 34(1) 2023; Margaret H Friedel, Stephen R Morton, Gary N Bastin, Jocelyn Davies and D Mark Stafford Smith, 'A history of CSIRO'S Central Australian Laboratory, 2: 1980–2018: interdisciplinary land research', *Historical Records of Australian Science*, 34(1) 2023.

12 HJ Frith, *Pigeons and Doves of Australia* (Rigby, Adelaide, 1982).

13 F Lewis, 'Notes on the Proper Protection of the Mutton Bird Rookery at Cape Wollamai', *Emu*, 23(10), 1923, pp. 61–4.

14 Letter to Mr Grey from Serventy (n.d., c. 1950), 'CSIRO Bird-banding Scheme', RAOU Archives, SLV MS 9247, Box 59(a).

15 'Banding Mutton Birds' [News and Notes], *Emu*, 47(1), 1947, pp. 77–8.

16 DL Serventy, 'The Banding Programme on *Puffinis tenuirostris Temminck*', *CSIRO Wildlife Research*, 2(1), 1957, pp. 51–9.

17 Serventy to Chandler, 30 August 1922, NAA (Perth).

18 BOC banding operations were confined to young birds on the nest, which would not work for passerine species.

19 Angus Robinson, 'The Biological Significance of Bird Song in Australia', *Emu*, 48(4), 1949, pp. 291–315.

20 Serventy to Grey (n.d., c. 1950), 'Bird-banding Scheme', RAOU Archives, SLV MS 9247, Box 59(a). See also Pauline Reilly, *Fairy Penguins and Earthy People* (Lothian in association with Esso BHP, Melbourne, 1983).

21 CO Fuller, 'The SAOA 1940–1960', in R Collier et al. (eds), *Birds, Birders and Birdwatching 1899–1999* (SAOA, Adelaide, 2000), pp. 60–1.

22 Libby Robin, 'Cane Toads as Sport: Conservation Practice and Animal Ethics at Odds', in Nancy Cushing & Jodi Frawley (eds), *Animals Count: How Population Size Matters in Animal-Human Relations* (Routledge Environmental Humanities, Abingdon-on-Thames, UK, 2018), pp 15–25.

23 Rick Shine, *Cane Toad Wars* (University of California Press, Oakland, 2018).

24 Robert Carrick, 'Australian Bird-Banding Scheme', *CSIRO Wildlife Research*, 1(1), 1956, p. 26.

25 Ibid., p. 27.

26 Ibid., p. 26. The Falkland Islands story is in *South Australian Ornithologist*, 23(3), 1960, p. 42.

27 DL Serventy, 'Angus Hargreaves Robinson' (obituary), *Emu*, 77(1), pp. 41–4. Angus Robinson, 'The Biological Significance of Bird Song in Australia', *Emu*, 48(4), 1949, pp. 291–315. Angus Robinson, 'The Annual Reproductory Cycle of the Magpie, *Gymnorhina dorsalis* Campbell, in South-western Australia', *Emu*, 56(4), 1956, pp. 233–336.

28 WB Hitchcock, 'The First Ten Years of the ABBS', *Australian Bird Bander*, 1964, pp. 38–42. Main, p. 33.

29 S Marchant, 'Obituary: Warren Billingsley Hitchcock 1919–1984', *Emu*, 85(1), 1985, pp. 51–2.

30 A major report on the silver gull work was R Carrick, WR Wheeler & MD Murray, 'Seasonal Dispersal and Mortality in the Silver Gull, *Larus novaehollandiae* Stephens, and Crested Tern *Sterna bergii* Lichtenstein, in Australia', *CSIRO Wildlife Research*, 2(2), 1957, pp. 116–44.

31 Alan J Leishman, 'Bill Selwyn George Lane 1922–2000', *Bird Notes*, March 2000, p. 5; Belinda Dettman, 'Obituary: S. G. (Bill) Lane, 1922–2000', *Flightlines*, 24, 2000, p. 3.

32 'Aims and Objects of the New South Wales Bird Banders Association', *Bird Bander*, 1(1), 1962, pp. 2–3.

33 HJ de S Disney, 'President's Message', *Corella*, 1(1), 1977, p. 19.

34 Hitchcock, p. 41.

35 SJ Wilson, SG Lane & JL McKean, 'The Use of Mist Nets in Australia', *Division of Wildlife Research Technical Paper* no. 8 (CSIRO, Melbourne, 1964), p. 26.

36 Marchant, 'A Brief History of the 1966 Proposal for Reform of the RAOU', unpublished typescript, 1998, p. 2. Steve Wilson, *Birds of the ACT* (COG, Canberra, 1999), p. 4.

37 Anne Kerle, email to the author, 1 June 2000.
38 Pauline Reilly & JA Kerle, 'A Study of the Gentoo Penguin *Pygosceles papua*', *Notornis*, 28, 1981, pp. 189–202.
39 Pauline Reilly, interview with Kate Gorringe-Smith, 1995, BirdLife Australia Archive. See also Kate Gorringe-Smith, 'Pauline Reilly: A Penguin Classic', *Wingspan*, 5(1), 1995.
40 Ian Rowley, interview with the author, 23 February 2000.

7   The Rest of the World Comes to Australia

1   Professeur Jean Dorst to Australian Academy of Science, letter of acceptance, 21 September 1970, AAS Archives, Canberra, 1225.
2   Allen Keast, 'The Evolutionary Biogeography of Australian Birds', in Keast (ed.), *Ecological Biogeography of Australia*, vol. 3 (Dr W Junk bv Publishers, The Hague, 1981), p. 1601.
3   Lack died before the Canberra IOC.
4   Dorst to Frith, 17 March 1971, IOC/20 'Advisory Council', SLV MS 11437, Box 19(a).
5   AAS 1225.
6   Minutes of the First Scientific Programme Committee meeting of the XVI International Ornithological Congress held on 9–10 August 1971 at CSIRO Division of Wildlife Research, Canberra, AAS 1226.
7   Frith to Serventy, 27 March 1973, IOC/20 'Advisory Council', SLV MS 11437, Box 19(a).
8   Dorst to Frith, 1 June 1973, IOC/20 'Advisory Council', SLV MS 11437, Box 19(a).
9   Frith to Dorst, 3 August 1973, IOC/20 'Advisory Council', SLV MS 11437, Box 19(a). International sanctions stopped visas for ornithologists from Rhodesia but otherwise did not affect the congress.
10 The Permanent Executive plus the Committee of One Hundred totalled 108, sixty-three of whom were from Europe and only forty-five from the rest of the world. France, Germany, the Netherlands and the United Kingdom alone accounted for 35 per cent. Dorst spoke German as well as English, and consulted widely and tactfully.
11 Jean Dorst, 'Historical Factors Influencing the Richness and Diversity of the South American Avifauna', in HJ Frith & JH Calaby (eds), *Proceedings of the 16th International Ornithological Congress* (AAS, Canberra, 1976), pp. 17–35.
12 HE LeGrand, *Drifting Continents and Shifting Theories* (Cambridge University Press, Cambridge, 1988).

13   Ernst Mayr, 'Geography and Ecology as Faunal Determinants', in
      KH Voous (ed.), *Proceedings of the 15th IOC 1970*, The Hague (EJ Brill,
      Leiden, 1972), p. 551.

14   Mayr, 'Geography and Ecology as Faunal Determinants', DL Serventy,
      'Causal Ornithogeography of Australia', and Allen Keast, 'Faunal Elements
      and Evolutionary Patterns: Some Comparisons Between the Continental
      Avifaunas of Africa, South America and Australia', in Voous (ed.), pp.
      551–61, 574–84, 594–622.

15   DL Serventy, 'Origin and Structure of Australian Bird Fauna', in
      JD Macdonald, *Birds of Australia* (AH & AW Reed, Sydney, 1973); Ernst
      Mayr, 'Continental Drift and the History of the Australian Bird Fauna'
      and Joel Cracraft, 'Continental Drift and Australian Avian Biogeography',
      Emu, 72, 1972, pp. 26–8 and 171–4.

16   First Circular, September 1972, AAS 1225.

17   HJ Frith, 'Achievement of Scientific Aims', typescript report to the AAS
      on the 16th IOC, 16 April 1975, AAS 1225, p. 5.

18   Lack to Frith, 30 July 1972, IOC/4/4 gives details of his 'totally
      unexpected operation' and recommends Keast for the task. By the end of
      that year, ill-health had forced his withdrawal from the IOC altogether,
      and he died on 12 March 1973.

19   Frith to Mayr, 2 December 1971, IOC/4/1 RAOU Archive, SLV MS
      11437, Box 19(b)(ii). Serventy's draft was in IOC/4/6 'Origin of the
      Australasian Avifauna'.

20   Direct quote from Sibley, as reported in Serventy to Frith, 19 December
      1972, IOC/4/6.

21   Serventy to Frith, 31 December 1972.

22   Mayr to Frith, 4 December 1972 and 7 February 1973, IOC/4/1.

23   Frith & Calaby (eds), pp. 103–70. The contributors were Allen Keast,
      SJJF Davies, GF van Tets, GT Smith, Richard Schodde (on birds of
      paradise, predominantly New Guinea), Allan McEvey and GR Williams.

24   Henry Nix, as director of the Centre for Resource and Environmental
      Studies (CRES) at the ANU and president of the RAOU, observed that
      he had more requests for the paper in the 1990s than in the 1970s and
      1980s. (Interview with the author, 15 December 1999.)

25   There is a whole file of letters to authors requesting that they shorten
      papers to meet the word limits. Charles Sibley, for example, traded off
      a shorter paper (5 pp.) in the Serventy symposium against a longer
      one (14 pp.) in his own. Correspondence on file IOC/25, 'Publication

Proceedings', SLV MS 11437, Box 19(b)(i). The next-longest paper was by Professor Finn Salomonsen, the previous president of the IOC, and was eighteen pages.

26   Maclean also contributed a paper on African birds in non-arid habitats in the 'Breeding of Birds' symposium.

27   Sibley to Frith, 15 March 1971, IOC/20 'Advisory Council', 11437, Box 19(a).

28   Ibid.

29   Frith to Mayr, 30 August 1971, IOC/4/1. This letter set out the parameters of the two different symposia. CG Sibley, 'Protein Evidence of the Relationships of Some Australian Passerine Birds', in Frith & Calaby (eds), pp. 643–54.

30   R Liversidge (Kimberley, South Africa) to Frith, 26/8/74, IOC/33 'Bouquets and Bitches', SLV MS 11437, Box 19(b)(ii).

31   Alexander F Skutch, 'Helpers at the Nest', *Auk*, 52, 1935, pp. 257–73.

32   Ian Rowley, *Bird Life* (Collins, Sydney, 1975), p. 77.

33   Minutes of the First Scientific Programme Committee meeting of the XVI International Ornithological Congress held on 9–10 August 1971, RAOU Archives, SLV MS 11437, IOC/20, Box 19(a).

34   Its final recommendation was 'That: The responsible authorities of all countries with a seashore be urged to encourage the establishment, if such is not already in existence, of a recognised central depository and archives for all forms of record of observation of seabirds, including photographs obtained during censuses and such samples as may be required in the detection and monitoring of contaminants and pollutants in the seabird environment.' Letter HJ Frith to WRP Bourne, 29 January 1975, IOC/25.

35   Keast to Frith, 16 August 1972, IOC/4/4 'Evolution of Island Land Birds'.

36   François Vuilleumier, 'In Memorium: James Allen Keast 1922–2009', *Auk* 127(4), 2010, pp. 952–4.

37   John Woinarski, 'James Allen Keast (DL Serventy Medal 1995: Citation)', *Emu*, 95(4), 1995, p. 301. Also unpublished curriculum vitae (1995) supplied by Keast (received 3 October 2000).

38   The congress was supported initially by CSIRO Wildlife, then hosted by the new Commonwealth Department of Environment and Conservation when Dr Joe Forshaw moved there.

39   ICBP, Summary of Resolutions (7 pp). Typescript in SLV MS 11437, Box 19(b) 'IOC/7 International Committee'.

40 Frith to Farner, 22 August 1974, SLV MS 11437, Box 19(b) 'IOC/7 International Committee'.

41 Serventy to Frith, 19 April 1974, SLV MS 11437, Box 19(b)(i).

42 Mike Fleming, interview with the author, 25 May 2000.

43 *Bird Study in Australia* (National Film and Sound Archive, ID 014615-02). Video kindly loaned to author by JD Macdonald (30 June 2000).

44 Wording from the report on the IOC by Walter Bock attached to a letter dated 16 December 1974 (IOC/33).

45 McClure to Frith, 27 April 1973 (IOC/20) SLV MS 11437, Box 19(b)(i).

46 Frith was elected Fellow of the AAS (and the Australian Academy of Technological Sciences and Engineering), but not until 1975.

47 Frith's IOC files 'Offers of help'. White's ornithological work focused on the variation of song in olive whistlers. On his distinguished scientific career in physics and in CSIR(O) see HC Minnett & Sir Rutherford Robertson, 'Frederick William George White 1905–1994', *Historical Records of Australian Science*, 11(2), 1996, pp. 239–58.

48 Registration numbers were allocated by the AAS in order of application from 1 to 642. According to final numbers, 677 people attended, but there were cancellations and changes and some numbers were issued to two or more people travelling together.

49 Storr to Frith, IOC/20 'Advisory Council', RAOU Archives, SLV MS 11437, Box 19(a).

50 J Deeble (executive secretary, AAS) to Dr A Graham Brown (president, RAOU), 3 August 1970. AAS Archives, 1225.

51 McEvey, transcript of February 1995 recorded interview with Norman Wettenhall, Kate Gorringe-Smith and Kate Fitzherbert (held at HL White Library), p. 21. Dates and venue from letters from Serventy to Hindwood, 9 and 23 December 1968, Hindwood Papers.

52 [Serventy and McEvey], 'Summary of the Review Committee's Report and Supplementary Report', MS 11437, Box 18(c), p. 6.

53 Ibid., pp. 2–3.

54 Pauline Reilly, transcript of interview with the author, 22 August 1998, p. 19.

55 Ibid., p. 21.

56 Pauline Reilly, interview with Kate Gorringe-Smith, 1995. Tape and transcript held at BirdLife Australia Library, p. 7. Serventy probably never had any intention of speaking. Because of his stammer he rarely spoke in public.

57 Norman Wettenhall, transcript of interview with the author, 10 March 1998, p. 4.

58 Reilly, transcript of interview with Kate Gorringe-Smith, 1995, pp. 9–10.

59 CH Tyndale-Biscoe, JH Calaby & SJJF Davies, 'Harold James Frith 1921–1982', *Historical Records of Australian Science*, 10(3), 1995, pp. 247–74. The authors argue (p. 253) that the accident affected Frith's self-confidence, which is consistent with the total denial of the accident in letters drafted by Frith in that period. (Frith's IOC files, RAOU Archives SLV MS 11437, Box 19(a), B, B(i), B(ii).)

60 CORESEARCH 1975 records that the lab itself suffered damage from a falling tree, but this was quickly repaired as it had to serve as a home for staff. All but two of whom had lost their homes in the terrible storm.

61 Robert Etchecopar, le Président, Société Ornithologique de France, to Frith, 24 September 1974 in IOC/33, 'Bouquets and Bitches', SLV MS 11437, Box 19(b)(ii).

62 Serventy to Frith, n.d., received 8 February 1971, IOC/20, 'Advisory Committee', SLV MS 11437, Box 19(a). In fact by 1974, the 'ladies' were referred to as associates. Although the majority of associates were wives, there were also husbands, daughters, sons and friends accompanying delegates, who enjoyed the program of art galleries, excursions and other non-ornithological activities offered.

63 Ian Rowley commented that working at CSIRO was 'hard on marriages', because of the expectation that an officer would be available to do his (in the 1950s and 1960s it was always 'his') private research (often on birds) after hours and at the weekend. (Interview with the author, 23 February 2000.)

64 Gove to Frith, 2 September 1974, IOC/33, 'Bouquets and Bitches', SLV MS 11437, Box 19(b)(ii).

65 Frith to the editor of *British Birds* (published in *British Birds*, November 1972) encouraging British ornithologists to make the long trip to Australia. Draft in MS 11437, Box 19(b).

66 Ibid. Cornell, Oxford and The Hague were the sites of the previous three IOCs.

67 Mike Fleming, interview with the author, 25 May 2000, p. 16.

68 Penny Olsen, pers. comm., 24 July 2000.

69 The letter was a response to WRP Bourne, *British Birds*, December 1971 pp. 548–51.

70 Gavin Souter, 'Did Australia's Birds Come from Gondwanaland?', *Sydney Morning Herald*, 9 August 1974.

71 Frith, 'Report on 16 International Ornithological Congress', 16 April 1975, AAS Archives, p. 6.

72 Letter of thanks from Frith to Mr M Darmody, 12 September 1974, for last-minute visit to his property. IOC/33 'Bouquets and Bitches', SLV MS 11437, Box 19(b)(ii).

73 Letters of thanks from Frith to Lendon, Corbett and Low, IOC/33 'Bouquets and Bitches', Box 19(b)(ii).

74 Henry Nix, pers. comm., 20 July 2000.

75 Letter JR Price to Frith, 23 August 1974 IOC/33 'Bouquets and Bitches', SLV MS 11437, Box 19(b)(ii).

76 Telegrams (undated) and letter (6/8/74) in SLV MS 11437, Box 19(b)(i), 'IOC/18 Pleas for Help'.

77 Frith's 'Bitches' file (IOC/33) contained other complaints. The Academy Report (16 April 1975) said that the matters were finally resolved during long nights on 10 and 11 August.

78 Correspondence on file IOC/25, 'Publication Proceedings', SLV MS 11437, Box 19(b)(i). The *Proceedings* sold for $50 instead of the $25–30 discussed with the Dutch publishers.

8   Noisy Scrub-bird

1 DL Serventy & HN Whittell, *Birds of Western Australia*, 5th edn (University of Western Australia Press, Perth, 1976; 1st edn 1948), pp. 314–20.

2 Graham Pizzey & Frank Knight, *A Field Guide to the Birds of Australia* (Angus & Robertson, Sydney 1997), p. 326. 'Zip da dee' comes from GT Smith & FN Robinson, 'The Noisy Scrub-bird: An Interim Report', *Emu*, 76(1), 1976, p. 40.

3 Quoted in Serventy & Whittell, p. 318. Gilbert collected four or five specimens including the type, and also saw and heard the bird at Augusta and King George's Sound.

4 EP Ramsay, Australian Museum, found the rufous scrub-bird in 1866.

5 AJ Campbell, 'Scrub Birds', *The Australasian*, 22 July 1899, in NMV/9/1 (i).

6 'A Missing Bird', *West Australian*, 5 November 1920. Cuttings file collated by Mr PE Petherick, Cottesloe, and deposited in the RAOU Archives, SLV MS 11437, Box 11(a), 'WA Visit and Conference Press Cuttings'.

7   E Sedgwick, 'Annual Congress', *Emu*, 48(3), 1949, p. 177. The memorial
      was also to commemorate the botanical collector James Drummond
      (1787–1863).

8   Serventy & Whittell, p. 33.

9   Ibid., p. 317.

10   Sedgwick, p. 178.

11   HO Webster, 'Re-discovery of the Noisy Scrub-bird, *Atrichornis clamosus*',
      Western Australian Naturalist, 8(3), 1962.

12   Webster field notebook, 17 December 1961.

13   HO Webster Collection, RAOU Archives, SLV MS 9247, Box 72.

14   Webster field notebook, 23 December 1961.

15   SJJF Davies, 'Obituary: Dr Julian Ford (1932–1987)', *Emu*, 87(2), 1987,
      p. 132.

16   *Emu*, 63(1), January 1963.

17   Letter to the Editor, *Albany Advertiser*, 19 July 1963, p. 4. The paper
      was running a story in connection with the bid to have habitat for the
      bird reserved.

18   From Webster's letter to the editor, ibid.

19   Webster, 'Re-discovery of the Noisy Scrub-bird', pp. 58–9.

20   AH Chisholm, 'The Story of the Scrub-birds', *Emu*, 51(2 & 3), 1951,
      pp. 89–112, 285–97, esp. p. 91.

21   The CSIRO Wildlife Section was created in 1949, with Francis Ratcliffe
      as officer-in-charge. It became the Division of Wildlife Research in 1962,
      when Harry Frith was appointed 'Chief', and changed its name many
      times after that.

22   Mary Heimerdinger Clench & Graeme Smith, *Records of the Australian
      Museum*, 37(3 & 4), special edition on the noisy scrub-bird, 1985,
      pp. 111, 113.

23   Ian Rowley, *Bird Life* (Collins, Sydney, 1975), p. 242. Smith & Robinson,
      pp. 37–42.

24   Alan Danks, 'History of the Noisy Scrub-bird', in the CALM-published
      children's book *Jeemuluk: The Young Noisy Scrub-bird*, 1999. Also Alan
      Danks, Sarah Comer & Lawrence Cuthbert, 'Trends in Four Noisy Scrub-
      bird Populations', presentation at the Southern Hemisphere Ornithological
      Congress, 29 June 2000 (see abstract in Lee B Astheimer & Michael F.
      Clarke (eds), *The Second Southern Hemisphere Ornithological Congress*, Birds
      Australia Report 9 (BA, Hawthorn East, 2000), p. 65.)

25   A Danks, AA Burbidge, AH Burbidge & GC Smith, *The Noisy Scrub-bird Recovery Plan* (CALM, Perth, 1996).

26   PJ Fullagar & HJ de S Disney 'The Birds of Lord Howe Island: A Report on the Rare and Endangered Species', *Bulletin of the International Council for Bird Preservation*, 12, 1975, pp. 187–202. Department of Climate Change, Energy, the Environment and Water, 'Species Profile and Threats Database: *Hypotaenidia sylvestris*—Lord Howe Woodhen', DCCEEW website, n.d. Penny D Olsen, 'Re-establishment of an Endangered Subspecies: The Norfolk Island Boobook Owl *Ninox novaeseelandiae undulata*', *Bird Conservation International*, 6, 1996, pp. 63–80. Penny Olsen, pers. comm., 28 November 2000. In this case it is a hybrid survival: the 'endling' Miamiti had not been heard since 1996, but her hybrid offspring fill the role of apex predator on Norfolk Island. Department of Climate Change, Energy, the Environment and Water, 'Species Profile and Threats Database: *Ninox novaeseelandiae undulata*—Norfolk Island Boobook, Norfolk Island Morepork, Southern Boobook (Norfolk Island)', DCCEEW website, n.d.

27   Population estimate comes from Danks, Comer & Cuthbert.

28   '24. Noisy Scrub-bird: *Atrichornis clamosus*', EDGE of Existence website, n.d.

29   'What is EDGE?', EDGE of Existence website, n.d.

30   Stephen Garnett and Gabriel Crowley, *The Action Plan for Australian Birds 2000* (Natural Heritage Trust, Canberra, 2000), p. 400, lists noisy scrub-birds as 'vulnerable', a less-threatened category than in earlier management plans, but this has been revised again in the two decades since.

31   Tjimiluk is now listed on the official Australian Government Species Profile and Threats Database: Department of Climate Change, Energy, the Environment and Water, 'Species Profile and Threats Database: *Atrichornis clamosus*—Noisy Scrub-bird, Tjimiluk', DCCEEW website, n.d. 'Jeemuluk' was the spelling used by Serventy around the time of the rediscovery in 1961. Serventy often used Western Australian Aboriginal bird names to label his own files, possibly because they were more stable than the official names (for example, the malleefowl file was labelled 'Gnow'; Serventy files, NAA Perth).

9   A Crisis in Conservation

1   The conference was led by Michel Batisse, head of UNESCO's Natural Resources Research, with partners the Food and Agriculture Organization

of the United Nations (FAO) and IUCN. Peter Bridgewater, 'The Man and Biosphere Programme of UNESCO: Rambunctious Child of the Sixties, But Was the Promise Fulfilled?', *Current Opinion in Environmental Sustainability*, 19, 2016, pp. 1–6. UNESCO, *Proceedings of the Intergovernmental Conference of Experts on the Scientific Basis for Rational Use and Conservation of the Resources of the Biosphere, Paris, 4–13 September, 1968* (UNESCO, Paris, 1970).

2   Barbara Ward & René Dubos, *Only One Earth: The Care and Maintenance of a Small Planet* (Norton, New York, 1972).

3   Bridgewater.

4   Original RAMSAR Agreement 1971, *Ramsar Convention on Wetlands of International Importance Especially as Waterfowl Habitat*, available on the 'Documents' page of the RAMSAR website.

5   In May 1972 membership was 845, and it had declined over the previous three reports; by December 1984, soon after the *Atlas of Australian Birds* was launched, it was 2015 plus 259 subscribers and increasing steadily (AGM reports).

6   M Blakers, SJJF Davies & PN Reilly, *The Atlas of Australian Birds* (Melbourne University Press, Carlton, Vic., 1984).

7   Pauline N Reilly, 'Introduction to Invited Papers on Ornithology in Australia: Practice, Prospects and Progress', *Emu*, 73 (supplement), 1973, pp. 203–5. Stephen Marchant, letter to Reilly, 22 May 1972, RAOU Archives, MS 11437, Box 16(a) (e) '*Emu*, correspondence'.

8   Allan McEvey, 'The Metaphysic of Ornithology', *Emu*, 73 (supplement), 1973, pp. 248–55.

9   Michael G Ridpath, 'Co-ordinated Research Overseas', *Emu*, 73 (supplement), 1973, pp. 213–16.

10   IOC *Daily Bulletin*, Thursday 15 August. This was one of many administrative meetings held in the evenings during the course of the congress.

11   With drawings by Rhyllis Plant. Penguin, Ringwood, 1990. First issued as *Learning about Australian Birds* (Collins, Sydney, 1980).

12   [Stephen Marchant], 'RAOU Nest Record Scheme', *Emu*, 63(5), 1964, pp. 424–7.

13   'Nest Record Scheme: David Thomas Takes Over', *RN*, 2, 1970, p. 3. Thomas ran the 'Individual Observation Points Scheme', starting in 1965–66 but discontinued it in 1969. Reports appeared in *Emu*, 68(1), 1968, pp. 42–84 and 68(4), 1969, pp. 249–71.

14   S Marchant, 'Third Annual Report: RAOU Nest Record Scheme', *Emu*, 68(4), 1969, pp. 243–8.

15   Reilly, interview with Kate Gorringe-Smith, February 1995, BirdLife Australia Library. Not all atlassers became members of the RAOU, but many did.

16   Davies, interview with the author, 3 October 1998.

17   A one-degree square is 1 degree of latitude by 1 degree of longitude.

18   'Members Invited to Submit Information for the Atlas from Their Own Notes', *RN*, 26, March 1976.

19   There were also other 'regulars' in and outside the office, including Tess Kloot, the honorary RAOU archivist, and Cecily Allen, the assistant librarian from 1971 until 1985.

20   'Atlas Field Work to Go Ahead', *RN*, 27, June 1976, p. 1.

21   For a full account of Serventy's maps, see Anon. (probably Tommy Garnett), 'Distribution of Birds on the Australian Mainland: Dr DL Serventy's Maps', *RN*, 36, September 1978, p. 3.

22   Blakers, interview with the author, 17 February 2000.

23   Bennett went on to work for the RAOU in various capacities for nearly eleven years, earning the title 'Computer King of Moonee Ponds', before leaving to set up his own consultancy in 1987: Margaret Cameron, 'Simon: Goodbye and Thank You', *RN*, June 1987, p. 4.

24   'From All of Us—Thank You', *RN*, 51, March 1982, p. 14.

25   *RN*, 37, 40 and 41, December 1978, June and September 1979, especially 'Institute of Field Ornithology in Being' in the first, and picture captioned 'Institute of Ornithology' in the last. Tommy Garnett was the secretary who worked on the landing on his regular visits to the North Melbourne office from his country home, the Garden of St Erth, in Blackwood.

26   Blakers, interview with the author, 17 February 2000.

27   'From All of Us—Thank You'.

28   There was also a composite newsletter, containing selected articles from the first eight issues of *Atlas Newsletter*, produced for the information of people who joined the project later on. The *RAOU Newsletter* (nos 47–51) took over after 1980.

29   'RAOU Camp-out', *RN*, 50, December 1981, p. 11.

30   Wettenhall, interview with the author, 19 March 1998.

31   Ibid.

32   *RN*, 50, December 1981, p. 9.

33 Fleming, 25 May 2000, and Erlich, 26 February 1999, interviews with the author. Also *RN*, 50 and 51, December 1981 and March 1982, pp. 9 and 15 respectively. The survey was completed on 6 November 1981.

34 A URRF was sent to observers who sent in a record of a species way out of range or of a very rare or enigmatic species (e.g. night parrot). It asked for more corroborative details.

35 Blakers, interview with the author, 17 February 2000.

36 Blakers, Davies & Reilly. Douglas D Dow, 'President's Report', in *Annual Report* (RAOU, Moonee Ponds, 1984), p. 2.

37 *RN*, 70, 1986, p. 14.

38 Michael F Clarke, Peter Griffioen & Richard Loyn, *Australian Bird Count: Where Do All the Birds Go?*, colour supplement (16 pp.) to *Wild: Australia's Wilderness Adventure Magazine*, 19(9), 1999 (funded by the Norman Wettenhall Foundation).

39 Michael E Soulé, 'What Is Conservation Biology?', *Bioscience*, 35(11), 1985, pp. 727–34.

40 Michael Soulé (ed.), *Conservation Biology*, 2nd edn (Sinauer Associates, Sunderland, MA, 1986), p. 117.

41 Libby Robin, 'The Rise of the Idea of Biodiversity: Crises, Responses and Expertise', *Quaderni* (Journal of l'Institut des Sciences Humaines et Sociales du CNRS) [Special Issue: *Les Promesses de la biodiversité*], 76(1), 2011, pp. 25–38.

42 Soulé, 'What Is Conservation Biology?'

43 RA Kenchington, 'Conservation and Coastal Zone Management', in C Moritz & J Kikkawa (eds), *Conservation Biology in Australia* (Beatty, Chipping Norton, UK, 1994), pp. 245–51.

44 Dolly Jørgensen, 'Extinction and the End of Futures', *History and Theory*, 61(2), 2022, pp. 209–18.

45 Kenchington.

46 Timothy Farnham, *Saving Nature's Legacy: The Origins of the Idea of Biodiversity* (Yale University Press, New Haven, CT, 2007).

47 Libby Robin, *Defending the Little Desert: The Rise of Ecological Consciousness in Australia* (Melbourne University Press, Carlton, Vic., 1998).

48 CI now has regional branches with their own websites. Australia's is at https://www.conservation.org/australia.

49 Conservation International, 'Partnering with Communities', CI website, n.d.

50 From 1993 the Australian Nature Conservation Agency and from 1997 Environment Australia.

51 David Purchase, 'Banding of Birds and Bats', *Biannual Report*, CSIRO Division of Wildlife and Rangelands Research, 1982–84, pp. 23–4.

52 Excerpt from the report of 1980, quoted in George Main, *Of Beauty Rich and Rare: Fifty Years of CSIRO Wildlife and Ecology* (CSIRO Wildlife & Ecology, Canberra, 1999), p. 38.

53 Minton was not the first to use cannon-nets in Australia. CSIRO Wildlife and Ecology had been using the nets in studies of magpie geese and other species since the 1950s. But they were new for many of the RAOU banders.

54 It is a 'special interest group' of BirdLife Australia and has its own website.

55 This project was launched late in 1979 and managed by the RAOU's Field Investigation Committee (*RN*, 42, 1979, p. 4). There were occasional general reports from the field. See, for example, Simon Bennett, 'The Search Continues for the Very Elusive Night Parrot', *RN*, 47, 1981, p. 10.

56 John Martindale & Clive Minton, '40,000 Great Knots', *RN*, 50, 1981, p. 8.

57 'New Bird Observatories', *RN*, 69, 1986, p. 1.

58 Plaque, Broome Bird Observatory.

59 28 March 1990, opened by the Hon. Ian Taylor, Deputy Premier of Western Australia. The plaque lists the sponsors as Lord Alistair McAlpine; Participants in the North West Shelf LNG Project; Department of Conservation and Land Management, Western Australia; BHP Petroleum; Rural and Industries Bank, Western Australia; Lister-Petter Australia P/L; Television New Zealand; Australian Broadcasting Commission; and the Shire and People of Broome (pers. obs., October 1998). The status of Roebuck Bay as Australian Ramsar Site no. 33 was ratified on 7 June 1990. BirdLife International factsheet for Roebuck Bay, 2022, http://datazone.birdlife.org/site/factsheet/roebuck-bay-iba-australia.

60 Serventy to Ratcliffe, 20 May 1955, pp. 1–2, Ratcliffe–Serventy correspondence, Ratcliffe Collection, NLA.

61 Ratcliffe to Serventy, 17 May 1955, p. 2, Ratcliffe–Serventy correspondence, Ratcliffe Collection, NLA.

62 Serventy to Ratcliffe, 20 May 1955, pp. 1–2, Ratcliffe–Serventy correspondence, Ratcliffe Collection, NLA.

63 Stephen Marchant, 'Introduction', *Handbook of Australian, New Zealand and Antarctic Birds, Volume 1: Ratites to Ducks* (Oxford University Press, Melbourne, 1990), p. 13.

64   Viola Temple Watts, *The Quintessential Bird: The Art of Betty Temple Watts*
     (NLA, Canberra, 2011). HJ Frith (ed.), *Birds in the Australian High
     Country*, illustrated by Betty Temple Watts (Angus & Robertson, Sydney,
     1969, and subsequent revised editions in 1976 and 1984).
65   The FIC considered the proposal in April 1980 and council approved it on
     28 February 1981, appointing a subcommittee in June 1980.
66   'The Handbook of Australian Birds', *RN*, 54, 1982. See also 'Stephen
     Marchant', *Wingspan*, 16, 1994.
67   Cramp, 'Introduction', in his *Birds of the Western Palearctic, Volume 1:
     Ostrich to Ducks* (Oxford University Press, Oxford, 1977), p. 2, lists Field
     Characters, Habitat, Distribution and Population, Movements, Food,
     Social Pattern and Behaviour, Voice, Breeding and Plumages.
68   Ibid., p. 13.
69   'Australia within the limits of the continental shelf, north to 10ºS or the
     Queensland–New Guinea political border, whichever lies further north, but
     excluding the eastern end of New Guinea and adjacent islands above 10ºS;
     New Zealand and its islands from the Kermadec Group to Campbell Island;
     the Antarctic Continent; the subantarctic islands (Marion, Prince Edward,
     Crozet, Kerguelen, Heard and Macquarie, and islands of the Scotia Arc:
     South Georgia, South Sandwich, South Orkney and South Shetland Islands);
     Cocos-Keeling, Christmas (Indian Ocean), Lord Howe and Norfolk Islands;
     reefs and islands of the Coral Sea', according to Marchant's introduction in
     Handbook of Australian, New Zealand and Antarctic Birds, p. 14.
70   Oxford University Press published the whole set (1990–2006) and paid the
     cartographer, but Birds Australia funded the artists and editors through a
     separate fundraising campaign that included selling the artwork after each
     of the seven volumes was published in nine parts (volumes 1 and 7 were
     both two books thick): vol. 1, part A: Ratites to Petrels; vol. 1, part B:
     Australian Pelican to Ducks; vol. 2: Raptors to Lapwings; vol. 3: Snipe to
     Pigeons; vol. 4: Parrots to Dollarbird; vol. 5: Tyrant-flycatchers to Chats;
     vol. 6: Pardalotes to Shrike-thrushes; vol. 7, part A: Boatbill to Larks;
     vol. 7, part B: Dunnock to Starlings.
71   L Christidis & WE Boles, *The Taxonomy and Species of the Birds of
     Australia*, Monograph 2 (RAOU, Hawthorn East, 1994).
72   Boles, interview with the author, 7 February 2000.
73   Christidis, interview with the author, 6 March 2000; Boles, interview with
     the author, 7 February 2000.

74   Moors, interview with the author, 28 February 2000.

75   Stephen J Ambrose, *Australian Bird Research Directory 1996*, Birds Australia Report no. 2 (BA, Hawthorn East, Vic., December 1997), p. 5.

76   Stephen J Ambrose, *Australian Bird Research Directory 1997*, Birds Australia Report (BA, Hawthorn East, Vic., April 1998), p. 7.

77   Environment Australia, 1999, p. 22.

78   See Chapter 12.

79   By 1952, ninety people were involved in the work, and 330 birds had been 'ringed', according to WR Wheeler, 'Altona Survey Group Report no. 2', *Emu*, 53(1), 1953, p. 30.

80   WR Wheeler, 'A Review of the Altona Survey Group', *Emu*, 52, 1952, pp. 206–8.

81   A major report on the silver gull work was R Carrick, WR Wheeler & MD Murray, 'Seasonal Dispersal and Mortality in the Silver Gull, *Larus novaehollandiae* Stephens, and Crested Tern *Sterna bergii* Lichtenstein, in Australia', *CSIRO Wildlife Research*, 2(2), 1957, pp. 116–44.

82   Benjamin Preiss, 'Peter the Penguin Protector Finishes Up at Phillip Island', *The Age*, 24 June 2022.

83   Peter M Dann, 'Distribution, Population Trends and Factors Influencing the Population Size of Little Penguins *Eudyptula minor* on Phillip Island, Victoria', *Emu* 91, 1992, pp. 263–72.

84   ABC Radio Melbourne, 'Researchers Use Heat Mapping to Protect Phillip Island's Little Penguins from Hot Weather', ABC Melbourne, 25 April 2022.

10   Watching and Observing

1   Edmund Selous, *Bird Watching* (JM Dent, London, 1901). Available online at Project Gutenberg.

2   Frederick Courtney Selous, Macmillan, London, 1908.

3   Selous, *Bird Watching*, pp. 335–6 ('fatigable' original emphasis; 'as the toys of … grown man', my emphasis).

4   Tom Griffiths, 'The Natural History of Melbourne', in *Hunters and Collectors: The Antiquarian Imagination in Australia* (Cambridge University Press, Cambridge, 1996), pp. 121–49. They were in fact a nature writer, a photographer and a dentist, but chose Scribe, Artist and Doctor as their nicknames for Woodlander business.

5   Ibid., p. 149.

6   Constable, London, 1931.
7   Julianne Schultz, *The Idea of Australia: A Search for the Soul of the Nation* (Allen & Unwin, Sydney, 2022), p. 233.
8   New Zealand nearly federated, too, and Western Australia nearly didn't.
9   Libby Robin, 'Being First: Why the Americans Needed It, and Why Royal National Park Didn't Stand in Their Way', *Australian Zoologist*, 2013, pp. 321–9.
10 Margaret Cameron, interview with the author, 3 September 1999.
11 One of the academics who taught the course, Andrew Fisher, by email, 31 July 2000, kindly supplied its short history, including the comments about students. Other teachers included Al Gibbs, Elizabeth Date and Iain Taylor.
12 Rick Allen, Charles Sturt University, Albury. Comment made at meeting about professionals in the RAOU/Birds Australia held during the Southern Hemisphere Ornithological Congress (hereafter SHOC 2), Griffith University, Brisbane, 29 June 2000.
13 Roy Sonnenburg and Peter Vaughan were also among those who led the field trips and walks for the international groups at SHOC 2 in June/July 2000.
14 Charles Sturt University, 'Graduate Diploma of Ornithology', CSU website, 2022.
15 David Goldney, *The Planning Implications of Greenhouse: Proceedings of a Seminar to Alert Town and Country Planners to Climatic Change and Its Implications for Land Use Planning* (Open Learning Institute CSU, Bathurst, 1992).
16 Matt Watson, 'CSU's Adjunct Professor David Goldney Receives AM', *Western Advocate*, 11 June 2018.
17 Richard Jordan, 'Twitchers and Ringers', *RN*, 52, 1982, p. 9.
18 Annie Rogers, *Addicted to Birds* (The author, St Andrews, NSW, 1992), pp. 193–4.
19 Sean Dooley, 'I Only Started Birdwatching to Get on My Teacher's Good Side …', *The Guardian*, 14 February 2019. ABC broadcasts: 'Sean Dooley Talks Comedy, Bird-watching, and Family Life', *Conversations*, 7 August 2009 and 'The Strange Life of the Twitcher', *Conversations*, 18 October 2017.
20 Sean Dooley, *The Big Twitch* (Allen & Unwin, Sydney, 2005).
21 Peter Slater, Raoul Slater & Sally Elmer, *Visions of Wildness* (Reed New Holland, London, 2016), pp. 268–9; Peter Slater, *A Field Guide to*

Australian Birds: Non-passerines (Rigby, Adelaide, 1970) and *Passerines* (Rigby, Adelaide, 1974).

22 CFH Jenkins, 'The Gould League in Australia', in Jenkins, *John Gould and the Birds of Australia* (Gould League of Western Australia, Perth, 1983), p. 38.

23 'Early Diary of Natural History, Winter 1919', Sharland Papers, AMS/191.

24 DL Serventy & HM Whittell, *Birds of Western Australia* (University of Western Australia Press, Perth, 1976), pp. 68–9.

25 SJJF Davies, 'Aspects of a Study of Emus in Semi-arid Western Australia', *Proceedings of the Ecological Society of Australia*, 3, 1968, pp. 160–6; SJJF Davies, 'The Natural History of the Emu in Comparison with Other Ratites', in HJ Frith & JH Calaby, *Proceedings of the 16th International Ornithological Congress* (AAS, Canberra, 1976), pp. 109–20.

26 PC Morrison, 'Stocktaking', broadcast 4 April 1946 (Wild Life Script no. 149), Morrison Archive, SLV, p. 4.

27 Proceedings of Annual General Meeting, *Emu*, 45(3), 1946, p. 201.

28 See extended discussion (based on a report from Michael Sharland in Tasmania) at the Perth Congress. E Sedgwick, 'Annual Congress', *Emu*, 48(3), 1949, pp. 201–2.

29 Johann Knobel, 'The Conservation Status of the Wedgetailed Eagle in Australian Law and Thoughts on the Value of Early Legal Intervention in the Conservation of a Species', *De Jure*, 2015, pp. 293–311.

30 Houghton Mifflin, Boston, MA, and Riverside Press, Cambridge, MA, 1962.

31 Ioan Fazey, Joern Fischer & David Lindenmayer, 'Who Does All the Research in Conservation Biology?', *Biodiversity and Conservation*, 14, 2005, pp. 917–34 and 'What Do Conservation Biologists Publish?', *Biological Conservation*, 124, 2005, pp. 63–73.

32 Peter S Alagona, *The Accidental Ecosystem: People and Wildlife in American Cities* (University of California Press, Oakland, CA, 2022), p. 10.

33 Jens Lachmund, *The Greening of Berlin* (MIT Press, Cambridge, MA, 2012), pp. 166–7.

34 Richard Mabey, *The Unofficial Countryside* (Pimlico, London, 1999; 1st edn 1973), p. 7.

35 Celeste Mitchell, Katie Gannon & Krista Eppelstun, *Life Unhurried: Slow and Sustainable Stays across Australia* (Hardie Grant Explore, Richmond, Vic., 2022), p. vi.

36 Mabey, p. 11.

37 Ibid., p. 12.

38 David M Richardson & Petr Pyšck, 'Fifty Years of Invasion Ecology: The Legacy of Charles Elton', *Diversity and Distributions*, 14, 2008, pp. 161–8. Charles Elton, *The Ecology of Invasions by Animals and Plants* (Methuen, London, 1958).

39 Angus & Robertson, Sydney, 1947.

40 Emily O'Gorman, *Wetlands in a Dry Land: More-than-human Histories of Australia's Murray Darling Basin* (University of Washington Press, Seattle, WA, 2021).

41 *Emu*, 2(1), April 1902, pp. 112–18; *Emu*, 1(4), January 1902, p. 74 also includes a note from 'a lady correspondent' in Queensland.

42 Marcie Muir, 'Catherine Eliza Somerville Stow (1856–1940)', in *Australian Dictionary of Biography*, National Centre of Biography, Australian National University, 1990. Patricia Grimshaw & Julie Evans, 'Colonial Women on Intercultural Frontiers: Rosa Campbell Praed, Mary Bundock and Katie Langloh Parker', *Australian Historical Studies*, 106, 1996, pp. 79–95.

43 Selous, *Bird Watching*, p. 336.

11 Raven

1 Richard K Nelson, *Make Prayers to the Raven: A Koyukon View of the Northern Forest* (University of Chicago Press, Chicago, 1983), p. 14.

2 There are several Alaskan flyways—see Bureau of Land Management, 'The AK Flyway Exhibit', US Department of the Interior website, n.d.

3 Hank Lentfer, *Raven's Witness: The Alaska Life of Richard K Nelson* (Mountaineers Books, Seattle, WA, 2020); Encounters North website; *The Singing Planet* by filmmaker Liz McKenzie, The Wild Chorus website, n.d.

4 'Listening to the Land: *Encounter* Documentary: Zebra Finches at Ocean Bore' (interview with Richard Nelson and Steve Morton), interlude 4 (CD) in Libby Robin, Christopher R Dickman & Mandy Martin (eds), *Desert Channels: The Impulse to Conserve* (CSIRO Publishing, Melbourne, 2010); Steve Morton, 'Rain and Grass: Lessons in How to Be a Zebra Finch', in Libby Robin, Robert Heinsohn & Leo Joseph (eds), *Boom and Bust: Bird Stories for a Dry Country* (CSIRO Publishing, Melbourne, 2009), pp. 45–73.

5   In vernacular English Waa is crow, but for technical ornithologists the
     corvids of the Koories (or Kulin nation) are Australian ravens.

6   Museums Victoria, 'Wominjeka: Welcome', Museums Victoria website,
     2022.

7   Jaara caption on Waa 2013 *Fire Sculpture in River Redgum* by Romanis-
     Trinham Collaborations and inspired by 'the many stories of Waa',
     Bunjilaka Centre (pers. obs.).

8   Ellen Vrana, 'Ted Hughes: *Crow*: From the Life and Songs of the Crow',
     The Examined Life website, 2022.

9   *The Crow: Poems from South Australia*, online journal, published by
     Ginninderra Press, Canberra, since 2020.

10   Backyard Buddies, 'Crows and Ravens', Backyard Buddies website, n.d.

11   All quotes from ibid.

12   Tony Hughes-d'Aeth, *Like Nothing on this Earth: A Literary History of the
     Wheatbelt* (UWA Press, Crawley, 2017).

13   RJ Hobbs & KN Suding (eds), *New Models for Ecosystem Dynamics and
     Restoration* (Island Press, Washington, DC, 2009).

14   DA Saunders & JA Ingram, *Birds of Southwestern Australia: An Atlas of
     Changes in Distribution and Abundance of the Wheatbelt Fauna* (Beatty &
     Sons, Chipping Norton, UK, 1995), p. 3.

15   Saunders, interview with the author, 3 December 1999.

16   Alex Wm Milligan, 'Notes on a Trip to the Stirling Range', *Emu*, 3(1),
     1903, pp. 9–19 (quote p. 11).

17   Saunders & Ingram, p. 12. Simple 'presence or absence' on historic bird-
     lists has given later observers a sense of a significant increase—for example,
     in silver gulls (*Larus novaehollandiae*) and 'twenty-eight' parrots (Australian
     ringnecks, *Barnardius zonarius*) in inland areas—and a corresponding
     decrease in species dependent on native vegetation, such as honeyeaters.

18   See Chapter 7.

19   'The Australian Raven' and 'The White-winged Chough', in Ian Rowley,
     Bird Life (Collins, Sydney, 1975), pp. 80–8 and 98–106 respectively.

20   Robert Heinsohn, 'Cooperative Enhancement of Reproductive Success in
     White-winged Choughs', *Evolutionary Ecology*, 6, 1992, pp. 97–114.

21   Robert Heinsohn, 'White-winged Chough: The Social Consequences
     of Boom and Bust', in Libby Robin, Robert Heinsohn & Leo Joseph
     (eds), *Boom and Bust: Bird Stories for a Dry Country* (CSIRO Publishing,
     Melbourne, 2009), pp. 223–39.

22 The Australian magpie, also with an extraordinary song, moved the other way. Magpies were right next to Raven in the 1926 Checklist, because the (unrelated) European magpie is in the corvid family.

12 Birding Abroad and at Home

1 Kerryn Herman & Katherine L Buchanan, '*Emu* evolves', *Emu*, 117(1), 2017, pp. 1–3.

2 BirdLife Australia, 'Publications: Our Members' Magazine', BirdLife Australia website, n.d.

3 Michael Rands, 'BirdLife International: Who We Are and Where We Have Come From', *Ostrich*, 71(1 & 2) 2000, pp. 148–9.

4 Paige West, *Conservation Is Our Government Now: The Politics of Ecology in Papua New Guinea* (Duke University Press, Durham, NC & London, 2006).

5 Ibid., p. 237.

6 Libby Robin, 'Wilderness in a Global Age, Fifty Years On' (Special *Wilderness Act* Retrospective Forum), *Environmental History*, 19(4), pp. 721–7.

7 Department of Climate Change, Energy, the Environment and Water, 'Indigenous Protected Areas', DCCEEW website, n.d. IPAs account for just over 49 per cent of the National Reserve System, which is a network of formally recognised parks, reserves and protected areas (including state-managed reserves) across Australia.

8 Vanessa Barnett, 'Rewilding lungtalanana: Returning Nature, Culture and Sovereignty to the Wilds of Bass Strait', WWF-Australia website, 2 July 2022.

9 Ibid.

10 Charles Massy, *The Call of the Reed Warbler: A New Agriculture, a New Earth* (University of Queensland Press, St Lucia, 2020).

11 Kate Dooley, Zebedee Nicholls & Malte Meinshausen, 'Carbon Removals from Nature Restoration Are No Substitute for Steep Emission Reductions', *One Earth*, 5(7), 2022; Kate Dooley & Zebedee Nicholls, 'No More Excuses: Restoring Nature Is Not a Silver Bullet for Global Warming, We Must Cut Emissions Outright', *The Conversation*, 4 July 2022.

12 BirdLife Australia, *Bird Conservation Strategy 2022–2032*, as endorsed at the board meeting on 20 August 2022 (BirdLife Australia Member Communiqué, p. 1).

13   BirdLife Australia, 'Indigenous Grant for Bird Research and Conservation', BirdLife Australia website, n.d.

14   Michael Westaway et al. (eds), *Kirrenderri: Heart of the Channel Country* (University of Queensland Anthropology Museum, Brisbane, 2022).

15   Christopher R Dickman & Libby Robin, 'Putting Science in Its Place: The Role of Sandringham Station in Fostering Arid Zone Science in Australia', *Historical Records of Australian Science*, 25, 2014, pp. 186–201. Libby Robin, Christopher R Dickman & Mandy Martin (eds), *Desert Channels: The Impulse to Conserve* (CSIRO Publishing, Melbourne, 2010).

16   Ann Jones, 'The Night Parrot and the Scientists, Indigenous Rangers and Naturalists who Search for Australia's Most Elusive Bird', ABC Science/ The Chase, 10 February 2019.

17   As stated on ABC TV (*The Drum*) during NAIDOC Week 2022 (6 July). Actual figures vary depending on what is included.

18   Robert Hall, *The Insectivorous Birds of Victoria: With Chapters on Birds More or Less Useful* (The author, Melbourne, 1900), quotes p. 2.

19   Libby Robin, *Building a Forest Conscience* (NRCL, Springvale, 1991).

20   Tess Kloot & Ellen M McCulloch, *Some Garden Birds of South East Australia* (illustrated by Rex Davies), (Collins, Sydney, 1970), p. 7.

21   Densey Clyne, *Wildlife in the Suburbs* (illustrated by Martyn Robinson; Oxford University Press, Melbourne, 1982).

22   Bill Middleton, radio scripts (loaned to the author), and annotated curriculum vitae.

23   Jonathan Starks, 'Celebrating Two Decades of Growth', *Park Watch*, 13 June 2017; see also the Hindmarsh Landcare Network website.

24   SGAP soon spread to other states. By 1962 an Association of Societies for Growing Australian Plants was established (now known as the Australian Native Plants Society), and today there are groups in all states and the ACT. Its interest in propagation made it distinct from earlier groups such as Miss Winifred Waddell's Native Plants Preservation Society (est. 1949). For current information on the Australian Native Plants Society, refer to https://anpsa.org.au/.

25   Kloot and McCulloch also produced *Birds of Australian Gardens* in 1980 (with paintings by Peter Trusler) (Rigby, Adelaide). George Adams, *Birdscaping Your Garden* (Rigby, Adelaide, 1980); Adams, *Birdscaping Australian Gardens: Using Native Plants to Attract Birds to Your Garden* (Viking, Sydney, 2015).

26 Zoë Wilson, organiser, interview with the author, 31 August 2000. 'BOC Birds and Gardens Survey 1988', *RN*, 76, 1988, p. 11.

27 Adams, 2015, p. 49.

28 Chloe Hooper, *Bedtime Story* (Scribner, Cammeray, NSW, 2022).

29 Philip Moors, 13 March 2012, announcement of his forthcoming retirement in 'Biographical Notes', Council of Heads of Australasian Herbaria, Australian National Herbarium website, 13 March 2012.

30 Sharon Willoughby, *Gardening the Australian Landscape* [PhD thesis], Australian National University, 2020.

31 Libby Robin, 'The Red Heart Beating in the South-eastern Suburbs: The Australian Garden, Part of the Royal Botanic Gardens Cranbourne', *reCollections*, 2(1), 2007.

32 Sharon Willoughby, pers. comm., 1 August 2022.

33 Ibid.

Epilogue: The Canary in the Coalmine

1 NLA Trove: DL Serventy and KA Wodzicki at Middle Harbour, April 1941. PIC/5989/172 LOC Album 1094/2.

2 University of Washington Press, Seattle, WA, 2021.

3 Daniel Pauly, 'Anecdotes and the Shifting Baseline of Fisheries', *Trends in Ecology & Evolution*, 10, 1995, p. 430.

4 Erin Lennox, 'I Used to Call Myself a Birdo. Now I Just Notice Birds', *The Guardian*, 24 October 2019.

5 United States Environmental Protection Agency, 'Participatory Science for Environmental Protection', US EPA website, n.d.

6 David Lindenmayer, 'The Distribution of Birds in Eucalypt and Exotic Pine Forested Landscape Mosaic: Novel Findings from the Tumut Fragmentation Experiment', Seminar, 23 March 2000, Centre for Resource and Environmental Studies, ANU.

7 David B Lindenmayer, Chris R Margules & Daniel B Botkin, 'Indicators of Biodiversity for Ecologically Sustainable Forest Management', *Conservation Biology*, 14(4), 2000, pp. 941–50.

8 David Lindenmayer, Emma Burns, Nicole Thurgate & Andrew Lowe (eds), *Biodiversity and Environmental Change: Monitoring, Challenges and Direction* (CSIRO Publishing, Melbourne, 2014). See also the TERN website.

9 Rosslyn Beeby, 'Giving Back to the Land', *Canberra Times*, 30 September 2006.

10 Ibid.
11 Anthony Hall-Martin & Jane Carruthers, *South African National Parks: A Celebration* (Horst Klemm, Johannesburg, 2003). Lesley Head, *Second Nature: The History and Implications of Australia as Aboriginal Landscape* (Syracuse University Press, Syracuse, NY, 2000).
12 David Lindenmayer & Joern Fischer, *Landscape Change and Habitat Fragmentation* (Island Press, Washington, DC, 2006).
13 Jo Stewart, 'Do Birders Make Good Tourists?' *The Guardian*, 2 May 2022.
14 Robert Nugent (director), *Night Parrot Stories* [independent documentary film], Canberra, 2016.
15 Libby Robin, 'On the Verge of Isolation', in John Dargavel & Ben Wilkie (eds), *Restoring Forests in Times of Contagion: Papers to Celebrate John Evelyn on the Occasion of His 400th Birthday* (Australian and New Zealand Environmental History Network, Canberra, 2020).

INDEX